Smart Business, Stupid Business

Smart Business, Stupid Business

What School Never Taught You about Building a
Successful Business – Make More Money and Pay Less Tax

Diane Kennedy, CPA
Megan Hughes

New York

Smart Business, Stupid Business
What School Never Taught You About Building a Successful Business
Make More Money & Pay Less Tax

ISBN 978-1-60037-743-3

Cover Design by: Rachel Lopez
Rachel@r2cdesign.com

Library of Congress Control Number: 2009943572

MORGAN · JAMES
THE ENTREPRENEURIAL PUBLISHER

Morgan James Publishing
1225 Franklin Ave., STE 325
Garden City, NY 11530-1693
Toll Free 800-485-4943
www.MorganJamesPublishing.com

In an effort to support local communities, raise awareness and funds, Morgan James Publishing donates one percent of all book sales for the life of each book to Habitat for Humanity. Get involved today, visit **www.HelpHabitatForHumanity.org**.

Dedicated to every entrepreneur who hangs in there, against all odds, for the sake of the most precious thing there is—a dream that things could be better.

Foreword

Congratulations. You've made the decision to start your own business and take responsibility for creating the lifestyle you and your family deserve. Give yourself a pat on the back. You are to be commended. Because most people never make it this far.

But now you find yourself at a crossroad. Will you build a "smart business" or a "stupid business"?

If you build a stupid business, chances are high your business will fail within the first five years. In fact, according to SCORE, the Service Corps Of Retired Executives, 627,200 new businesses were created in 2008, 595,600 businesses closed their doors and 43,546 suffered bankruptcy. So the odds are definitely stacked against small business success.

The good news is you can dramatically increase the odds for success by simply building a smart business from the beginning.

Which means beginning with the end in mind.

Assume your business is a success financially. Can your business survive an IRS audit? If so, you have built a smart business. If not, you may find yourself closing your doors.

Do you have a business license, liability insurance, and a good bookkeeping system to document all of your expense and sales? If so, you have built a smart business. If not, your new business could be classified a hobby and you risk losing everything.

The devil is in the details. And within the pages of this book you will discover exactly what you need to do to build a smart business rooted on solid ground that can withstand virtually any assault. Civil, judicial or legal.

Megan Hughes has helped thousands of new business owners set up and maintain the best business structure, paperwork and formalities needed to ensure success. She is a master of sorting and sifting through all the critical details required by all the various local, state and federal government agencies and provides you with a step-by-step blueprint to ensure your business is operating in good standing. She has helped me set up three distinct businesses and it's a comfort to know she has me covered.

Diane Kennedy, CPA is often referred to as the Millionaire's Mastermind. The go-to person of record for tax strategies that can make and save you a substantial amount of money and take your business to the next level. She has coached millionaires, brainstormed with millionaires and helped create millionaires. So Diane knows smart business, and you could not be in better hands than you are right now.

The strategies, skills and techniques you are about to learn have empowered the world's most successful business owners to achieve their dreams and now it is your turn. As you use these strategies, skills, and techniques, you will begin your journey with a new found confidence you can and will succeed because you are building a smart business. A business that will serve you versus being served by you.

Begin with the end in mind.

Are you seeking time and financial freedom?

Then do not become the technician in your new business. Hire people to produce the work. Create systems that can produce a result entirely independent of your active participation once established.

Are you seeking to create a multi-million dollar international business?

Then make sure you have the right business structure to support that growth and minimize your taxes. Make sure you study the intricacies of scaling up your business by leveraging the cash flow cycles within your industry.

Are you seeking to create a legacy you can pass along to future generations?

Then focus on building multiple streams of income. Don't build your business with one major customer and lots of vendors or a lot of customers with one major vendor. Because what happens if you lose the customer or the vendor? What happens if new technology reduces or completely eliminates the need for your primary product or services?

Think multiple markets. Multiple customers. Multiple products and multiple, very distinct sources of income.

Are you looking to build your business fast?

Then it is important that you only seek out mentors who are truly qualified in the business arena you intend to do battle. Bad advice is often worse than getting no advice. Yet good advice can be the springboard to a fortune.

Study the strategies, skills and techniques Diane and Megan are about to share with you as if your financial future depends on it. Because it does. It most certainly does.

Be blessed and great marketing,

Rob Fore
Six Figure Marketer
http://blog.robfore.com

Acknowledgements

We thank our clients who have taught us, the challenges that have molded us, and the changing laws that keep us on our toes.

Specifically, we thank Marco Carbajo and Cyndi Finkenbinder, CPA for their help with this book, Scott Bradley (Rapid Results Marketing Group, LLC), Rob Fore (Listech, Inc.), David Hancock (Morgan James Publishing) and Jorge Manzitti (LatAmConnect), who believed in the book and Eva Brunette (Apex Design) for her gorgeous designs.

Diane also gives a big 'thank you' for the continuing patience, love and support to hubby Richard and son David.

Megan thanks her family for their unconditional love and unwavering support, even when things get crazy.

Table of Contents

Section Four: Financial Statements Made Easy (and What You Can Do with that Knowledge)

Section Five: Advanced Tax & Asset Protection Strategies

Section Six: Make More Money, Pay Less Tax

Section Seven: The Next Stage

Introduction

I f you ask a dozen business owners why they started their first business, you'll hear a dozen different stories, but most stories boil down to just one overwhelming reason: They had no choice.

That first business might have been a way to put food on the table or to create some extra income for the family. It might have been an answer to an unexpected job loss. Or, it might have been because you couldn't stand one more day of being told what to do.

Every business owner has a story. Here are the stories of how we started our first businesses.

Diane's Story

My dad was a serial entrepreneur. Every few years, he moved our family to another small town in Oregon to work in a new business that he'd bought. The businesses were always failing before my dad got hold of them. He understood numbers. He also knew how to work hard, and he expected us to do the same.

My mom, dad, and I (and later my younger sister) all put in long days at the various businesses, mixing in school and a few social activities when we could.

My dad worked more than any of us. He was usually up and gone by 5 am, and we were lucky to see him by 9 pm for dinner. Eventually, he started taking two half days off per week. And, by the way, a week was 7 days, not 5.

My dad had his first heart attack before he was 40, and by 47, he had to retire. Luckily, he had always invested responsibly, and he was able to retire well.

I learned two things from my childhood: Owning your own business meant you had to work really hard, and, secondly, there had to be a better way.

So, I went to college, got my degree and my CPA certificate, and started working in public accounting. For some reason, I thought being a CPA meant shorter hours. I learned how crazy that plan was during my first tax season.

Eventually, I left to go to work for my biggest client: a master planned community in Reno. This took place at the end of the 1980's, when the ramifications of the 1986 Tax Reform Act had really hit real estate hard. The tax write-offs were largely gone, and the value of real estate had dropped. As property values dropped, mortgage holders defaulted and banks, primarily in the Southwest, folded.

I'll never forget the day that I heard that all of my employer's lines of credit had been frozen. Dropping values. No credit. Business looked bleak. And, personally? I'd just gone through a divorce, and I had been ordered to pay alimony to my ex-husband. Meanwhile, not only was there no net worth, but we were upside down. We owed more than we were worth, and I was given the sole responsibility on all of the debt.

It was clear my current plan wasn't working out too well. So, I took even more dramatic action. I quit my job. I bought a small tax practice, and I jumped into it with both feet, marketing like crazy and working day and night to fulfill on the business promises.

The business flourished. I made some powerful connections and learned, from my multi-multi-millionaire clients, important lessons on business building, investing, and the need for strategic thinking.

That was my first business, started back in 1991. Things rolled along until I found myself almost 2 decades later, having to re-invent myself.

I lost sight of my fundamental core competence in 2003. I let go of the CPA practice and took my attention off my tax education company to follow a business I was passionate about. It flourished, and I felt that I was doing important work in the world. Unfortunately, I had partners who didn't share my rather idealistic approach, so we parted.

In 2008, I started over again. And that meant, for me, the beginning of a business. It wasn't my first business. But it was my first business of a comeback.

"It's never too early, or too late, for a comeback."

Lessons:
- Owning your own business can be a lot of hard work in the beginning, but it's up to you whether that hard work continues.
- There are three types of business income:
  (1) Active: You work for the money.
  (2) Leveraged: You still need to work, but use others to fill in the gaps (getting you much higher value for your time).
  (3) Passive: Income that you don't need to work for at all.
- Stay true to your core competence.
- Don't ever sell your value short.
- It's never too late for a comeback.
- Never bring on a partner who doesn't share your stated values and that you could hire instead.
- "Don't let a hungry dog guard the smoke house." – Reverend Ike

Megan's Story

I grew up as a first-generation immigrant. My parents came from England. Growing up, my family was working middle-class. So, I grew up expecting to work hard for a living, for someone else. That was what I saw in my family, in the families of my friends, neighbors, and so on. I also figured that my hard work would be rewarded by employer loyalty, job security, and a good income.

Out of high school, I landed a position in the legal field. It turned out to be a great fit. Law appealed to my core values of justice and fair play. Over the next 20 years, I worked and educated myself from a junior legal secretary to a senior paralegal. My field was securities law, so I knew a lot about Wall Street. As a career employee, though, I didn't know very much about Main Street.

The summer of 2003 was my "summer of enlightenment." I was unexpectedly laid off. But, after I got over the initial feelings of hurt, betrayal, and fear, I started to look at it more like an opportunity than a curse. I had a couple of clients who wanted me to continue providing the same services as a freelancer. All those years as a paralegal had given me knowledge that I could leverage in a business as an independent service provider. In fact, there was nothing barring me from going into business for myself, other *than* myself.

So I did it. I figured, if things didn't work out, I could always go out and get another job.

Six years later, I'm still here. I've made a TON of mistakes. It's taken me a long time to learn to think like a business owner, instead of someone who is self-employed and has simply created her own job. It took time to learn how to manage a business budget and to make sure the daily things got done. It took time to learn how to grow my business effectively and where to concentrate my efforts. And it took time to learn that I didn't have to know everything to succeed.

I know a lot more about Main Street these days.

> "There's nothing barring you from going into
> business for yourself, other *than* yourself."

Document your first business story.
Every business has a story: What's yours?
Take a few minutes, and grab a pad of paper and pen. By the time you've finished this book, you'll have created systems, marketing copy, tax strategies, asset protection plans, a business valuation formula, and an exit strategy.

Now, write down your business story. This will be the story that others can relate to and that can go on to become part of your "business legend."

The Six Inches That Determine Whether This Book Will Be Valuable to You

Combined, we've worked with business owners for over 40 years. In that time, we've seen people who've gone on to succeed phenomenally well and those who've gone from failure to failure. We've also seen people experience a single failure and disappear, never to be heard from again.

What is the difference? It's just six inches, and no, this isn't a spam ad for an enhancement drug.

Six inches is the average width of a human head, from ear to ear. In other words, it's the size of your brain. But, in this case, we're not saying that success or failure is determined by how smart you are. Instead, we're saying it's determined by your mindset.

Starting a business takes a special type of person. You're going to have to make decisions based on sheer gut response sometimes. You're going to get some things right and some things wrong. In the early days, you're probably going to get lots of things wrong. So you'll need the discipline to go back and look at what worked and what didn't. The secret is to do more of what works and to stop doing what doesn't work.

There is no failure, only feedback.

Some of your mistakes may be excruciatingly painful. You might have to rebuild your company entirely with different marketing, products, services, fulfillment, and brand new employees. It takes drive and commitment to see things through to accomplish that.

It also takes a different kind of mindset. An entrepreneurial mindset is fundamentally different than the mindset of a good, albeit unhappy, employee. It's that mindset that makes the difference and it resides, or is created, in those all-important six inches.

You're also going to have to be ready for some hard work. While it is possible to get rich quick, it's rarely possible to get rich quick AND be lazy. Later, as your business matures, you'll be able to shift to passive income. But, in the beginning, you'll need at least one asset to start, and it usually boils down to one (or both) of two things: your time or your money.

Participation = Value

> In the beginning, business owners trade time for money. Later on, you can trade that money for time.

The hard work and a need to delay gratification are often the most critical differences between someone with an entrepreneurial mindset versus someone with an employee mindset. Later on, the ability to develop systems and build infrastructure will determine whether your business can turn the corner into leveraged and passive income. But, in the beginning, it's all about getting paid for what you do. Only, this time, you don't need to do it as an employee.

An Entrepreneurial Parable

There was a village that was at the bottom of a hill. At the top of the hill was a spring. Every day, the people of the village made the long trek up the hill to get water for the day. It was a long, hard walk, and it took the time that most people didn't have.

Three different men figured out a way to make money off of this opportunity.

The first man picked up two buckets and started trudging up the hill. He made the climb many times in the day, and every time he came back with his two buckets of water, he was able to sell them for a few cents.

He was an entrepreneur! He made his money by actively working in his business. He was rewarded immediately for each trip.

The second man picked up two buckets and started trudging up the hill as well. Then, he realized that he had 4 more buckets lying around. He could hire two other people to make the trip as well.

In the beginning, he walked with the other two people. Then, he realized that he could stay with the buckets at the bottom of the hill, build a little stand, pour the contents into sanitary bottles, and make more money. So he hired another guy to walk up the hill to replace himself. He made more money, plus he didn't have to make the trip himself. He hired younger people to make the trip so that they could travel faster.

He was an entrepreneur as well. He made his money by leveraging other people's time and abilities. He earned leveraged money.

The third man waited a little bit before he jumped into the water business. He studied the first and the second entrepreneur, and he realized there was still a high demand in the village for the water. People had money that they were willing to pay for the convenience of water. So he hired an engineer and a contractor who designed a pipeline from the spring. He hired the workers to build the pipeline.

He had to wait to get paid, and he actually had to invest his own money first in the pipeline. There was a risk, but if this paid off, he'd get paid every time somebody turned on a faucet.

Eventually, the pipeline was built. People signed up for the water. It was easier to get, and it was cheaper. The third man was also an entrepreneur, but he made all his money passively after first investing his time and money into the project.

There are three types of income: active, leveraged and passive. What kind of income are you building?

This book is written for those starting, or re-starting, a business. It's going to be basic for some, especially if you've been through it before. But it'll also include foundational information for those of you who've done it the old fashioned way, through the school of hard knocks, and feel like you may have missed out on some of the tricks. If you've ever wished you could get a tax and/or legal advisor who really "gets" what it means to be entrepreneurial, then you're going to love this book.

But not everyone feels that way. If you've got an employee mindset, where you want complete certainty and rock solid answers that everyone, including all tax courts, the IRS, your high school economics teacher and the neighbor next door, will agree on, then you're probably not going to like this book. In fact, we can almost guarantee it. You might want to consider saving yourself a lot of grief and ask for your money back right now.

Are you an Employee or an Entrepreneur-in-Waiting?

Are you currently an employee who yearns for the freedom and control of your own business? Check in with some of the classic differences between employee and entrepreneurial mindsets. If you're currently an employee who wants to build a business and the distinctions with employees make you uncomfortable, then that's great news. Congratulations! That means you don't WANT to fall into the employment trap.

Employee vs. Entrepreneurial Mindset	
Employee Mindset	**Entrepreneur Mindset**
• Short-term	• Long-term
• Works for a paycheck	• Works to build assets
• Instant gratification	• Delayed gratification
• Time-focused	• Value-focused*
• Company owns him/her	• He/She owns company
• Needs a job	• Creates jobs
• Commitment to paycheck	• Commitment to customer
• Wants to be protected	• Knows security is his responsibility
• Powerless	• Creates what he/she wants
• Waits for opportunity	• Creates opportunities
• Inflexible to changes	• Flexible
• Replaceable	• Unique
• Feels he/she is owed	• Knows reward comes from creating value

* Some entrepreneurs may sell their time by the hour, not by the value they create.

Now, let's get started!

Section One:
Getting Your Business Off to the Right Start

Chapter 1:
Why Your Own Business Is the Only Answer

How are you feeling about your current finances and your financial future these days? Stock prices are volatile. Real estate, after experiencing record declines, is, at best, uncertain. Pension plans are decimated. Employers are shedding jobs. Depending on your age bracket, you might be facing 25% or more unemployment rates. Where do you go when everything you believed in is letting you down?

For many of you, the answer is starting your own business. But, even if the only reason you're thinking of starting a business is the current economy, here's something to think about. The "work for someone else plan" never did work that well, even in the best of times.

The 5 Step Lies You Were Told

There's a 5 step financial life-story you may find familiar. It goes something like this: "Study, get a job, work hard, save, and retire." Yet, ironically, employee status only became desirable during the Industrial Revolution. Before that, people were small business owners: craftsmen, tradesmen, farmers, artisans, and professionals. There were no handouts. You weren't guaranteed anything. Success meant creating a product people wanted and doing it better than your competitors. In today's world, we've come full circle. We're going back there again.

Take a look at each of these 5 steps, first from an employee mindset and then from an entrepreneurial mindset.

The Five Lies You Were Told

Study, get a job, work hard, save, and retire. Those five steps are built upon this grand ideal that you should sacrifice everything so that someday you can retire in luxury, or at least not work so hard.

The truth is that those five steps are five lies. They aren't the steps to your fortune. They are simply the steps to becoming and staying an employee.

Employee Perspective	Employer Perspective
Study academics	Study practical applications
Get a job	Create jobs
Work hard	Work smart
Save	Invest
Retire	Create legacy

The reward at the end of all of this, for you as an employee, is a retirement that often means you settle for less than you had while you were working. Retirement on these terms means just making do. And that's if you get lucky. Look at how many retired people are now working for minimum wage as greeters at big chain stores or working at local fast food places.

In 1996, in the heart of our last economic boom, the Workplace Pulse[1] released its 4th annual study. It had surveyed a sample of workers, regarding their retirement plans. Most felt that they had put enough away for retirement. In actuality, less than 2% had. Think about that: when the economy was strong, over 98% of us were not ready for retirement. What do you think it looks like now, after the real estate bust and stock market meltdown have decimated personal fortunes?

In contrast, most entrepreneurs never retire. Instead, they learn how to maximize their skills to create leveraged and passive income. Entrepreneurs eventually can move to creating passive income solely as they build their legacies. They don't retire from making money; they just move on from having to work so much actively.

---

1   The telephone survey of 1,000 full-time workers was conducted Nov. 7-10 by Pulse Surveys of America Inc. for Colonial Life & Accident Insurance Co. and the Employers Council on Flexible Compensation.

It's a Brave New World

If you're an employee (or if you recently lost your job), you may already have found that the 5 step plan isn't the way to success, even in the best of times. But those aren't the only forces working against employees. To understand what those forces are, we'll have to look back a little into history.

In 1989, two very significant events occurred:

1. The Berlin Wall came down; and
2. The commercialized Internet was born.

The impact from those two seemingly unrelated occurrences continues to dramatically change how we live and how we work.

The Berlin Wall collapse was a very public symbol of the decline of the Eastern bloc communist nations. Within two years after the fall of this wall that divided Germany into two philosophically different nations, the entire Eastern bloc had collapsed. The Cold War between the then Soviet Union and the US was done. It was a final hurrah for a power struggle between sovereign nations.

In *The Sovereign Individual*, by James Dale Davidson and Lord William Rees-Mogg, the consequences and aftermath are clearly foretold as the world changed from Age to Age. We saw how dramatically the political and social climate changed as the Agrarian (Agricultural) Age gave way to the Industrial Age. During the Agrarian Age, the Church State was most powerful. In the Industrial Age, the Nation State became the domineering force. In the Information Age, which was born in 1989, the individual became sovereign. And in that year, 1989, the fall of the Nation State's extensive control began.

In the Information Age, innovators have begun to move beyond geographic constraints. Businesses are no longer bound by international boundaries. If you don't like the tax system where your internet company is based, move it! It might be as simple as switching servers and hosting companies over a long weekend. And, voila! You are no longer under the power and control of a country.

The world's nations will react to these changes no differently than you would. Let's say you're holding a precious vase. You feel it slipping through your fingers. What do you do? You grab on tighter. That's a basic instinct. If you feel something you're holding start to slip, your natural reaction is to grab more tightly. And that's exactly what is happening in countries around the world. Governments are watching businesses move to more economically and politically friendly climates. They're seeing declining tax revenues, so they're grabbing on tighter.

If you have a US-based business, you're not hearing anything new. You've felt it yourself in the increased tax rates, larger tax base, and the overreaching of neighboring states. All of them have two goals: your wallet and nailing you down so you can't move your business elsewhere.

But, even as governments try to hang on to you and the tax you pay, you also have an unprecedented opportunity to create new streams of income in a different way. You can set up income to be earned in other states and even other countries.

In *Smart Business Stupid Business*, we'll show you how you can take charge of your income and how you can actually decide where you pay tax, how much, and when.

The job controls an employee (or someone with an employee mindset). The entrepreneur (or someone with an entrepreneur mindset) controls the job.

Economic Changes

How we make money and how countries tax that income is changing. And, perhaps even more personally impactful to you, the economy has been running the boom-bust trend in shorter time cycles.

When the economy, and especially real estate, was booming, there was a saying that "a rising tide raises all boats." It was easy to make money through business and real estate. People got to the point where they even felt they were entitled to easy money and that it would always be there.

And then it wasn't.

The economy, just like the tide, went out, and for a while, it looked like there was nothing left. But, if you look closely, there is still life. In fact, some of our clients are prospering in unprecedented ways. Some have businesses that work best in down markets, others have made use of new technology to reach new markets, reduce costs, and increase efficiency. All of us have less competition. The marginal business with poor practices is gone.

The economy didn't destroy business. It revealed business: its challenges and its opportunities.

The economic downturn also revealed that it has never been more important to pay attention to the numbers of your business.

Smart Business or Stupid Business?

There are two kinds of money problems that you can have with your business: Too much money and not enough money. In a rapidly growing economy, it's sometimes too easy to make money. Systems get lax, because if you waste a little, it doesn't matter. Employees get lazy because the owners are too busy to really pay attention to what they are doing. The money is too easy, and it's very tempting to get sloppy.

In an economic downturn, the reality of the business is revealed. If there are no real economic projections or financial check-ups, the business will probably crash. You've lost all the easy money flow that covered the multitude of sins.

An economic upturn can bring huge opportunities and a chance to build something fast. An economic downturn can bring much cheaper resources and less competition. A smart business prospers in either economic climate. It's built on solid fundamentals and the ability to quickly adapt with good information

---

Too Busy to Save Money

Diane is a CPA, but is better known as a Tax Strategist because she saves her business clients so much tax money.

When the economy was going non-stop, one of Diane's new clients was making money hand over fist. It was the end of 2007 and she had to make some changes to her tax structures before year-end or face some pretty dire tax consequences. Diane and her staff called the client at least a dozen times, trying to schedule the time to talk about what needed to happen. She never made the time.

One phone call and signing a few forms could have saved her $100,000 in taxes. And she knew it. Her answer? I can make that amount of money in less time than it would take me to save it.

Now that the economy has slowed, that statement seems really outrageous. But that's the risk of over inflated economic surges! All businesses make money. Stupid businesses make money. Smart businesses make money.

Smart Business often acts opposite of what you think are normal trends. When the economy is great and making money is easy, it's the time to save. When the economy is slow, it's time to spend and invest in the business.

Make More Money or Pay Less Tax?

Every dollar you save in taxes is worth more than a dollar you earn. Here's why:

Earn $100, pay $30 in taxes.	You have $70.
Save $100 in taxes.	You have $100.

When given the choice to "make more money" or "pay less tax", choose both! Tax savings is money that goes directly in your pocket.

But maybe it's not concerns about your financial future, the economy, or global changes, making your job obsolete that have you concerned. Maybe you've simply had it with working for someone else.

True freedom and security can only come from your own business. You're even going to get an unexpected surprise when you start your business and start paying attention to the bottom-line. You're going to have a lot more to show for it after the tax man is done!

A business owner will always pay less tax than an employee.

Whatever your personal reasons for picking this book up may be, we're glad you did. If you have a business, we can save you taxes, help you protect your assets, and learn what's next for building your business.

Action Steps

Action Step 1: Often the things that stop us are the things we don't even think about. What have you been told about business? In this exercise, you'll need to complete the sentence quickly. Don't stop and think or rationalize. Grab your Smart Business notebook, and write down this phrase 10 times:

A business is: _____.

Now complete the sentence as quickly as you can. Don't think, just write. Some of the answers might seem crazy, but that's okay.

Now go back and look at your answers. What trends do you see? Are your answers more positive or more negative? What is your biggest fear? What is your biggest dream?

Write down the three things you want to either avoid with your business or achieve with your business. What do you want your business to stand for? And what do you want it to never stand for?

(1)

(2)

(3)

Resources

Grabhorn, Lynn. 2003. *Excuse Me, Your Life is Waiting.* Hampton Roads Publishing; 1st Trade Paper Ed edition

Hill, Napoleon. 2004. *Think and Grow Rich.* Aventine Press

Kiyosaki, Robert. 2000. *Rich Dad Poor Dad.* Warner Press.

Robbins, Anthony. 1992. *Awaken the Giant Within : How to Take Immediate Control of Your Mental, Emotional, Physical and Financial Destiny!* 1992. Free Press

Tolle, Eckhart. 2004. *The Power of Now.* New World Library

And for those who want to take it up a notch or ten, go to www.MySmarterBusiness.com and receive a special introductory offer when you click through to investigate 'Frontier Trainings'–a great business training program. You can find Diane, Richard, and their son David at most of the events.

Chapter 2:
Creating Meaning with Your Business

Y ou might have picked up this book because you wanted the nuts and bolts or the "how to" of accounting, business structures, and tax strategies. We'll get there, but this chapter isn't it.

This chapter isn't about the "how." It's about the "why." You'll find there are days when you question whether you want to stay in business (and maybe even question your sanity) and why you left your safe, secure job for the ups and downs of running your own business. There are plenty of glowing stories about the good times of having a small business, but not that many about the tough times.

Do you have a story that is more about the meaning of your business? Why do you have a business instead of a job?

During the hard times, you need to remember what it really means to you to have the freedom to determine your own course and to make a difference in other people's lives.

And, during the good times, it's even more important. That's because you'll be hit with so many choices that you might be tempted to chase the next shiny nickel.

The challenge for the Smart Business owner is not lack of opportunity, it's choking on opportunity.

So take a minute and think about the meaning that is behind what you're doing.

Why do you want your own business?

We've asked our clients that same question. Here are some of their answers:

- I get to choose when and how much I work. (Freedom of time)
- I am building something to leave to my children. (Legacy)
- I am doing what I'm passionate about. (Emotional connection)
- I am making more money than I could by working for someone else. (Financial freedom)
- No one is telling me what to do. (Independence)
- I enjoy the freedom of delivering a service in my own way. (Independence)
- I like the challenge of building something that is mine. (Accomplishment)
- My skills and knowledge are now benefiting me and my clients, rather than my employer. (Building a future)
- I like knowing that I'm setting a positive example for my children. (Legacy)
- I wanted to prove to myself that I could do it. (Confidence)
- No-one else was doing what I wanted to do, and I saw an opportunity. (Visionary)
- I wanted a way to work AND to watch my children grow up. (Freedom of time)
- I was tired of punching a clock. (Control)
- I was tired of other people taking credit for my work and my ideas. (Impact)

Take a minute and think about why you want a business. In fact, better yet, grab the notebook that you are using to journal in as you work through this book.

Write down the top three reasons why you want your own business. Or, if you're questioning that yourself right now, what were the top three reasons why you wanted it before?

In the next chapter, we're going to get into the e-center of your business. That's the intersection where (1) What you do best (Entrepreneurial Abilities), (2) What you are passionate about (Emotional Charge), and (3) What your customers want and need (Economic Marketplace), all meet.

Your Business eCenter

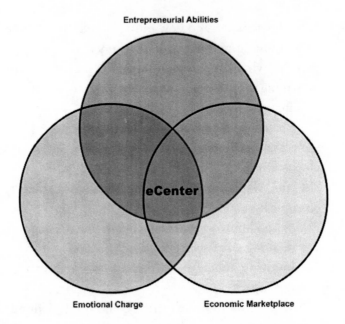

Without these three things, you'll struggle with the ability to keep going when times are tough. If the business is hard, and you hit a rough spot, you might question whether you even want to keep going with it. Wouldn't it be easier to just get a job and forget all this? That's the real reason most businesses fail. The owners just get tired, and they give up.

Without passion and meaning, you'll also struggle when times are good.

Stop a minute, and read that sentence again.

You will struggle just as much when times are **good** as when they are bad, unless you have <u>passion and meaning</u> in your business.

Without passion and meaning, you could find yourself in one of the traps that stop business owners cold. When business is too easy, you might find yourself asking, "Is this all there is?" You might look for meaning by trying to find out what's next, instead of paying attention to the business you have. Or, you might sabotage your business with unnecessary changes, just for the thrill of building again.

In both cases, the solution to keeping your Smart Business on track is the same. It's getting in touch with your own "why" for your business.

If your purpose with your business is bigger than you are, then you will survive both the good times and the tough times as well.

What does business mean for you? What is the "why" behind what you do? We call that your business vision.

Vision-Mission-Values

Vision

> ## Diane's Story
>
> A little over 10 years ago, I went through an intensive, one-on-one business training with Renie Cavallari, a corporate strategist extraordinaire. It was brutal, but enlightening.
>
> Over 10 years later, I still follow the processes she taught me, with a little refinement that's come over time, of working the system.
>
> I've found the "why" of my business and my passion.

Your business vision is the "why" that will sustain you through the rough patches.

Diane's Vision: To empower individuals to maximize their net worth.

Mission

The more clearly you can define and talk about what your business is, the more focused your business will be.

Your business mission is the "what" that defines what your business is.

The mission of your business is the "what" of your business. There is a famous story about the importance of having a clear mission statement:

During the Tylenol® scares of 1982, Johnson & Johnson, the company that makes Tylenol, held an emergency meeting.

Someone had tampered with their product. People were dying from the contaminated pills. But, if they stopped production and pulled back their entire inventory, they would face financial ruin. How could they handle this crisis as prudent business leaders?

Someone pointed to the mission statement on the wall, which basically said: Put the needs and well-being of the people we serve first.

Johnson & Johnson had no choice. To honor their mission statement, the "what" of what they do, they had to pull their inventory. They had to protect human life. If they betrayed their mission, their business would be gone ultimately anyway.

Today, Johnson & Johnson is still around. Lives were saved. Tylenol is still one of the best-selling over-the-counter drugs in the country. The Johnson & Johnson campaign is legendary in marketing circles, and it is widely seen as one of the most effective PR campaigns in history.

If someone tells you, "It's nothing personal. It's just business" then they don't understand business. If you're doing it right, business is always personal.

What does your business do? State your business mission clearly so that your employees, vendors, and customers understand who you are and what you do.

> USATaxAid Mission: Provide tax education in plain language through coaching, books, teleseminars, and home study courses that teach clear cut legal tax strategies to reduce taxes.

You may have one central theme for your vision with multiple businesses supporting it.

Keep the focus clear for your business and investments. Stick to one vision that all businesses support.

> USTaxAid Services Mission: Customized cutting edge tax strategies, plan development, implementation, and tax preparation that give clients massive ROI. (Return on Investment)

> High Touch Marketing System Mission: Provide easy and affordable systems to grow businesses fast.

DianeKennedyOnline.com: This isn't a company, per se, but a website with Diane's identity as a tax communicator and business builder who is actively involved in community and family.

Megan's Business

I work in an industry that is filled with misinformation and outright falsehoods. It was vital to me that my company maintains solid ethics that stand for honesty, quality of service, and accurate information. My company's mission is to provide quality service and quality information at a fair and reasonable price. There are no gimmicks, games, and strategies that don't add value to a client's business.

Does your business support your one big vision?

Values

Values are the "how" of what you do. If you've ever struggled with the idea of how you'll handle growth and the stepping away from the day to day routine, worried that customer service may falter and your company may become something different, then you need to look at the values you have for your company.

If you don't clearly communicate these values, you can't expect others to follow them. In the absence of a value-driven leadership, there will be other leaders that emerge with agendas and values of their own.

Take the time to write out these values, and then come back to them every year or so. You'll find that there are certain core values that are always important to you, and you will take those from one business start-up to the next business start-up. They will become part of the essence of who you are as an entrepreneur.

Diane's Company Values

- Tell the truth in a helpful and empowering way
- Deliver more than we promise
- Positively impact others
- Inspire customer confidence
- Say "please and thank you." Be polite
- Make only agreements we intend to keep
- Answer or acknowledge all requests within 1 business day
- Admit and correct mistakes quickly
- When problems arise, first look to the system, then go directly to the source and look for the solution
- Honor, validate, and support the brand, vision, mission, values, and team
- Take responsibility for completing your own communication
- Commit to on-going personal growth and financial education

It's very tempting in the beginning of a new venture to just dive in headfirst. There will be a hundred distractions and emergencies in the early days.

But, without a vision, you will fragment and start a dozen things. They'll all become greedy little children, wanting every bit of your attention.

Without a mission, your business will wander; seizing on every new opportunity, you will spend your days chasing shiny nickels.

Without a stated value system, you won't get to choose what your corporate culture will be. In that void, someone will always step in and decide for you. And, most likely, you probably won't like the results.

"Those who think, govern those who labor" – Marshall Sylver

Action Steps
Action Step 1: What are the three biggest reasons for why you started (or want to start) your business?

1.
2.
3.

Action Step 2: Go through the exercise in Chapter 2 to create your own Vision, Mission, and Values Statements. List them here:

Vision Statement:

Mission Statement:

Values Statement:

Now consider all the places you can use these statements to make them come alive in your business. You probably want to post them on a wall, a website, or your employee manual. You may even want to include them in service contracts for your clients or service providers.

How can you make these statements an integral part of your business as it grows?

Resources

www.ManagementHelp.org: This website provides one of the world's largest collection of resources regarding the leadership and management of you, other individuals, groups and organizations.

http://www.managementlogs.com: Another resource website, this one features links to over 30 different discussion forums on a wide range of management topics.

Register your book at www.MySmarterBusiness.com with the special registration code found in the Bonus section of this book. You can sign up for 3 FREE courses on topics that will make your Smart Business even better.

Chapter 3:
Setting Up Your Business to Win Big

We asked our most highly successful clients what made their first business a success. They identified these seven traits:

- Passion
- Hard work
- Perseverance
- Persistence
- Not accepting, "I can't"
- Listening to your customers
- Connecting with others

First on the list was passion, but that's not enough by itself to be successful. There are plenty of people wandering the streets who are passionate about something, yet no one is giving them any money for that passion.

There are actually three key ingredients to finding that sweet spot in the market where making money becomes effortless: Your Entrepreneurial Abilities, Your Emotional Charge, and the Economics of Your Marketplace.

When you find that sweet spot where all three intersect, you can focus on that spot as the core competency of your business. There, you'll be able to find that your work days feel like play while the money rolls in. It's only when you forget one of those three key ingredients that your business will feel like drudgery or that you are always struggling for money.

Finding Your Business's eCenter

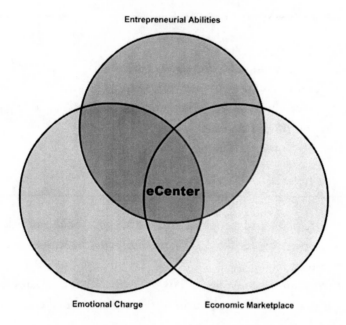

Finding Your e-Center

Your Entrepreneurial Abilities: What can you do best in the world?
First, what is it that you do that you do extraordinarily well? Or, what is something that you could be phenomenal at with some practice and training? In *Good to Great*, author Jim Collins referred to this entrepreneurial quality as being the "best in the world." That's probably the best definition that there is.

What do you, and your company, do that is best in the world? Where do your unique talents and abilities lie? What are the things that you do, or your company does, that others notice as extraordinary and different from the average, run of the mill accomplishments?

If you don't know what that is, or what that could be, here's an exercise to help you to get started.

Identify 10 people that you work with or who have been customers in the past. Then, simply ask them. You might be surprised by the response that you get back.

Here's a sample letter or email that you can send:

> Dear XXX,
>
> I'm going through an exercise as part of Smart Business Stupid Business, and I could really use your help.
>
> As you've observed me in my current business (or at my job), what do you think I do best?
>
> Thank you for your help.
>
> Warmest regards,

That's it, plain and simple. Don't be afraid. You're not asking for criticism or negative feedback. We predict you'll be astounded by the positive results.

As the responses come back, look at them. What resonates for you? What is it that you and your business do that could make you the best in the world?

Your Emotional Charge: What are you passionate about?

Now, look at what you're passionate about. It's okay if it's something wildly different from the items in your Entrepreneurial Abilities circle. Passion isn't a mild, "I like doing this." Passion is jumping out of bed, alive every morning, excited to be doing the work you're doing. Passion is knowing that what you do is important to you and to others as well.

Have you ever had a day where you worked really hard, yet you had more energy at the end of the day than you did when you started? That's the type of passion that we're talking about. What is it that gives you that kind of fire? What are you passionate about?

> ### Megan's Story
>
> I know it may sound goofy in this day and age, but I love the law. I love the tradition behind it, and I love what it stands for: justice. If we don't have justice in our society, then we have nothing. And, if we can't trust in our justice system, then we have worse than nothing. But it's a complex system, and it's not always easy to understand.

There are people out there who know that and who make a living out of twisting the law to suit themselves. Their actions pollute our perception of law and people in it, and I really hate that.

So, when I see scams being perpetuated on business owners, it makes me angry. In my business, I see it ALL the time. One of the things I love blogging about is how you can spot the scams and not be taken in by them.

Not too long ago, I wrote about a company that was sending out bogus notices to business owners. I got a huge response. Thousands of people read the blog entry, and hundreds have commented or emailed, saying that they had received the notice, were about to pay, but found my blog entry first.

Every single one of those comments put a smile on my face. I may be a romantic idealist, but any time that I can help people to keep money in their pockets, it's a good day.

Your Economic Marketplace:
What do your customers want and need?

There are books on the marketplace that will tell you that if you simply do what you love, you'll get rich. The problem with that is, no matter how much you love it, if you can't convince your prospective customers that you can give them something they want or need, nobody's going to buy it.

It's possible to create marketing campaigns that build demand for something brand new. For example, who knew you would need a Pet Rock˚, until Gary Dahl told us about them in 1975? Or for that matter, who had even heard of an iPod˚ or the concept of one, prior to 2001?

In both cases, though, there was a human need or want that was just waiting to be fulfilled.

The easiest way to sell something is to offer a solution for something that people already know they need or want. In other words, you don't have to spend as much money building the demand. You may have to work at getting the word out about your product or service, but at least you don't have to explain to people why they need your solution.

As you look at your Entrepreneurial circle and your Emotional circle, what do you see that intersects? How can this be turned into a product or service that customers want or need?

Find the spot where your Entrepreneurial Abilities, Emotional Charge, and Economic Marketplace intersect. That's the Sweet Spot of your business.

There are three strategies, once you have identified the Sweet Spot, for your business:

Sweet Spot Strategy #1: Keep your business focused. Use the Sweet Spot as your business's focus. If your business gets off that spot, your financial numbers will show it. Continue to fulfill within that one spot, and you'll prosper. Remember, you only need to focus on three things:

1. Entrepreneurial Abilities: What do you do best in the world?
2. Emotional Charge: What are you passionate about?
3. Economic Marketplace: What do your customers want and need?

Sweet Spot Strategy #2: Keep yourself focused. It's said that it takes 10,000 hours to master a skill or subject. Once you have that mastery, there are dozens of strategies to create products and services that your customers want and need.

For example, Diane is a CPA/Tax Strategist. In the beginning, she had clients that she worked with one-on-one. Today, she still does. Only now, years later, the number of clients she chooses is much smaller. And, Diane's time is expensive because they get unlimited consultation time. For others, there are still services available that are custom-tailored to their needs. For still others, they want coaching, not consultation, so that they can do-it-themselves with some guidance. Diane's company does all of that. She provides books like this one, online study guides, webinars, live seminars, free teleseminars, and the list goes on.

Diane has a lot of companies and a lot of different products and services, yet all are staying inside that sweet spot.

That's because when you're doing what you're good at, what you're passionate about, and what your customers want and need, there is an abundance of wealth, fun, and good that you can accomplish in the world.

Sweet Spot #3: Create synergy. Quite frequently, we see new clients making the fatal mistake of "I can do it all!" For example, let's say that you start a business selling products online, and then you decide to get involved in a network marketing juice company. Oh, and then how about selling a prepaid service company through another network marketing opportunity? And wait, there is affiliate marketing, too! Oh, and you read that the real estate crash had created some great buying opportunities for buying and flipping. Plus, you'll want to hang on to a few and become a landlord extraordinaire.

The problem with all of this is that you're going in too many different directions. You'll likely find yourself flitting from one project to another, trying to keep all the balls up in the air. Every so often, one will fall and hit you in the head, but as long as it's not a bowling ball, you reason, you'll be okay.

You're quite likely to succeed with one of the businesses. You may be able to succeed with a few of the businesses. But you're not going to succeed with all of them. However, you will have worked yourself to death and distanced yourself from friends and family. That's because you simply don't have enough time to accomplish everything.

You will also have lost the opportunity of the biggest benefit of all when you use the e-Center Sweet Spot strategies. You will have lost the ability to have synergy within your e-Center.

For example, let's say that you currently work as a consultant. You provide a service, and you probably have a specialty. In fact, it's because of that specialty that people hire you. That means that you have information other people want. You could write articles, a book, host a seminar, or even host a webinar about what you do. You could find other services and products that your clients need and that align with the vision you have for your businesses. And you could make a little bit of money from each of those items.

Even better (because remember we are all about saving you taxes), you're going to discover how those little bits of money here and there can wind up being a huge tax strategy later on.

Make more money, pay less tax. That's our goal for you.

Action Steps

Action Step 1: What are your Entrepreneurial Abilities? What is it that you do better than anyone else?

Action Step 2: What makes you want to jump out of bed in the morning, excited to take on the day? Where do you get your Emotional Charge? If it's been awhile since you've felt that way about your business, think back. When did you have that feeling, and what was it that you were doing that made it so exciting then?

Action Step 3: What is your Economic Marketplace? What do your customers want and need? What problems are you solving for your customer? What further needs do they have that you can take care of?

Action Step 4: Look back through the previous Action Items. Where is your business' e-Center?

BONUS: What do you want to focus on to grow your business? Is your business working in areas that are outside its e-Center?

Resources

Collins, Jim. 2001. *Good to Great*. Harper Business.

www.sba.gov: The US Small Business Association is an excellent resource center for new business owners, with coaching, information on business loans and financing, and much more.

www.asbdc-us.org/: The American Small Business Development Center Network helps new entrepreneurs realize their dream of business ownership, and to assist existing businesses to remain competitive in the complex marketplace of an ever-changing global economy.

Are you ready to take it up a notch? One of the strategies that big businesses use to keep their businesses on the leading edge is to bring in top talent for their board of directors. A mastermind can give you the same results.

When you go to www.MySmarterBusiness.com to register your book, you'll receive a free online workshop full of tips for forming and running your own mastermind group.

And, as a special thank you for being part of the Smart Business community, you can also download your own copy of Business Alchemy™. This game has been used at Diane's live events, and it is always fun. You'll learn what is most important to you and your business and create a fantastic mastermind as an added bonus.

Section Two: Eliminate the Biggest Risks to Your Business Right from the Start

Chapter 4:
Does the IRS Know You're a Business?

The title of this chapter, "Does the IRS Know You're a Business?" might invoke a powerful response. In fact, we run into people all the time that answer, "I hope not!"

Although that's an understandable sentiment, in this chapter, we're going to look at why you want the IRS to know you're a business and, then, how you go about making that happen.

Believe it or not, the IRS is not a particular threat or risk to your business.

The three biggest risks to your first business are (1) not knowing your business, (2) lack of cash flow, and (3) other people's bad intentions.

If you're truly operating your business as a business, it can be quite beneficial to avoid those three risks.

When it comes to profit and your business, one of three things is going to happen:

(1) You're going to make money;

(2) You're going to lose money; or

(3) You're going to break even.

If you make money, the IRS will be happy to take your money. If that's the case for your business, this chapter is going to be less significant for you.

If you break even, the IRS may want to make sure you really did take all of the business's deductions correctly, but generally, they're happy with that too.

But, if your business loses money, and you take that loss against other income on your tax return, the IRS is going to want to make sure you really do have a business. This chapter is for you.

If your business continually has a loss, the IRS may determine you don't have a business. Instead, they will determine you have a hobby. Having a hobby business means that you pay tax if you make income, but if your business loses money, you can't take that loss against other income.

Does the IRS know you're a business? If the answer is "yes", you'll save on taxes.

So, if you have a loss for your business, be prepared to prove that it is a real business. This is especially true if you're involved in something like dog breeding, horse training, sponsoring race cars, or even a network marketing company. Those are some of the industries that have abused the business loss rules in the past, and the IRS now looks closely at them[2].

If you have a loss, it's up to you to prove you have a real business. Don't assume the IRS is going to help you.

You might have heard that you need to show income for 3 out of 5 years for your business. This is just one test. If you pass this, the chances are good that you won't have a problem with the IRS.

But, just because you have a loss for more years than that, don't assume that you can't pass the IRS test. After all, consider Amazon. com. That company was started in 1995 and lost millions each year, before posting its first-ever profit in the 4th quarter of 2002. Yet the IRS never questioned those huge losses, year after year. Why?

Amazon was run like a business with a clearly defined profit-purpose.

Here are the 9 factors that IRS will use to assess your business. Next to each item, we'll give you tips on what you need to pass this part of the test.

1. **You carry on the activity in a businesslike manner.** That means having a separate company bank account and taking it seriously. Don't use the company's account as your own piggy bank when you need some extra cash. Keep your accounting

---

2   When you register your book at www.MySmarterBusiness.com, you will be able to download a list of business types that are currently being scrutinized by the IRS.

records and business paperwork separate in some kind of filing system. Take your business's debts and receivables seriously. It's hard to tell the IRS your business is taking losses when you aren't making any effort to collect debts that are owed to it.

Each business owner is going to maintain his own books and records in a way that's congruent to his own business style. The IRS even admits that in their audit instructions to their auditors. They also know that if you're serious about business you need financial statements that tell you how your business is going, whether you're making any money and what changes you should make to improve your business.

These are red flags for the IRS:

- Not maintaining a separate business checking account
- Not maintaining a log tracking business miles driven
- Inability to determine success of business
- Customer files not maintained
- Continued expenditures in activities that show little or no profit potential (such as craft shows and exhibitions)
- Bartering transactions

2. **The time and effort you put into the activity indicate you intend to make it profitable.** With this factor, the goal is to keep a record of the time you are spending in the business. Some people keep a time card, or record their weekly activities. A schedule of business appointments is very helpful here, along with notes of conversations or other communications with clients. It's also a great idea to keep documentation of your communications with people who can help you to grow or improve your business such as your lawyers, CPAs, business builders, marketing experts, and so on. Plus, if you are attending night school classes or other education activities, like seminars, keep records of what you have done and when you've done them.

3. **When trying to combine business with pleasure, remember that making money IS part of the plan! You depend on income from the activity for your livelihood.** This one is going to be different for everyone. In the early days, you may have a day job and are starting a business on the side. You're not necessarily going

to factor that income into your living expense budget because it will probably be irregular. But, as your business matures and the income stream becomes more and more dependable, it will begin to factor into your budget. Hopefully, there will even come a point where you leave your job and depend entirely on the income from your business (or businesses).

The IRS is okay if you have a job in addition to your business. They want to know how you're spending time and that you ARE spending productive time on your business. Here are some question the IRS auditor is likely to ask you:

Do you know how the use of your time is helping your business? In other words, what is your personal return on investment (personal ROI)?

Do you determine what activities you should keep doing and which ones you should stop? Do you ride the winners and cut the losers?

Are you working at growing your business?

4. **Your losses are due to circumstances beyond your control (or are normal in the startup phase of your type of business).** Remember, it's okay to have a loss, as long as you can provide a reasonable explanation. What the IRS wants to see here is documentation and an explanation. Are these losses typical for your business industry? Have others experienced the same types of losses? What have you tried to do to offset the losses?

5. **You change your methods of operation in an attempt to improve profitability.** This factor goes hand-in-hand with #4, especially if you have losses for several years in a row. There comes a point where the IRS is going to take a look at what you're doing to improve your business. Improvement may be attained by engaging business consultants or other experts to help you better your business, or it may be a demonstration of self-education, like buying business books, attending seminars, and the like.

Losing money in business is okay. Losing money for years is okay. Losing money for years + no effort to improve = not okay.

6. **You, or your advisors, have the knowledge needed to carry on the activity as a successful business.** This is a factor that gets more important as time passes. There comes a point where talking things over with a beer with your neighbor, who has no experience in your field, doesn't qualify as self-education. If you don't have experience in your field and your business continually loses money, you need to get yourself to an experienced advisor for help.

Fishing for a Deduction, but Coming Up Empty

There was a taxpayer who loved to fish. He wanted to combine his love of fishing with a business opportunity. So, he began putting himself out there as a professional sports fisherman. He bought an expensive boat and fishing equipment, and he attended all the tournaments he could.

Unfortunately, he wasn't very good at competitive fishing. After 3 or 4 years of reporting losses in the $30,000-$40,000 range each year, the IRS pulled his returns for review. They noted that he didn't keep any type of business records for his fishing activities, and he had never tried to improve his technique by working with other fishing sportsmen or guides. He had never won a tournament or even placed in the top 20 in a tournament. He had no sponsors. When the IRS added it all up, they found a guy who liked to fish. An enjoyable pastime, yes. Deductible business expenses, no.

The IRS wants to see that you have taken actions to become profitable. They want to know that you've adjusted your business with an intention to increase sales, decrease expenses, or both. If your business is selected for audit, expect the IRS auditor to ask you for specifics on what you've done to improve your business.

The IRS does allow you a 'get out of jail free card' under IRC Section 183(d) applies. You may file Form 5213, Election to Postpone Determination, if an activity has not been carried on for a 5-year period. The IRS will generally postpone its determination of whether your business is engaged in for profit and will not restrict deductions during the 5-year period.

In order to take advantage of this election, Form 5213 must be filed within 3 years after the due date of the return for the first year of the activity, or, if earlier, within 60 days after the IRS issues a written notice proposing to disallow deductions attributable to the activity. Filing the form automatically extends the period of limitations for tax assessment on any year in the 5-year period until 2 years after the due date of the return for the last year of the period. The period is extended only for deductions attributable to the activity and any deductions that are affected by changes made to adjusted gross income.

7. **You were successful in making a profit in similar activities in the past.** This one can be applied in different ways. For example, did you (or do you plan to) leave a job to provide the same service on your own? If you worked for a successful company, you can use many of the same methods to demonstrate an attempt to be profitable. If you have run other businesses before, and those businesses have succeeded, you've got a great argument that you know what you're doing. And, if you've never run a business before, then you'll need to pay more attention to Factors 2, 5, and 6, by trying to learn and getting help from others who have relevant experience.

8. **The activity makes a profit in some years (how much profit it makes is also considered).** Good years and bad years are normal, especially in the early days. What the IRS is looking for here is evidence of efforts being made in the down years. They're also looking to see that the profit you make in the good years is reasonable. Is the profit in the good years enough to make running the business in the bad years something the average person would consider? (This is where those with passion and not much else often get trapped).

The difference between a business and a hobby is intent. If your intent is to make money, you've got a business.

9. **You can expect to make a future profit from the appreciation of the assets used in the activity.** Ahh, the payoff. In this case, there is evidence of something coming. Can the company be positioned to go public? Does it look like a company someone else would want to acquire and sink money into? If it's real estate, is there a market for the land or buildings? Is it a company with a product about to go to market and has a good expectation of profitable sales?

The type of business activity and the taxpayer will dictate which factors are more important in relation to each other. Factors 1, 3, 6, and 8 are generally dominant, Factors 2, 5, and 9 less important, and Factor 4 will rarely come into play. Factor 7 (amount of occasional profits) deserves special note and applies in all situations.

These questions are applicable only when you have a business that is continuing to run at a loss, particularly if there is other income that is high. It doesn't mean you don't have a business, it just means that you might have to prove you do.

When Do You Have to Report Business Income?

At the other end of the spectrum, you may have a few sales from an outside activity and wonder when you have to report them on your tax return.

For example, let's say you inherited Great Aunt Betsy's attic full of treasures and/or trash. You sell some of it at a garage sale, some of it on eBay® and the rest you give away to a local charity. Does that mean you have a business?

If it's a one-time sale, you don't have anything taxable to report. If you had a sale to report, you'd have an offsetting expense for the cost of the item. Since you inherited Great Aunt Betsy's stuff, you get to take a step-up in basis. That means the basis is what the value is. The value is what you sell it for. So, the basis equals the value.

The same thing is true if you clean out your garage and put your own treasures and/or trash for sale. The basis of the items will be equal to their current value if you had purchased them personally first.

At some point, you may decide that this is a great way to start your own business. There isn't any bright line definition of when you go from selling a few personal items to having a business. The federal government will require merchant account providers like PayPal to report any sellers who sell over $20,000 per year starting in 2011.

Another way to look at this, though, is not "When do I have to start reporting my business?" Instead, ask yourself, "When do I get to start reporting my business?" That's because if you truly have a business, and not a hobby, you'll get to take deductions that reduce your taxable income.

Business today, less tax tomorrow. Just make sure the IRS agrees you have a business.

Action Steps

Action Step 1: If your business has a taxable loss, go through the Nine Factors. List all that could be a concern.

Action Step 2: Review this list with your tax expert. How can you make a solid case?

Action Step 3: Even if your business is, and has been, profitable, go through the Nine Factor list. Are there any suggestions that could make your business stronger?

Resources

IRS Audit Guides. You can search for them at www.irs.gov, or we have the information at www.MySmarterBusiness.com when you register your book.

Smart Business, Stupid Business: Chapter 11: All You Need to Know About Bookkeeping and Record Keeping from Day One
Smart Business, Stupid Business: Chapter 12: You Can't Keep Good Books without Good Records
Ilasco, Meg Mateo. 2007. *Craft, Inc.: Turn Your Creative Hobby into a Business*. Chronicle Books.

Chapter 5:
Cash flow Needs Throughout Your Business Lifecycle

It's easy to get caught up in the excitement of your business, especially in the beginning. And it's tempting to ignore the numbers. As long as the customers are flooding in, they are happy, and there is money in the bank then life is good.

That's the trap of the economic good times. You can get lulled into not thinking about the fundamentals of your business. When times are bad, you need good reporting and cash. And when times are good, you need it even more.

Your business has cash flow needs based on where it is in the normal business lifecycle. Every new project, new location, and even every ad campaign effects your cash.

Now imagine you had a way to know what the outcome of every decision was. You'd know which project would succeed and which would fail.

If you can't have that, how about if you had a way to know that your business was prepared for the worst case and the best case? That's what a good business projection can do for you. A business projection is part science and part skill. And that skill depends on you and your abilities to accurately assess the impact of possible scenarios. It's a skill that you can develop over time, and one that you will especially need as your business grows beyond its beginnings.

The better the projections are, the stronger the company will be.

Creating Business Projections That Work

The business term for a budget is a projection. You have a personal budget; your business has projections.

They're not exactly the same, though. Your personal budget is limited. You have a hard limit on the amount you earn each month. As an employee, that's your paycheck. What you can spend depends on what you earn.

With a business, a projection looks at what the business expects to earn. That's the top-line. It also looks at the take-home profit at the end of the day. That's the bottom-line. The biggest difference between a business's projections and your personal budget is that with a business, you can move your top-line.

Making projections is often a big challenge the first few times. This is where you begin putting the hard parts of your business together. What do you anticipate your first few months of sales will be? For a service-based business, you'll be looking at attracting customers. How many customers do you plan to attract in the first 6 months of operation? How much will the average customer spend? And how much will you spend to capture those customers?

Want more money in your pocket? There are two ways to do that:
    (1) Increase your income, and/or
    (2) Decrease your expenses.

If you are an employee, you can find another job, ask for a raise, or get a second job. Alternatively, if you want more cash, you cut your expenses.

In business, you can still cut expenses, but you've got a lot more options when it comes to increasing your income.

When creating your projections, use a 3-sided approach. What are your absolute best case and worst case scenarios? And where is the middle? Where is your most likely case scenario?

Each projection should have 3 sides:

(1) Best case,

(2) Worst case, and

(3) Most likely case.

Get started with your business projection by first looking at your business past, if you can. If your business has been around for a few years, you can compare your income statements on a yearly basis. For more detail, break it down into a monthly basis. You may be able to spot trends. For example, we know our business is slow in the summer. Our busy periods are the fall and the spring. That's normal for a tax practice. Knowing this trend, we can plan for the slow months better than we would without having run projections.

If your business is newer, then you can begin fleshing out a basic projection by gathering some the following information:

- List of known income sources from sales (this is guaranteed income, like a long-term contract, monthly recurring billings, etc.)
- List of anticipated income sources from sales (this is income you're hoping to get)
- List of known income sources from credit (line of credit, credit card, personal money available to the business, etc.)
- List of anticipated income sources from credit (this is additional credit you're hoping to get, but it hasn't been confirmed)
- List of known expenses (these are your fixed operating costs, like rent, mortgage, heat, light, internet, phone, and so on)
- List of anticipated expenses (these are costs that vary, like equipment purchases, office supplies, auto expenses, and so on)

Be realistic with your numbers, especially for the worst case scenario! This isn't where you fudge your numbers, or are overly optimistic. However, don't take the easy route, either. Obviously, the worst case for any business is lots of expenses and no sales; however, that doesn't take any work to figure out. You may want to start with your expenses. How many sales do you need to cover your business expenses? Are you going to be able to meet that minimum? Can you arrange loans or other forms of credit to cover those shortfalls?

If you are realistic with a worst case scenario and your business can survive it, you're already head and shoulders above most business owners who start business on a hope and a wish and have no real plan. There's a reason that the SBA (Small Business Administration) insists that business owners, looking for a loan, must create a plan first, before the SBA will even considers providing funding. Without a plan, success is unlikely. It's no wonder that the majority of businesses fail within the first 3 years.

On the other end of the projection spectrum is your best case scenario. That usually means you sell more than you really think is possible. What will you do to staff up? Will you have to invest in more equipment or inventory? How will you cover the expenses to hit the best case? Unexpected success can kill your first business just as fast as a worst case scenario.

Overnight Success Almost Causes Meltdown

A group of 4-5 friends worked together to create an online business selling teddy bears. They pushed the button to launch their website and clustered around a computer screen to see what would happen next. There was a brief pause, and then a sale popped up. The group cheered and high fived each other. A second sale came in, then a third ... and then the order counter began running more and more quickly until it was a blur of motion.

The energy went out of the group as they slumped into their chairs. They were completely unprepared for that level of success, and they had no idea how to fulfill the orders bombarding their site.

This story illustrates a very valuable point. Unexpected success can kill your first business just as fast as a bad year. Of course, it's a great problem to have. But it's still a problem.

In between the worst case and the best case scenarios is the most likely case. This represents the sales and the expenses you reasonably expect for your business.

A projection is not quite a financial statement because it's still just a best guess. That means you don't know if it'll be accurate. The assumptions you make with your projection are critical. If you've never done this exercise before, it's even more vital that you carefully document your assumptions.

Later, go back and compare the actual results with your projection. Which of your assumptions were correct? Which ones were off? As you go back and look, you'll be able to refine your own projection abilities. That is one of the critical entrepreneurial skills that can make you a fortune throughout your business life.

The ability to project worst case, most likely, and best case scenarios for projects & businesses is a critical entrepreneurial skill.

There's no question that creating a financial projection is daunting in the early days. Fortunately, most business plan software that is available commercially today has a built-in ability to create projections. You'll also find resources at www.MySmarterBusiness.com on creating projections.

Creating Your Own Three Stage Plan

Big projects are always easier when you chunk them down into manageable pieces. And building your business empire definitely qualifies as a huge project.

So, let's break this down into three stages for your business.

Stage One: Working your business part-time.

If you are still working a full-time job, your biggest challenge with Stage One will be time. How can you juggle a new part-time business with the same full-time demands you've always had?

If you've got a family, things will get tougher still. A new business is going to demand a lot of your time. Yet your family also has needs. There is undoubtedly going to be times when the two will collide, and they will leave you facing some very hard decisions. This is a great place to get your family involved. If you're going to be less available while you begin this new venture, talk to everyone about your goals and plans and how everyone as a family can help to make the changes needed to get the new business off the ground.

The other concern is cash flow. You may choose to jump in with both feet right from the start, and that's okay. But it also means that you'll need to make sure you have cash flow coming in right away or have some money squirreled away for the beginning times of a business. Most businesses struggle in the beginning. You need to build inventory, products, market share, websites, and so forth. That takes cash. And you're building your reputation, client base, and brand identity, and that takes time. There are some tricks to jump start cash flow that we'll talk about later, but for the most part, plan on having a good reserve and quick sales if you immediately are planning to quit your day job.

Either way, if you haven't done so already, it's important to first figure out what your monthly budget is. How much do you need to make to cover your regular expenses? What can you do to cut back? What other income could you make? In the beginning, the secret is to put all the resources you can into your business. It'll grow faster and bigger, and it will provide even more as it matures.

**Starting your first business? Cash flow is critical.
Think big, but act small.**

Stage Two: Going into Your Business Full time

This is an exhilarating and terrifying time for your business. You've quit your day job, and you're going to take your shot at being a business owner.

At first, it's all about survival. You'll need to do what it takes to pay the bills. Often, that means you're doing all (or most) of the administrative work. Plus, you'll be working long hours, providing the product or service that your customers want. And, don't forget: marketing and sales! You'll probably be wearing that hat as well. All this makes for long, hard days.

Whatever It Takes

One of our clients told a story at a seminar recently about her first year in business. She was doing medical transcription work, which meant big print jobs. The technology of the day was dot-matrix printers, which meant long print jobs, too. She remembered lying on a hard concrete floor while the jobs printed. Anything softer and she would have fallen sound asleep, something she couldn't afford to do at the time. But she was so exhausted she couldn't stay upright any longer. The concrete floor allowed her to catnap during these long print jobs.

Today, this client is the owner of a multi-million dollar company. She's long past the stage of sleeping on the floor, but she has never forgotten the hard work that went into making that business a success.

Hard work is noble, but it's also dangerous. It can lead to the most common trap entrepreneurs fall into.

In the beginning, you do everything for your business because you can't afford to pay someone or because you want to really understand the business before you turn any part over. At this stage you're not so much a business owner as you are self-employed. You've created your own job, with very long hours, lousy pay, and questionable benefits (at least that's how it will feel some days).

There is a HUGE difference between being self-employed and being a business owner.

Then, your first big breakthrough: You need help and you follow through on getting some. In other words, you make your first hire. You bring someone else in to play with your baby, and invariably, they goof up at some point. That person doesn't care as much as you do. They don't do things as well or as fast as you would. You find yourself with your first customer challenge, an inventory issue, or who knows what. The one thing you do know is that it's going to cost you a bunch of money to get it fixed.

And this is where the trap lies. You fix the problem, and vow, "Never again!" Boom! The trap closes. You're stuck now. Every time a problem comes up in the future, you'll be the one fixing it. Until you can take a step back and create a system and a training opportunity, you've just created one more item on your to-do list.

At Stage Two, your biggest challenge will be fighting the need and the desire to do everything for yourself.

This is also where you first really begin to bump into the difference between working on your business versus working in your business. It's where many would-be entrepreneurs get stuck. They like what they do, but they didn't like working for someone else.

Stage Two is a place where many businesses and business owners stay. In a sense, it's easy. You are doing something you like to do, but you're doing it on your own terms. The business may or may not expand beyond a certain point, but you're okay with that. You don't really want to expand beyond a certain point because you like things the way they are.

This is what we call working in your business. You are doing the work involved to create the product or provide the service. The downside here is that your expansion potential is limited. You can't do anything more than you are prepared to do on your own. Your earning potential becomes limited too. You're stuck with charging more or cutting costs.

Working in your business also limits your freedom. Imagine trying to take a 2-week carefree vacation, while tethered to your phone and laptop. Now, imagine your spouse's reaction. If you aren't thrilled by that prospect, that's good. That means you've got a much better chance at becoming a successful business owner, and moving into Stage Three: working on your business.

The cash flow is tempting at Stage Two as well. You're hitting your stride, and you get paid for your time. To move to the next step means hiring your replacement(s), and that means your cash flow is going to dip for a while. You'll need to be able to run some business projections to determine who you need and how much it's going to cost.

For every additional person or expense you take on so that you can move beyond doing all the work, you need to calculate a return on investment (ROI). For example, if you hire a bookkeeper so that you don't have to do the bookkeeping, what does freeing you up from that task mean for the business? How much more in revenue can you generate for the business by letting go of that task?

Unless you're trained as a bookkeeper, that's usually a pretty easy task to let go of. But what about letting go of the things that you do well? It's the reason your clients come to you, and no one else does it better. In fact, your clients are clamoring for you, and only you, to work with them. That's when you need to resolve to keep going, using the Ultimate Systems at Chapter 27 to build your business.

Meanwhile, though, you need good business projections at this stage as well. Determine the best, worst, and most likely cases for each person you add to your team.

Stage Three: The Move to Working on Your Business
When you get to Stage Three, the work begins all over again. Now you're looking at replicating yourself so that you can take yourself away from the daily business work and begin to look at the bigger picture: growth and development.

Stage Three is all about building systems. Chances are, at Stage Two you already knew how to do everything, so you just did it. To succeed with Stage Three, you're going to have to now document everything you have been doing in such a way that other people can do it.

This stage is guaranteed to challenge you! Designing systems isn't easy if you're more of a big-picture person and aren't at your best when caught up in details. It's also hard if your business is rocketing along and the work is coming fast and furious. The temptation to run with it and catch up systems at a later date is alluring.

The payoff is money and time. As you replicate yourself, your revenues will increase, but so will your costs. So it's still not time to take your eye off the bottom-line. But making the move to working on your business also gives you the time to look around to see what else you could do. Perhaps there's another income source you've wanted to explore. Maybe there's a product or service that meshes nicely. Maybe you see a new market that needs some nurturing. Or, maybe you see the writing on the wall for your business, and you need to retool to meet a coming demand or challenge.

As your business matures through Stage Three, the challenge of complacency comes into being. When the systems are clicking and you have your market dialed in, it's easy to get lulled into thinking it will be like that forever. It won't. The market is changing, new competition is coming, and technology changes everything.

Inevitably, things will change. Continue to assess each product line, project, and employee/independent contractor contribution. Business is changing at a faster rate than ever before. If you wait around for the good old days, you may be waiting for a very long time.

If you're waiting for your business to come back, you're missing the point. It's never coming back. It's moving forward. Are you?

Action Steps

Action Step 1: If you've never done a business projection before, this is a great time to start! Go to www.MySmarterBusiness.com and look at a few sample projections. Your first business projection doesn't need to be perfect. You'll learn as you go along. Just get started!

Action Step 2: Grab your calendar and book the time for when you will review your actual results with your projections. The better your projection skills get; the better your business decisions will be. And the only way to hone those skills is to compare what you thought would happen with what actually happened.

Resources

Smart Business Stupid Business: Chapter 20, Financial Statement Basics.

www.score.org. SCORE is a resource partner with the US Small Business Administration. It's a nonprofit association dedicated to educating entrepreneurs and the formation, growth and success of small business nationwide. You'll find an extensive list of templates and resources to help you create your own business projections.

www.planware.org. Offers a comprehensive selection of different planning tools for financial projections, marketing, cash flow and more.

Chapter 6:
Funding Your Business

Now let's look at the next big risk to your business. It is second on the list, but it is probably the most important. Money. Cash flow. It's the lifeblood of your business. Without it, you don't have a business. You need cash flow to start your business. You need cash flow to sustain your business. You need it if times get hard, and you really need it if you have explosive growth.

Most small businesses fail because of a lack of cash.

Over the next few chapters, we're going to talk about three strategies to find money for your business:

(1) Bootstrapping,

(2) Business Credit, and

(3) Other People's Money.

Let's start with bootstrapping. That is just as it sounds: the ability to pull yourself up by your bootstraps. You use your business's cash flow to build and grow. Bootstrapping your business isn't easy. A lot of times, it limits the growth that your business can achieve and the size of your ultimate business. On the other hand, it can be intensely satisfying emotionally to know that your business got there on its own merits.

Here are some tips to get your business off the ground using the bootstrapping method:

(1) Stick to what you know best. If you're bootstrapping, you don't have time for a big learning curve. You need to hit the ground running. This is one of those ready, fire, aim,[3] or maybe even fire, fire, fire type of scenarios. Cash flow is the lifeblood of your business, and you need it now.

---

3   *Ready, Fire, Aim: Zero to $100 Million in No Time Flat*, by Michael Masterson

> What unique abilities do you possess? What do you know or have that others want or need? How can you package it for a quick sale? Or, how can you design and sell your unique abilities in advance to create the cash flow to use for development.

(2) Keep costs under control. At this point, your money will be more important than your time. Start with as little of your own capital as possible and no borrowed money. It's sink or swim time. Watch every dime.

(3) Don't buy ahead or invest for the future. If you don't need more office space (or for that matter, ANY office space) don't spend the money. Jeff Bezos of Amazon.com started out with an old door on two filing cabinets for a desk. Now think: do you really need to go buy a bunch of office furniture?

(4) Remember, the purpose of your business is to make money. You can find cheaper ways of killing time or meeting new people than starting a business. Be ruthless when it comes to examining your business.

Most business owners hang on to losing propositions way too long. Shoot the losers. Ride the winners.

(5) Create a worst, most-likely, and best case scenario for your business. How will your business survive each eventuality?

(6) Get noticed. Small business often start with an entrepreneurial urge to do something better than anyone else has done it before. That's working in the business. And to a certain extent, you need that. But, in today's world, it's highly unlikely that the world will beat a pathway to your door based on something great you've done that no one else knows about.

(7) Each product and product line must stand on its own merit. There is no room for dogs in a company that is bootstrapping. Unless, of course, you have a pet grooming business.

(8) Create a sales funnel. The sales process resembles a funnel. At the top end, the widest part, are the people who are just finding you, checking out their options, considering using your services,

buying your product, etc. If you can adapt your product or service to match the funnel, you can often pick up sales. For example, at the top, where the funnel is widest, you may want to offer an entry level product or a special report for free or at a reduced price. This may help you to retain some of those people who otherwise may not have gone past the looking point.

(9) Can you create some kind of recurring business model, where you receive automatic monthly payments? This is a great way to generate steady cash.

Stylist with a Style That Pays

A San Diego hairdresser uses the recurring business model to great advantage. By offering his clients a discount in return for scheduling regular bookings every 2-3 weeks, he's able to generate a much more secure income stream.

---

(10) Create different service levels. Not all clients want the same thing. Can you create a premium service level that allows you to charge a higher rate for some of your current clients? What are the things that would make your service more valuable? Increased access to you personally? Front of the line option?

(11) As you create a product or a service, think about what other products or services could be offered to complement and augment it. What else do your clients or customers need? What other services can you give them to create additional streams of income for your business?

(12) Strategic relationships. When you focus on a niche, you often find that there are things you can't do, but are things that augment your service perfectly. By affiliating with other service providers, you can create a bigger, higher-value product that benefits everyone.

(13) Create a high-end and low-end solution. One of our new passions is talking about the bi-modal graph. Imagine a two-hump camel. One hump represents the people who want hands-on, concierge service. The other hump represents people who want the lowest-cost solution. The depression in the middle is

what used to be our target market: people who wanted a little of both. Today, that market is largely gone.

(14) Bill and collect in advance. It's much easier to collect money up front then it is afterwards. It might be a little harder with the first sale, because your customer doesn't have any experience with you, but after that, you've actually got to question why they don't pay you in advance. If you are willing to extend credit, make sure you bill at a premium. There is a cost to carrying debt, especially in a tight credit market.

(15) Give a discount to those that pay in advance. Instead of charging a premium to carry, give a discount to pay in advance. If you assess a late fee, the chances are you're going to upset your client and never get the fee paid anyway. But, if you offer a discount for early payment, on the other hand, you've got a much better chance of being paid.

(16) Take credit cards. Whenever a new business is established, set up a credit card processing option right away. There are so many options out there; you can find one for your business, no matter how large or small it may be. For example, PayPal® offers a credit card processing service for $30 per month, plus a small percentage of the amount charged. QuickBooks® offers something similar, meaning you can take payment right through your accounting software.

(17) Give a thank you discount. The best customer is a repeat customer. So, send a thank you note when someone buys. Then, a few weeks later, send them a discount that encourages the next purchase. Make sure the purchase is related. You'll probably find that you pick up an additional 20% in sales using this one technique alone. If you have a big ticket item that you sell, what related item can you sell at a discount? Always think of how you can enhance your relationship with your customer.

(18) Give free information. Become an expert in your field by writing ezine articles or Knols. This is free promotion, and it is powerful one. Think about it for a second. If someone searches a subject and your name pops up on articles over and over again, then who looks like the expert here?

(19) Get a website. Here's an amazing stat. Did you know that 44% of small business owners don't have websites? Now contrast that with 82% of consumers who say they only find places to spend their money on the internet. There is a big gap between small businesses on the internet and where the consumers are. Don't waste money on other forms of advertising until you've firmly established your web presence. Setting up a simple website can cost less than $1,000, yet bring in huge rewards. Go to where the prospects are!

There's one more source of money for your business: the government. But it's not government grants; it's even easier than that. It's all the tax savings you're going to get with your business.

You probably didn't get into business with the sole purpose of paying less tax. On the other hand, having a business means you will save money on taxes. It's not a bad side effect!

But the knowledge that having a business will save taxes is something that the wealthy have known about for years. The savings lie in the deductions. These are deductions that are created by the government and intended to be used not just by the wealthy, but by all business owners.

A loophole is an incentive provided by the government to promote a specific public policy.

Maybe you've heard the term "loophole" before and wondered whether it really was safe. Let's talk about that first. A loophole is a government incentive to promote a specific public policy. It is not a dodge or an illegal, immoral, unethical, elitist, anti-social, pro-corporate culture, forget-you-I've-got-mine action or attitude. In this instance, the public policy being promoted is the creation and operation of business.

Business drives this country, along with most other countries. Businesses provide jobs and income for their workers. Businesses drive the economy by producing saleable goods and services that are bought, sold, and taxed. Economically, there is a direct correlation between business growth and economic growth as a whole. And the better the economic growth, the more jobs and money that is available for everyone.

As a result, the government rewards businesses and those who start them with tax breaks. As a business owner, you hire employees and employ advisors. You invest capital in your business. You stimulate the economy. The country is stronger because of strong businesses.

And tax breaks are for ALL businesses, not just the big ones. There's nothing in the Tax Code that says only businesses that have profits of $1 million or more get tax breaks. That's the secret that the wealthy know and one of the things that most wealthy people have in common. The wealthy know that business ownership provides better tax breaks. So, if you want more out of your life, take control of your business and push it to the next level. The more you push, the more your business succeeds, and the more you will save.

The Three Ways a Business Saves You Tax Money

There are three main ways a business saves you tax money:
- increased access to tax deductions,
- lower tax rates (depending on the business structure), and
- increased management and distribution of income

Increased Access to Tax Deductions

When you are an employee, your deductions are limited. That's because the government looks at employment as "safe." We're putting the word safe in quotation marks for a reason: when you can be fired or laid off at the drop of a hat, how safe are you? However, the government views it as safe because you aren't risking the same things that business owners risk. As an employee, you aren't putting your savings into a job or taking out a second mortgage to help fund your employer. Business owners fund business development.

As a business owner you can deduct just about anything you can think of. It's got to pass the "reasonable" test though. In other words, to successfully write off a business expense you have to be able to explain why it was a necessary and reasonable expense for your type of business.

With a business, it's also possible to move many deductions that you pay with after-tax dollars (as an employee) to deductions that you pay with before-tax dollars. Two common examples are auto expenses and telephone expenses. As an employee you can't write off your car or your phone. As a business owner, both things are deductible since they are vital to your ability to run your business and earn income.

Each expense that you successfully move to "above the line" (meaning it's paid with pre-tax dollars) decreases your overall tax bill. It decreases the profit your business has, so it's taxed at a lower rate. That allows you to rearrange how money flows into your pocket. Again, if it's reduced, you will pay less tax. But it doesn't mean less lifestyle. You've still got the car and the phone; you're just paying for things differently with pre-tax dollars. In the extra online material, you'll find a worksheet to help you take a look at your current expenditures. You may find some expenses you can move to become above-the-line deductions.

A former client made about $50,000 a year as an employee. He converted to being an independent contractor, and he began maximizing his tax savings through deductions and tax planning. The funny thing was that after becoming an independent contractor, he still grossed about $50,000 a year. The difference was, as a business owner, he was paying about $10,000 LESS in tax on that $50,000.

There are a couple of ways you can shoot yourself in the foot with your business, and one of them is using the wrong structure. Not only can it leave you with more legal liability than you need, it can also increase your tax bill. There are business structures out there that can cause you to pay more in taxes if you use them in the wrong situation. Used correctly, on the other hand, they can save you thousands.

The final way that a business can help you to save taxes is by increasing your ability to manage and distribute your income. As an employee, you receive a salary. You pay income tax on that entire amount, along with payroll taxes, Medicare, unemployment, and so on. With a properly structured business, you can control how your income is distributed. You can even control how much of your income is distributed, depending on the business structure you choose. There are also other methods, like pension plans and defined benefit plans, that can help you park currently unneeded income for use in investments while saving taxes.

Control, freedom, less taxes, and more income: Having your own business can give you all of these things.

Action Steps

Action Step 1: What bootstrapping methods can you use to build your company without debt or investors?

Action Step 2: Start a Cash Flow Sunday. Diane started Cash Flow Sunday as a family project when the recession first hit. They still do it. Her family (husband Richard and son David) get together and come up with 10 things they can do to bring in cash flow within the next week. Open up your mind to the question, "How can I (or my business) get cash flow over the next week?" You'll be surprised at the answers. Oh, and, by the way, they also added the parameter that it must be fun, healthy, and legal! Get your team and/or family together and do your own Cash Flow Sunday.

Action Step 3: One of the quickest and easiest sources of cash is the government. Are you paying too much in taxes? Find out for free! Contact Diane's full service tax practice for a FREE CPA review of your past return to find out how much money you've been leaving on the table. Get started by contacting Diane's firm at 888-592-4769 or via email at Richard@USTaxAid.com.

Resources

www.USATaxAid.com. Diane's flagship information website, offering a forum, blog, video and audio workshops, business coaching and more.

www.USTaxAidServices.com. Download free tax-saving reports and more at Diane's resource web site. Updated constantly, there's always something new to discover.

Gold, Steven K. 2006. *Entrepreneur's Notebook: Practical Advice for Starting a New Business Venture*. Learning Venture Press.

Swanson, James A., and Baird, Michael L. 2003. *Engineering Your Start-Up: A Guide for the High-Tech Entrepreneur*. Professional Publications, Inc.; Second Edition.

Chapter 7:
Building Business Credit

Most small business owners build their business based on their own credit. In the beginning, you probably found it simpler to use your personal credit card for charges, and over time, you just kept using that. Maybe your bank eventually gave you a credit card with your business name on it, but you needed to personally guarantee it.

Or, maybe you're like the hundreds of thousands of business owners who take out personal loans or home equity loans in order to fund a business. If something happens to the business, you lose your house.

That's not a good plan. The answer is to build business credit from day one. We asked our friend and business credit expert Marco Carbajo to help us out with this chapter. He's got years of experience showing business owners how to build business credit of $100,000 or more in less than a year.

From Marco Carbajo
www.nationalentrepreneurclub.com

During the early stages of starting and operating your business, you may have become accustomed to using personal credit cards to finance purchases, equipment, and even payments to suppliers or vendors. What's even more alarming is if you personally guaranteed each and every credit card, credit line, or loan for your business then you are putting your personal assets and family at risk!

Statistics show that over 65% off all small businesses use credit cards on a regular basis; but the problem is that less than half of those credit cards are actually in the business name.

The single greatest challenge facing small business in America is awareness. Less than ten percent of business owners in America know about, let alone understand, how business credit is established or how to even generate a business credit rating. You're about to discover what the majority of entrepreneurs in our country do not know about and that is building business credit separate from personal credit.

So what is business credit?

It's the ability to obtain financing under the name of your business entity without using your personal credit or personal guarantee. Business credit should be separate and based on the corporation's credit worthiness not yours! Recently Entrepreneur Magazine was quoted as saying "You should differentiate your personal credit from your business credit."

If you own a separate legal entity for your business than you have a unique opportunity that no other individual or sole proprietor has. It's the ability to establish a business credit profile that is completely separate from a personal credit profile.

If you think your business is doing just fine and you don't need the credit think again! The reality is that your business will at one point require an influx of cash in order to cover unforeseen operating expenses, development, expansion, legal fees, inventory, or a range of other items that a business may require in order to grow.

One of the key advantages of having business credit is that instead of putting your personal credit and assets at risk every time your company requires financing, you would now be in a position to secure the financing you need with your businesses' credit. Some other benefits you can expect, include:

- Any debt you accumulate for your business would only report to your business credit file not your personal credit file.
- Eliminating the co-mingling of funds, and this includes the "co-mingling" of credit profiles, so you won't jeopardize the protection of the corporate veil.
- Protecting you and your family from personal liability when you get approved solely on your businesses' credit file.

- Increase your businesses' ability to obtain cash credit 10 to 100 times greater than you can obtain personally.
- SAVING MONEY! For example, an individual might pay up to 13% interest on a $100,000 line of credit whereas a business could qualify for an interest rate of 7%. That would save you almost $40,000 in interest alone.

So how do you get started? Setting up and establishing business credit for your business can be broken down into eight steps:

(1) Corporate Conformity. This is where you will set up your business entity whether it's an S-Corp, C-Corp, LLC, or Limited Partnership. This is the foundational part of your business credit, so taking short cuts or side steps can result in poor ratings and reduce your chances for funding.

(2) Business Plan. This is not a mandatory step, but it's necessary for your overall business success as well as a door opener for some specific lenders.

(3) Business Credit Profile. Once you have completed corporate conformity you'll be ready to set up your business credit profiles.

The next 5 steps have to do with trade accounts also known as vendor credit lines. There are over 500,000 vendors extending credit to businesses, but less than 6,000 of them report your payment history to your business credit profile. Choosing the right vendors is also a critical part of the process.

(4) Tier 1 Trade Accounts. This is the first step where you set up trade accounts for your business that are known to grant small amounts of credit to businesses that have no credit history.

(5) Tier 2 Trade Accounts. At this point, you set up business trade accounts for your business that are known to grant credit to businesses that have little business credit history. Because most Tier 1 accounts will now be reporting on your business credit profile, you can now apply for Tier 2.

(6) Tier 3 Trade Accounts. These companies will grant credit in higher amounts than what was granted from Tier 1 and Tier 2 accounts.

(7) Tier 4 Cash Credit Accounts. Tier 4 accounts consist of creditors who will grant your business cash credit cards, typically with a Visa or MasterCard logo. Benefits at this step include no personal guarantees and impact on your personal credit profiles.

(8) Advanced Business Financing. At this stage of the process, your business credit file is built, you have history, business scores, rating, and access to funding; and you can continue to obtain even larger amounts of financing by following some advanced business credit building strategies.

After the recent economic downturn, small business owners, like you, are facing a new era when it comes to business financing. Banks, lenders, suppliers, leasing companies, and others are making adjustments, adopting new rules, and facing new regulations in the lending arena.

Now more than ever, you need to be proactive and establish a new level of financial preparation, which includes establishing a strong business credit profile, a favorable business credit rating, and a solid bank rating. I encourage you to start building your business credit today, and you can enjoy the benefits and peace of mind that comes with it!

Action Steps

Action Step 1: Go to www.MySmarterBusiness.com and listen to Diane's teleseminar with Marco Carbajo. It's free and full of information you can use to build your business credit.

Action Step 2: After listening to the teleseminar, what steps do you need to make right now to start building your business credit?

Resources

www.nationalentrepreneurclub.com. Marco Carbajo's website features a wealth of articles, programs and resources to help you build business credit the smart way.

www.dnb.com. A DUNS number and registration is one of the first steps your business should take.

www.DKTeleseminars.com. Join Diane and a wide range of business experts and leaders. Learn to succeed with these free teleseminars.

Chapter 8:
Using Other People's Money

After bootstrapping and business credit, the next avenue for raising cash is through other people. That could mean a simple loan from friends or family, a public offering, or getting a government grant.

For many people, that means looking to close friends and family for a loan. It's important that all loans be documented properly and the terms clearly spelled out. Many people use unsecured promissory notes (essentially a 1-page promise to pay), but they don't set repayment terms. In that case, it becomes a demand note. This means the owner can ask for it to be repaid at any time. That could create a problem for you and your business if the demand comes at a time when you can't really afford to pull the capital out of the company[4].

Sometimes friends and family may want a piece of the company as security for the loan. In other words, they want to invest in your business rather than giving you a loan and have some equity. In that case, all of the same things apply that we'll talk about in Chapter 9: Good Partner, Bad Partner. Anyone coming into the company as an owner becomes your partner. You're joined together even after the loan is repaid, which isn't always a great move. Plus, there are legal issues involved every time someone buys a piece of your company. The United States has very tight securities law regulations around buying into companies, even if they are privately held by just a few people.

---

4   You can find templates of the most common business forms needed as part of the 97 Contracts Your Business Can't Live Without product we offer at USATaxAid (www.USATaxAid.com).

$7,000 Mistake Sinks Company

There was a company that got into serious trouble by taking money from investors without following the rules. The founders were raising money through friends and family. They brought 30-40 people into the company. The investments were all relatively small, and no one investor had come in for more than $10,000.

The problem was that the investors were considered unaccredited investors under federal securities laws. They didn't meet the legal guidelines to buy stock without the company first going through the expensive process of having a private placement document prepared and having its financial statements audited. Without those two things, companies are not allowed to sell to investors who don't meet the federal government's accredited investor guidelines. Accredited investors are individuals with a high net worth and income, who have experience in private investments.

The company was surviving (barely) and trying to raise money to launch business operations when one of the early investors asked for his money back. He wanted to withdraw from the investment entirely. If the company had done a private placement document, he wouldn't have been able to ask for the refund. That's because a proper private placement document explicitly sets out the risks of private investments and states flat out that there are no refunds. But the company didn't have a proper private placement document. The founders didn't know they needed one, and they had simply gone around and asked people for money.

When the company couldn't pay him fast enough, the investor made a complaint to his state's Securities Division. In addition to the federal securities agency, each state also has a government authority that looks after investments at a state level. At the state level, there is a whole other vetting process for investors.

The state Securities Division came down on the company and its officers like a ton of bricks. Sales of unregistered securities can result in huge fines or even jail time. The company couldn't take the strain and collapsed. One founder's marriage broke up, and he declared bankruptcy.

The amount of the investment was about $7,000. Doesn't seem like much, but it was enough to kill the company. The lesson to take away here is very simple: no shortcuts when it comes to raising money through equity sales!

Take no shortcuts when it comes to raising money through equity sales!

Accredited Investors in a Nutshell

Accredited investors are defined as:

- A bank, insurance company, registered investment company, business development company, or small business investment company;
- An employee benefit plan, within the meaning of the Employee Retirement Income Security Act, if a bank, insurance company, or registered investment adviser makes the investment decisions, or if the plan has total assets in excess of $5 million;
- A charitable organization, corporation, or partnership with assets exceeding $5 million;
- A director, executive officer, or general partner of the company selling the securities;
- A business in which all the equity owners are accredited investors;
- A natural person who has individual net worth, or joint net worth with the person's spouse, that exceeds $1 million at the time of the purchase;
- A natural person with income exceeding $200,000 in each of the two most recent years or joint income with a spouse exceeding $300,000 for those years and a reasonable expectation of the same income level in the current year; or
- A trust with assets in excess of $5 million, not formed to acquire the securities offered, whose purchases a sophisticated person makes.

If you don't have a full offering document and financial statements, then stick to raising money from accredited investors. It's safer and you'll sleep better at night.

Government Money

There's also the government money option. The Small Business Administration works with lenders to offers loans for companies that meet certain standards. Companies are required to have a detailed business plan prepared ahead of time, and the SBA won't guarantee 100% of the loan. As an owner, you can expect to guarantee part of the loan repayment and be asked to put up collateral to back up your application.

SBA loans were hit hard by the economic recession. Because the loans are actually made by commercial banks (with the SBA guaranteeing a portion of the repayment), lenders were much less likely to lend than in previous years, and loan requirements toughened up as a result. Changes in 2009, as a result of government intervention, loosened things up a little but you still will need a good plan before approaching the SBA.

Applying for Grant Money

Grant money is another source of income. Unlike a loan, grant money isn't repaid. However, it's not that easy to get either. The late-night infomercials don't present the truth or the whole story. Grant money is given out to fulfill a stated public purpose. It's meant to do something specific. Grant money isn't meant as a way to develop a business idea from concept to reality.

If you review the federal government website, www.grants.gov, you'll notice that most eligible organizations are either governmental or non-profit. You may be able to qualify for a grant if your business offers a service that the grantor is specifically looking for and fits the profile. Most federal and state governments are looking for businesses that fit the SBA's profile. That means, if your business doesn't qualify for an SBA loan, it probably won't be suitable for a grant either.

Funding your dream business will take some hard work and effort. Most likely, you will find your business money through a combination of personal funds, bootstrapping, and business credit. It's definitely something you want to be clear about from the start. Your business dream will die if you wait for funding to magically arrive. Take some time to create your funding plan before you jump in.

Action Steps

Action Step 1: Now that you've seen three possible strategies for funding your business, what plans do you want to pursue to raise money? (Don't raise money just because you can. This assumes that you've already calculated what your return on additional funding would be.)

Action Step 2: What are your next action steps for raising money?

Action Step 3: If you have, or are planning to, take money from friends, family, or other investors review this chapter carefully to make sure you are compliant with the rules. Do you need to improve your paperwork?

Resources

Kawasaki, Guy. 2004. *The Art of the Start: The Time-Tested, Battle-Hardened Guide for Anyone Starting Anything.* Portfolio Hardcover; 1 edition.

Nesheim, John L. 2000. *High Tech Start Up, Revised and Updated: The Complete Handbook For Creating Successful New High Tech Companies.* Free Press; Rev Upd Su edition

Turner, Robert P. and Hughes, Megan. 2001. *How Your Company Can Raise Money to Grow and Go Public.* SuccessDNA, Inc.

Chapter 9:
Good Partner, Bad Partner

We've talked about the IRS, and we've talked about money. Now let's talk about people. Ask most business owners and, chances are, they have a bad partner or bad employee story. In the next two chapters, we're going to talk about things you can do to reduce the risk that comes from picking a wrong partner or employee.

Many business owners think of themselves as rugged individualists. In a Smart Business, though, you will need to know how to work and play with all kinds of people.

This is especially true if you are thinking of going into business with one or more partners. Is it a good idea? Well, it depends.

Is a partnership a good idea?

Ask most business people their most horrendous business story, and it will almost always involve a partner. A partner is someone who becomes even closer than a spouse. Yet you're with that person in a relationship that doesn't always have clear cut guidelines on how to deal with change. When that inevitable change occurs, there can be a lot of upset. This is especially true in regards to money. Having a partner withdraw from a business at a critical time can kill a business that otherwise would have been successful.

Before you go into business with a partner, consider why you want a partner. Here are some common reasons we've heard:

I need this person as a partner because she has abilities I don't have.

Never partner with someone for her abilities when you can simply just hire her instead.

An employee will always be cheaper. If someone absolutely insists on receiving a profit share in the company, give him a percentage of net profit. If all that a person brings to the table is the ability to do a job, then you do NOT want him as a partner. You can hire that skill set instead.

Remember, a partner owns part of the company. As the business grows and becomes more valuable, he will share in that as well. You could do the same thing with an employee, but do it simply by giving him a raise or a bonus.

I need this person as a partner because he is bringing needed money to the business.

If you have a surefire business going, you likely have two options to raise money: equity and loans. Most people think of banks when they think of loans, but if you have someone who wants to invest in your company, you may be able to turn him into a lender instead.

If you have a choice between borrowing money and selling off part of your business, consider the long-term benefits of each. If you borrow money, you'll repay it with interest. But, when the money is repaid, your relationship with the borrower is over. On the other hand, bringing an investor into the business as a part owner means that even after the money is repaid that investor still has a say in how decisions are made and how the company operates. You could also find yourself locked in a power struggle, as a repaid money partner adjusts to a lesser level of control.

What if a potential partner has knowledge, needed skills, and cash? Things begin to change a bit. Now you have someone who brings more than just one element, and maybe that is enough to welcome a partner into the fold.

On the other hand, if your potential partner has cash flow problems, think twice. His cash flow issues can well transfer over to your business. Money rarely solves money problems. There is often something bigger and more fundamental that is wrong. And secondly, a successful business' bank account can look very tempting to someone who is struggling to pay the bills.

Considering a partner? "Never let a hungry dog guard the smokehouse." – Reverend Ike.

I need to partner with this person because she's a key employee, and I don't want to lose her.

Pay her a profit percentage instead. If money is the motivator, she'll make the same amount as if she were a partner. Only, you don't have to worry about all the headaches that go along with having a partner, and she won't have a vote in how the company is run.

I want to partner with this person because I owe him.

Send him a fruit basket. You're in business. If he is helpful to the business, then it's a business decision. He will help the business in a way that an employee cannot or will not. But, if you want to make him a partner to pay a past debt, do it with cash, not with a part of your company.

I want to partner with this person because she is just like me. We think exactly alike.

If you and your partner think exactly alike that's the perfect reason to not be partners. Being exactly alike means, you have the same faults and the same strengths.

Sales versus Operation

Dennis was an extraordinary sales guy. Put him in front of a room, and he'd consistently close the highest percent. He also hated details.

He failed miserably in his first business, which was a product-oriented company. He spoke at other people's seminars and events, and he sold them his product, which he would ship later. He gave a cut right off the top to the people putting together the events, so they were happy, too.

There was one problem. Dennis was horrible at details. The products never got shipped on time. He often didn't have enough in stock. He didn't get good addresses or send via freight companies with tracking. In the end, there were lawsuits against him and Better Business Bureau complaints, and he owed more than he owned. Unfortunately, it also spilled over on to other people that he joint ventured with.

When you partner your business with someone else, you're taking a huge chance on them. Don't do it lightly!

He learned from that. He didn't like or know how to run the back end of a business. So, for his second business, he partnered up with someone who was great at that part of it.

For a time, they made a lot of money. But, it was never that much fun because there was a constant push-pull of sales versus administration. And Dennis felt sales were always more important. Soon, he got to the point where he resented the costs involved in running a company and so he and his partner split. And it wasn't a good split.

Dennis partnered up with the top sales guy from the old company and launched a new company. And he fell flat on his face. They could generate sales, but because both were super salesmen and neither could do the fulfillment, it didn't take long before they had a lot of angry customers.

Thinking alike doesn't mean you don't share the business dream or goal. That's essential. Instead, it means that the partner you choose should be someone who has strengths where you have weaknesses and weaknesses where you have strengths. If you're not detail oriented, your partner had better be. Your task is to find a way for you to work together in an atmosphere of mutual respect and trust.

If you decide you want a partner, put it in writing.
Perhaps the most effective partner relationships are those where expectations are clearly spelled out. If you are considering bringing a partner into your business, either at the beginning or later on after the business is up and running, take the time (and possibly spend the money) to have a formal, legally-binding agreement prepared. These are typically called a Buy-Sell Agreement. They set out how you will work together and how you will resolve issues. The agreement will also set out how you can dissolve the partnership if you can't resolve your differences. You need an exit strategy from the partner relationship, and it needs to be one that won't break your company. That means thinking about things like:

- Work. How do you make sure you both make a proportional contribution to the business, either financially or through providing know-how?

- Compensation. If you've got a money partner, this will look different from a "sweat equity" partner (that's someone who works for their share). The money guy has far more at risk.

- Death, Divorce and Disability. These are commonly called the "3 D's" in the legal world. How do you handle your partner's death? Most assets are passed on to family members, meaning that your partner's husband, wife, or children could become your new partner. Are you okay with that? The same question needs to be asked for divorce. If your partner leaves his wife and she gets half of his stuff, she becomes your third partner. Are you okay with that dynamic in your meeting rooms?

- Disability is the third D, but it's more of an internal issue. If your partner is injured or becomes seriously ill and can't contribute to the company, someone's got to pick up the slack. That someone needs to be compensated for their efforts (ideally out of your partner's share of the profit), right at a time when revenues may be down or when your partner may need every cent she can get her hands on. With a long-term illness, it could be months or even years before someone recovers, if they recover at all. At what point do you make the decision to move on without that person?

- The Buy-Out. The honeymoon is over, and you and your partner have decided to go your separate ways. Perhaps you want your partner out. Perhaps your partner wants you out. How are you going to do that? And, more importantly, how much is your company really worth?

- This is the big one. There's more litigation on this one point than all of the others, combined. How do you value a company that hasn't made a dime, but you expect it to make millions one day? And you (or your partner) were an integral part of getting it there? Paying someone a buy-out fee based on projections can be a tough prospect. It also depends on what side of the table you are on. If you are the one being bought out, you're looking for the highest possible dollar amount. The other side of the table is not.

- Financing the Pay-Off. Assuming you make it through points 1-4, you've now got to figure out how you pay off a former partner, if it comes to that. Early stage companies don't necessarily have deep pockets. There is often a profit share or other form of payment schedule that continues on long after the partnership is over. Looking for business financing is hard. Looking for business financing to pay off a partner is even harder.

- To learn more about the steps you need to take to create a legal and binding Buy-Sell Agreement, go to www.dkseminars.com and listen to a free teleseminar led by Megan Hughes.

One final note on the Buy-Sell Agreement: wherever possible end on good terms. A nasty partnership break-up can ruin the chances of ever having a partnership again. After all, if you come off as a 'win at all costs' type of guy, who is going to want to go into a partnership with you?

A partner can make or break your business. If in doubt, don't form a partnership. Find a way to joint venture on a specific project or pay an income or equity portion.

Who Are You Partnering With Anyway?

This is a true story about two partners who went from fortune to failure all over a bad partnership agreement. We can't use their real names, so we'll just call them Larry and Curly.

Larry and Curly had a successful contracting company. They took it big-time, and they had created a business where neither of them had to work very much. They made the crucial decisions and reviewed the results, and they, otherwise, just collected their high six figure checks.

Then, Curly got in a nasty divorce. It went on for months, and in the end, his wife ended up with his percentage of the business. It was an asset of their property, and the court awarded it to her. Now there was a real problem.

Curly's wife, Sue, hated Larry with a passion. She had 50% ownership of the company and purposely voted opposite of him on everything.

The business was stuck, and they were closed in less than two years.

Remember, you're forming a partnership not just with one person but also her spouse and her heirs. Don't assume things will always stay the same.

There are lots of fantastic partnerships in business. The purpose of this chapter isn't to make you run screaming for the hills at the thought of having a partner. It's not a decision you can rush into either. Before you take the step of working with other people, you've got to think through the potential consequences if things don't work out the way you have planned. And, above all else, make sure you have the right paperwork in place. You don't want to be putting together paperwork after the fact, as a partnership is dissolving.

Action Steps

Action Step 1: If you have decided to work with a partner, go to www.MySmarterBusiness.com to listen to the free audio seminar with Megan Hughes on "Buy-Sell Agreement Basics".

Action Step 2: Have a frank conversation with your partner(s) on how you will handle disagreements and a possible dissolution. Do they have a commitment to work through problems, or are they viewing the partnership as a short-term proposition?

Resources

Fleming, Quentin J. 2000. *Keep the Family Baggage Out of the Family Business: Avoiding the Seven Deadly Sins That Destroy Family Businesses*. Fireside, 1st Ed.

Gage, David. 2004. *The Partnership Charter: How To Start Out Right With Your New Business Partnership (or Fix The One You're In)*. Basic Books

Goleman, Daniel. 2006. *Emotional Intelligence: 10th Anniversary Edition; Why It Can Matter More Than IQ*. Bantam; 10 Anv edition.

Chapter 10:
Are Your Employees Ripping You Off?

You're working hard to build your business. You've finally reached the point where you have some employees to give you a little time off, and you even have some extra cash to enjoy that spare time.

That's when you realize that you have a whole new issue to deal with: your enemy within. No, this is not about saving you from yourself. It's about saving you from your employees and an occasional partner or two.

Employee theft and embezzlement can run the gauntlet from low-level employees stealing office supplies to partners who bankrupt companies. It's uncomfortable. It's unpleasant. And it's not something you want to think about. Yet it happens more than you might suspect.

Employee embezzlement is costing U.S. businesses $652 billion annually.

According to just one survey conducted by the University of Florida, employee theft was estimated to be responsible for 47% of all store theft. That adds up to about 17.5 billion dollars, and that's just in the retail industry.

On the other hand, when you compare medical offices and professional offices to retail, retail gets off easy. Over 70% of medical professional offices are embezzled from once. Over 60% are embezzled from twice. Embezzlement is a real problem.

An Atmosphere of Cheating

Cherise had years of experience as a bookkeeper when she decided to try something new. She had a long-time friend, Rick, with a thriving retail business in Michigan, near the Canadian border. He had both US and Canadian tourists filling his store on the weekends to buy his unique, hand-crafted items.

He had a huge facility and a lot of staff. The items had a low manufacturing cost, and they fetched a high price on the open market. Yet, for some inexplicable reason, Rick's business was always late paying its bills. He was now looking at some serious financial problems. Cherise bought in as a 50% partner for a song because her friend needed her expertise more then he needed the money.

The first thing Cherise noted was that they had a full-time bookkeeper on staff, but there hadn't been any financial statements issued in years. They had both a retail and wholesale business, so profit margins were all over the place. And without financial statements, no one could be sure what they were anyway.

The other thing she that found had her even more concerned. Her long-time friend was a tax cheat. Rick had a habit of not ringing up sales on the cash register when he was working. Instead, he'd put the money straight into his pocket. With his new partner, Rick wanted to keep things fair. So, he started a new system. For every dollar he put in his left pocket, he put another one in his right pocket for Cherise.

That's when Cherise called us. She needed some help showing Rick that there were plenty of ways to legally pay less tax. He didn't need to cheat to do that.

Rick listened. But now we needed accurate financial statements in order to do good strategic planning. Plus, Cherise wanted to find out why the company wasn't making more money.

Rick had been in business for over 30 years and for 27 of those years Barbara had been his bookkeeper. He trusted her with his life. Cherise couldn't stand her. She could never get a straight answer. Barbara hid the records every chance Cherise came around.

Finally, Cherise got fed up and told Rick that unless he ordered Barbara to start producing accurate financial statements, she had to go or Cherise was going to withdraw from the partnership.

First, Rick argued and cajoled. Barbara had been with him almost from the beginning. He trusted her with his life. Without her, he wasn't sure the company could even exist. But he finally agreed to Cherise's demand.

Rick put his foot down with Barbara. And that's when the rest of the story came out. She broke down crying. She had worked for Rick for 27 years. And for 24 of those years, she'd been stealing money. Because Rick had been "cooking the books" by stealing from the top-line of the business, it was easy for Barbara to steal money, too.

25 Embezzlement-Busting Strategies to Protect Your Business

You can do more to protect yourself from embezzlement than you might expect. Most of these strategies are things you can do without hiring any outside experts. Often, that's all you need to do to stop a big embezzlement plot cold!

Strategy #1: Hire the Right People

Do more than just check references. Do a background check on all employees who have access to inventory, accounting, or money. In fact, it is best to do a criminal check on all of them. You may also want to run a credit report on anyone who is charge of the accounting and money. Past mistakes are okay. Hiding them or lying about them is not okay.

If your prospect is going to lie on an employee application, he's going to lie about other things as well.

Strategy #2: Maintain an Ethical Management Climate

There is a saying that the fish rots from the head down. That's certainly true in a company. If the owners and managers are stealing from clients, vendors, or each other, there will be a climate of thievery. Only it's not Robin Hood and his merry men, it's a bunch of thieves who want your money. Set the standard and make sure your managers follow suit.

The best anti-embezzlement strategies start with you. Foster a no tolerance atmosphere.

Strategy #3: Make Anti-Fraud Policies Visible

As soon as you have more than a couple of employees, it's time to roll out some highly visible anti-fraud policies and procedures. Prevention is always cheaper in the long run.

Set the tone for new employees on their very first day. Include loss prevention education in the employee handbook. Hold regular meetings. And periodically talk about loss, and how it impacts the business. Loss means lost profits, adverse publicity, and decreased morale and productivity. Give employees a way to anonymously make suggestions for better control and prevention. Make them your eyes and ears in a non-accusatory way.

Your anti-theft program should include, at a minimum:

- A statement that fraud, waste, and abuse, occur in nearly all companies.
- A statement that such conduct costs the company jobs and profits.
- A statement that your business actively encourages any employee with information to come forward.
- A statement that your employees can come forward and provide information anonymously and without fear of recrimination for good-faith reporting.
- An exact method for reporting, including a telephone number, name, or other information. You may want to keep the exact method low-key and not have people reporting to their immediate superiors.

Strategy #4: Enforce Mandatory Vacations

Most embezzlement scams need the embezzler present. The scams generally aren't that sophisticated. Take the person out of the loop for a week, and the whole scam falls apart and is discovered. The enforcement of mandatory vacations will aid in the prevention of some frauds.

Strategy #5: Cross Training & Job Rotation

Cross training and job rotation also makes it hard for an embezzlement scam to work. Frauds are often detected during sickness or unexpected absences of the employee thief because the fraud requires continuous, manual intervention.

A middle manager of a successful company embezzled $1.6 million from his employer. Later, when asked what could have been done to prevent it, he replied, "If the company had coupled a two-week vacation with four weeks of rotation to another job function, my embezzlement would have been impossible to cover up." He had been stealing money for three years.

Strategy #6: Watch What Behavior Your Bonus Plan Rewards

You undoubtedly have the best of intentions with your company bonus plans. Be careful though. What type of behavior are you encouraging?

The best bonus plans are thought out in advance. Make sure your employees can control the result you want, and it's something that helps your business.

All too often, business owners offer bonuses without thinking them through. In the case of a jewelry store, sales associates got huge bonuses if they reached certain sales goals for the month. If they didn't hit the goals, they got paid practically nothing. In the beginning, the associates manipulated sales to make sure they were hitting the goal every other month. That way, they got a huge bonus on that month, and then, since they couldn't make it every month anyway, they had hardly any sales in the next.

Then they caught on to the idea of keeping copies of customer credit cards and making huge sales on the cards on the last day of the month. The sales were credited on the very next day, which put a negative sales figure in the next month. It didn't matter, though, because they never intended to hit the goal that month anyway.

The problem, of course, was that this was fraud, and it was a serious one at that.

Strategy #7: Watch Your Employees' Lifestyles

Generally, when employees steal, they leave a visible trail. Their lifestyle improves. Look for more expensive cars, extravagant vacations, expensive clothing, new or remodeled homes, expensive recreational property, and outside investments. Managers should be educated to be observant for these signs.

After seven years on the job, an employee suddenly started wearing expensive designer clothes and bragging about them. She also was sporting around in a brand new BMW. But she hadn't gotten any raises, didn't have any outside income from investments or another job, and hadn't won the lottery. Where had the money come from?

The owner asked his CPA to look into it. As soon as the employee realized that the owner was looking into her work, she confessed.

Over the past year, she'd stolen almost $100,000.

Strategy #8: Unhappy Employees Are More Likely to Steal

One of the common justifications by embezzlers for their actions is that the owner didn't appreciate them or treat them well. That may or may not be true in reality, but certainly, the perception is a powerful one. If your employees aren't happy and feel that they are taken advantage of, then they will find a way to make it right.

Every employee or business partner who steals from you, either is a complete sociopath or they have a way to justify it to themselves. And when it comes to employees, the most common justification is that they weren't treated well.

Rotten Fruit

The controller of a small fruit-packing company in California stole over $112,000. When asked why, he said, "Nobody at the company ever talked to me, especially the owners. They were unfair. They talked down to me, and they were rude. They deserved everything they got."

Strategy #9: Watch the High Risk Areas

Some areas in your business carry more risk than others. By developing an internal audit policy, you can often uncover evidence of wrongdoing. Some of the areas to concentrate your fraud audits on are:

- Expense reports
- Payroll
- Purchasing
- Sales
- Accounts receivable
- Customer complaints
- Cash
- Suspense accounts

Strategy #10 Watch the People Who Handle Your Money

Money, especially cash, is the most liquid asset you have. It's the most subject to embezzlement.

Pay attention to those that sign on bank accounts. If possible, each employee handling funds should be periodically removed from his or her job so that any scam is disrupted.

Strategy #11: Do Not Assume Any Employee or Partner is Beyond Theft

Things change. Even the nicest people may be subject to temptations and failures of character.

If you talk to most people who have survived embezzlement, they'll probably tell you that the thief was the last person that they would have expected to have stolen from them.

Strategy #12: Look for Sudden Increase in an Expense Line Item

This is where watching your ratios and comparing financial statements comes in handy. If you have double billing going on or someone has set up a fictitious company to siphon off money, you'll catch it by looking at the percentage of expenses.

Of course, not every increase means theft. An increase in the office supply account could just mean someone was stocking up on sticky notes. The fact that you ask, though, indicates you are watching. And often, that is all it takes to stop a future problem.

Strategy #13: Pay Only Original Invoices, Never Photocopies
Once you've signed the check, make sure your bookkeeper stamps "paid" on the invoice immediately. Watch for missing or altered documentation.

Strategy #14: Watch the Accounting Records
Look for out-of-balance accounts, unexplained adjustments to accounts, cash shortfalls, and confusing records. This might take a little skill in the beginning. Ask your outside CPA what records to request from your bookkeeper, and then get a quick lesson on what to look for. If you ask your bookkeeper about things that don't make sense, listen for unreasonable or convoluted explanations.

Strategy #15: Protect Against Computer-Aided Fraud
Change your passwords frequently, and keep track of who has access to what. All too often, theft continues after an employee is gone, simply because he still has access to the computer files. And, of course, remember to shred documents.

Strategy #16: Limit Access to Valuable Equipment
Don't get so caught up with protecting your bank account that you forget that you also have other things an employee might want to take. Keep a list of all assets.

Strategy #17: Backup Your Bookkeeping Records Regularly
Regular backups will save any "original" data entry that your bookkeeper has created, and it will also give you files that are easy to go through if you suspect embezzlement. Make sure you have a password and sign-in information to the accounting program that your bookkeeper does not know.

Strategy #18: Ask to See Your Company's Bank Reconciliations without Notice
With computerized banking and accounting programs in place, bank reconciliations usually take no more than half an hour to an hour to complete. If you don't know your bank balance, this is a big warning sign that something is not right. Periodically ask to see the most current bank reconciliations without notice. If your bookkeeper delays

production, stay alert. You could just have a lazy bookkeeper, or you could have money disappearing.

Strategy #19: Keep Copies of All Reports from Your Bookkeeper
In the hands of a smart operator, many accounting software programs allow changes without a good audit trail. That means, the statement you get today might be changed, after the fact, by entries later. Hang on to every report your bookkeeper gives you. At some point, you may need to hand these over to your CPA to investigate a problem.

Additionally, get a copy of the check register each month and keep it. Is there a gap in check numbers? Ask to see the copies of the voided checks that fill in the gap.

Strategy #20: Fill Out Your Own Credit Applications
It's very tempting to have your bookkeeper complete your personal credit applications. After all, they likely have access to all the information anyway. But, if your bookkeeper later fills out credit applications or merchant account applications, you can more easily prove you didn't do it if you have a pattern of always completing your own applications.

The Age of Electronic Signatures

It could be years later until you discover the full extent of the damage a dishonest bookkeeper makes.

Recently, we discovered that one of our friends with a successful internet business had her electronic signature used by an unscrupulous bookkeeper. His personal credit wasn't any good, and so he used her electronic signature on the faxed applications that he made for Merchant Credit Accounts for his side businesses. The Merchant Account Providers never asked for an original signature.

The only way she discovered that there was a problem was when she was talking to one of the Merchant Account Providers about another one of her accounts, and they asked about the forged one that had her name on it.

To this day, she doesn't know if she has found all of the accounts that illegally have her name on them.

Strategy #21: Make Sure You See Voided Checks
Always verify voided checks. A common way for a bookkeeper to take a few hundred extra dollars is to get the owner to sign a check made out to "cash," and then say he needed to void it. But, in reality, the check didn't get voided. It got cashed.

Keep the checks you void in case you ever get audited.

Strategy #22: Look for Gaps in Check Number Sequence
Make sure checks stay in numerical order. Look out for big jumps in the numbers. This could indicate that someone has some blank checks, just waiting for the time to run them through your account. If there are jumps, you should have voided checks for the skipped sequence.

Strategy #23: Check Your Credit Card Statements
This is incredibly important for you even if you don't have a business. Check your credit card statements! By looking over statements, you will catch any fraudulent charges instantly. Most credit companies only allow you to dispute fraudulent items within 30 days of receipt of statements. By not looking over the statement immediately, you are giving up your disputing rights and may get stuck with any fraudulent charges that have occurred in your name. So go over these statements carefully and contact your creditor immediately if anything is on there that should not be.

Strategy #24: Lock Up Your Credit Cards
Chances are, your bookkeeper knows your credit card account number, but that doesn't mean everybody in your company should. Keep your credit cards locked up, and check the monthly bills to verify that there aren't any unauthorized charges.

Strategy #25: Always Sign with the Same Felt Tip Pen
Forgers are getting good. And one of the easiest ways to forge a signature is to trace it. A regular ink pen won't show if someone went slow and carefully, tracing the letters. The end result will look just like your signature.

However, if you use a felt pen (like a Sharpie Ultra Fine pen), extra pressure or writing at a slower pace when tracing is going to show up as a fatter line. That can be enough to prove a forgery if you ever have to do so in court.

Watch Out for These Common Scams!

Embezzlers are often just taking advantage of the easiest possible way to get money. And the way they take it is often remarkably predictable. The most common embezzlement methods are:

- Failure to record cash transactions
- Diverting deposits
- Claims for false reimbursements
- Use of company accounts for personal transactions
- Payroll fraud
- Fraud through supplier accounts and other payables
- Kickbacks

Trust Your Instincts

A professional office can be especially susceptible to embezzlement because the profit margins are often so high. If it's a high volume practice, a little here and there is barely noticed on the financial statement.

For a few months, an owner felt something wasn't quite right. She asked the controller for some documents, and after about four weeks, of "I'll get it to you tomorrow," she knew it was time to get firm and demand that she get copies of the current financial statements.

She got the copies, late on Friday afternoon, via email, along with a note admitting that he had taken approximately $27,000 over the past three months. But that's just where it started. Over the next few months, she discovered that he had set up four different companies, all paying him money for work done. In other words, not only had he taken $27,000, he had been paid four times as much as he should have been. All told, the loss was closer to $100,000. And, that was just after three months.

Imagine how much more it would have been if she had waited a few more months.

Trust your instincts.

Watch for these potential problems in your sales cycle:
- Straight forgery using contractual adjustments to bury the embezzlement
- Stealing cash by never recording the sale into the accounting system
- Opening a separate bank account and depositing the checks

Here are some strategies for protecting against these problems:
- Reconcile your sales on a daily basis
- Investigate client, customer, or patient complaints related to payments immediately

Watch for these potential problems in your payment cycle:
- Employees creating fake companies to get paid by the company
- Employees including personal utility, phone, or credit card bills with office bills

Here are a few tips to avoid these problems:
- Stay familiar with the vendors that your business uses
- Watch the ratios of your financial statement
- Anyone signing checks (other than the owner) should be bonded

Most businesses are embezzled from once. Trust your instincts. If something seems wrong, it probably is.

Here are a few more common problems we've seen:
- Excess postage. Employee puts too much postage on outgoing mail, and then gets a cash refund at the post office.
- Post office checks. Employee has a signed check made out to the post office, supposedly for postage, stamps, or to fill up a postage machine. The check is exchanged for a money order made payable to the employee.
- Payroll taxes. Payroll clerk overpays payroll taxes and claims excess as withheld taxes to get refund later. Another version is to credit taxes that were withheld from other employee checks and claim them as their own. Again, the purpose is to get a government tax refund later.
- Sound alike companies. If you're doing all the check signing, chances are, there are some vendors you are used to paying. So, if you're used to signing a check to Apex Deliveries, Inc., you'll

probably sign a check made payable to Apex Del. The difference is, it is a completely different company, owned by the employee thief. It gets even more confusing with credit card bills. Let's say you have an American Express card. So, you'd expect to sign a check to pay your American Express card each month. But, in this case, the check is used not to credit your account, but instead the employee's.

- Look out for sudden, unexplained changes in revenue, cash flow, or profit. That could be a sign that something is wrong.
- Also, it could be a sign of trouble if you have increased accounts receivable write-offs.
- Investigate supplier complaints about slow payments or customer double-billing.
- A security breach in the company's computer system may also be a warning.

When Is It Time to Bring in an Expert?

If your business is growing and you feel a little out of control or something just doesn't seem right, it may be time for you to bring in an expert to help you out. There are a number of different examinations that a CPA can help pinpoint where you might have risk from employee theft.

There are four procedures your CPA might perform for you:

(1) Review,

(2) Audit,

(3) Internal Control Audit, or

(4) Agreed upon procedures.

These are all technical terms that mean specific actions that your CPA will take in an examination.

Review. A review is an analysis of your financial statements. Your CPA will look at the percentages of gross profit, various expenses, and ratios and compare these to prior periods for your business and against industry standards. This is a very effective way to spot fraud because it will always show up in the financial statements.

If an employee is double billing payroll, there will be a jump in the payroll numbers. If an employee is siphoning off cash from sales, the gross profit will drop.

Audit. An audit is often less effective at spotting irregularities. Although you may be more familiar with the term and actually request an audit, you'll find that the audit is more expensive and probably doesn't give you what you want. The audit is designed to make sure you are accurately reporting your financial results. So, an investor or lender in your company would love to see an audit. It isn't designed to look for internal irregularities.

Internal Control Audit. As your business grows, you may want an internal control audit just to determine whether the systems you have set up could be made better. For example, the most easily embezzled item is cash. Cash controls often include separation of duties so that no one person controls enough of a cash flow process that it would be easy to embezzle.

Agreed Upon Procedures. "Agreed Upon Procedures" is simply a term that CPAs use to describe everything else. If you have a real concern about a particular portion of your business, then you may want to have this area looked at closely by a professional.

Stupid Controller Not So Stupid After All

A very busy urologist hired a local CPA to perform an audit. He was so busy making money that he really felt he had no handle on his business at all. Furthermore, he really didn't want to. He just wanted someone else to say that it was okay.

He had a full-time controller, who was originally from Sweden. He was flamboyant with a crazy lifestyle, but always produced financial statements. The problem was that the doctor never had time to learn how to read them.

The audit team was comprised of a senior level CPA and a couple of juniors. They figured that they would be done with the audit within a day or two. Little did they know, the records were a complete mess!

They started on Thursday, and by Friday, they knew the books had to be completely redone. For example, the controller had been running cash deposits through the depreciation account. The senior CPA laughed about how bad the books were.

"I gave him a tough weekend," she explained back at the CPA firm on Friday afternoon. "I told him he had to provide back up on all those entries."

On Monday, the controller didn't show up. In fact, he was never seen again. He had gone back to Sweden over the weekend.

Over the next few weeks, it was discovered that he had embezzled over a million dollars from the urologist. How had he succeeded in doing that? No one had ever bothered to check the financial statements.

Diane was one of the junior accountants on that job, just right out of college. She learned a lesson there that she never forgot.

Don't expect an auditor to catch an embezzler. Sometimes it works, but more often, it's the questions that are asked and the breaking up of a routine that cracks the case.

As an owner, you can do much more to stop an embezzler cold. If something doesn't seem right, investigate. And always, always, always, get regular financial statements. They are your best defense against employee theft.

Action Steps
Action Step 1: Review the anti-embezzlement strategies in this chapter. Which ones do you need to implement in your business?

Action Step 2: Probably, the most important part of an anti-embezzlement program is awareness. How will you implement an employee program?

Action Step 3: What action steps do you need to take to protect your business?

Resources
Abagnale, Frank W. 2002. *The Art of the Steal: How to Recognize and Prevent Fraud--America's #1 Crime.* Broadway.

McMillan, Edward J. 2006. *Policies and Procedures to Prevent Fraud and Embezzlement: Guidance, Internal Controls, and Investigation.* Wiley.

Section Three: Survive or Thrive: Critical Decisions in the First Stage of Your Smart Business

Chapter 11:
All You Need to Know About
Bookkeeping and Record Keeping Day One

I f we had to sum this chapter up into a single idea, it would be this: if you aren't prepared to start and maintain good books and records, you're better off not having a business.

If you aren't ready to keep good records, you're better off not having a business.

Bookkeeping is recording the financial events in your business life. Money coming in, money going out, income, expenses, loans, monthly bills, bad debts, equipment bought and sold, supplies bought and consumed, and so on. Record keeping is maintaining all of the back-up documentation to support your bookkeeping data. If you have a sale, there should be an invoice documenting the sale, along with a purchase or sales order. If there's an expense, there should be documentation showing what it is, when it was paid, and so on.

Smart Business or Stupid Business?

For want of record-keeping, the bookkeeping was lost.
For want of bookkeeping, the accounting was lost.
For want of accounting, the planning was lost.
For want of planning, the business was lost.

There is one thing that most small business owners have in common:

Accounting is often the last thing on your mind.

The root word for accounting is account, just as it is with accountable. Stop there for a minute. Have you ever thought about how rare being accountable is in this world?

Avoid-Blame-Justify-Responsibility-Accountability

There are actually five levels of human empowerment and responsibility. For this exercise, let's look at this strictly from a financial perspective.

The lowest level of financial empowerment, in fact the most disempowering thing you can do, is to simply avoid the issue, similar to sticking your head in the sand like an ostrich. But that really doesn't do justice to the ostrich. The ostrich has a purpose. When he sticks his head in the sand, he's eating gravel to help digest his food. When you avoid a problem by metaphorically sticking your head in the sand, you don't have a purpose. You're just simply hiding.

This is especially true with small business owners. For whatever reason, it's easy to be too busy to deal with financial information for your business. As long as everything is running, it must all be going great, right? You've got money in the bank, sales are coming and you're going to be just fine. The accounting will get caught up when it gets caught up, and then you'll get to see all the money you made!

Unfortunately, ignoring your finances is the wrong answer. Increasing sales and advances and a booming economy can make a bad business look like a good one. All it takes is a downturn for the truth of the business to be exposed.

The "I'm Too Busy" Excuse

The most common excuse we hear for not keeping good records and accounting is, "I'm too busy."

We're not buying it.

Here's why: If you had a new client come to you with an offer of $100,000, but you had to devote 50 hours a week for the next two weeks to his project, could you do it? How could you NOT do it? That's $1,000 per hour.

Think about what you'd change to free up that time. What projects would you have to let go of or give someone else. What personal time would you cut back on? What would you do to make $1,000 per hour?

Or, would you simply say, "I'm too busy."

Chances are, you'd find a way to make an extra $100,000 in two weeks.

What this says to us is that you're not too busy. It just means that the bookkeeping is not enough of a priority for you yet. Or it means that the pain of doing the bookkeeping, and being face to face with the results, is greater than the pain of having a business fail. Is that really what you want?

Here's something else to think about: When you worked for someone else, you went in every day, did your thing, and went home. You probably weren't involved with the bookkeeping or had access to the finances of the business. You collected a check and didn't worry too much about where the money came from, as long as you got paid. If you've gone into business with the same thinking, watch out. You're heading for trouble.

Avoiding your financial stats is the lowest level of financial accountability.

The next step up the empowerment chain is blame. You know this one. You've probably met a few of these guys. Their bad financial state is always someone else's fault. Someone didn't pay. An employee dropped the ball and lost a client. They are glad to complain about that person, to the point that they maybe even sue that person.

As unpleasant as it is to be around someone who rolls around in blame, or even worse, decides to sue you because they refuse to own up to their own responsibility, imagine what it does to them.

Blame is disempowering. If the chief motivator behind the lowest level, (avoidance) is fear, then the chief motivator behind blame is a victim mentality.

A person who blames others is a person who doesn't believe he has any power in his life.

Five Levels of Financial Accountability

Accountability
Responsibility
Justify
Blame
Avoidance

Next level up is to justify. It's barely above blaming when it comes to empowering beliefs about your finances. In this case, it's never your fault because this happened or that happened. The economy hit a downturn, and that's the justification for why business took a downturn. Justification is nothing more than an enhanced version of blaming. It's just as disempowering, and at the end of the day, you're still a victim. That's because the best you can do is "try." You never just do something.

Moving past these three stages means making a commitment to change. For some, it won't be easy. These are deeply entrenched behaviors. On the other hand, if you do commit to change and stick with it, you may find that your business isn't the only thing that receives the benefit. For many of us, business and personal lives are wound together.

At the next step, though, things do change. When you reach the responsibility level with your business finances, you've risen above the victim mentality. You're saying, "I'm responsible."

When you began your business you were probably responsible for every aspect of it. Package didn't get mailed? That's on you. Rent didn't get paid. Oops, you didn't get that done. Whatever the issue, it was yours to deal with.

If you are still in business after the first few years, you've probably mastered this level, at least to some degree. (If not, your business probably failed, or it has come close to failing at least once.) Your bills get paid, the business tax returns are filed each year, your licenses are renewed, and you are getting it done on a daily basis. You are creating your financial future, not being buffeted around by the whims of an uncaring world (whine).

Even so, you still have a challenge. When you make yourself responsible for everything, you've created a need for you to watch everything. You are very involved in the daily operations of your business. You've succeeded in leveraging your time so that you're paid more than ever before, but you're not quite there yet. That's because at this level, when you are taking responsibility for everything, you're still, in essence, self-employed. You have to show up to get paid.

The next step for you is the final step: accountability. At accountability, you have ultimate responsibility, but you aren't personally responsible for getting the work done. This is the level of being a true business owner: Complete accountability without having to personally do each task. The only way that you can achieve accountability is with good accounting.

Accounting is being accountable with your finances. Your financial statements tell you whether your business is working or not. They tell you what you need to stop doing and what you need to do more of. The financial statements of your business are a scorecard for how effective you've been with your business management decisions.

Accounting simply means accounting for your income, expenses, assets, and liabilities. Bookkeeping is the first step. It's keeping the records so that you can prepare, or have prepared, financial statements that give you vital information about your business.

Using Computer Software to Track Your Income and Expenses

(The following section was written by Cynthia Finkenbinder, one of our CPA Tax Advisors at US TaxAid Services, LLC. Cynthia's passion is early-stage business owners. You can meet her at our website, and you can learn more about QuickBooks and QB training, by going to www. MySmarterBusiness.com).

By having accurate and organized information at your fingertips, it will not only help you to manage your company's financial information, but it will also help you to save money. You'll be able to make better informed financial decisions concerning your business, and you'll also be ready with more accurate information when it is time to work on your tax strategies.

There are several computer programs that allow you to track income and expenses as well as customer and vendor information. Your choice for tracking the information will depend on the type of business you have and your computer system. For PC users, some of the options include Intuit QuickBooks˚, Sage Peachtree˚, Microsoft Office Accounting˚, and Microsoft Excel˚ spreadsheets. Versions of all programs except for Microsoft Office Accounting are also available for Mac users. MS Office Accounting, Peachtree, and QuickBooks are all very similar software programs. but you'll want training to fully utilize the one you choose.

You very likely have a spreadsheet program on your computer already. Spreadsheet programs like Excel often have templates available for invoicing, check registers, inventory tracking, and creating financial reports. The problem with using just a spreadsheet program for tracking your business is the data is not integrated, making it easy to overlook important information.

When working with a complete accounting software package, such as QuickBooks, the first step is to choose the correct version for your type of business. QuickBooks comes in multiple "flavors." There's even an online version. The online version is useful if you travel a lot, have multiple locations, sales representatives, a virtual assistant, or bookkeeper; and you don't carry an inventory.

The advantage of using QuickBooks online is that you never need to purchase a new, updated version of the software. It will work with any computer with internet access, so you are not confined to a certain computer. There are some limitations for Mac users, but not many. Currently, you must have a PC environment to successfully operate the payroll feature. In either case, since the program is on a securely hosted server, you'll never have to worry about losing accounting data if your computer should crash.

Normally, I suggest using QuickBooks Premier˚ as it has been customized to be industry specific. There are versions for General Business, Contractors (includes specialized reports such as certified payroll and change orders), Manufacturing and Wholesale (managing inventories and customer orders), Professional Services (for lawyers, architects, and other professionals), Nonprofit, Retail (managing sales, inventories and pricing), and Accountant (which allows accountants to open any version of QuickBooks files). The software maker, Intuit, has other products available such as Point of Sale˚ and Cash Register Plus˚ for front end retail sales, and there is also QuickBooks Professional˚ and Simple Start˚. The Professional and Simple Start versions are cheaper, but do not contain as many reports and other helpful features for running your business.

Two main things to remember when using any computerized accounting system are:

- Back-up your data, and
- Choose a tax professional who is familiar with the software you use.

Data backup is often overlooked until it is too late, and you have a hard drive failure or a virus corruption. According to the National Computer Security Association[5], it takes 21 days and $19,000 to recreate 20MB of accounting data. And, according to another report, this one by PriceWaterhouseCoopers[6], 7 out of 10 small firms that experience a major data loss go out of business within a year.

Not backing up your data can be catastrophic to your business. Don't take the chance. Make sure you know a good computer specialist who can help you to make sure your backup system is not only in place, but that it is also working correctly and includes off-site storage.

Now I'll walk you through the basics of QuickBooks. The reason I recommend QuickBooks over other software programs is that it's a very powerful program with a quick learning curve. If you are at all familiar with programs such as Word or Excel, you can learn the basics of QuickBooks very quickly.

When you start QuickBooks for the first time, you'll be asked if you want to create a New Company, Open an Existing Company, or Open a Sample Company. Because you are just learning QuickBooks, you will want to open the sample file first and literally play around in it. The fastest way to learn QuickBooks is to try things out in the sample company. Never use a working file (like your own company file); you do not want to have made up information in your working file.

After you have familiarized yourself with the program and have taken a basics class, you are ready to get started. Create a new company and go through the interview process.

---

5   Newman, J. (2009, March 11). *Small Business Backup - data Loss Statistics.* Retrieved September 5, 2009, from SearchWarp.com: http://searchwarp.com/swa447993-Small-Business-Backup-Data-Loss-Statistics.htm

6   DTI/PriceWaterhouseCoopers. (2004). *2004 Information Security Breaches Survey.* Retrieved from http://www.entrust.com/resources/pdf/ukdti_infosecbreachessurvey2004_execsumm.pdf

You'll need to know the following information before you can begin using QuickBooks:

- The legal name and trade name of your business
- The Tax ID number for your business
- The State ID numbers (especially if you are doing payroll)
- Your business address, phone number, e-mail, and web site address
- Your business's tax classification (C Corporation, S Corporation, Sole Proprietorship, or Partnership)

The only piece of information required to set up your QuickBooks file is the trade name. The other information, however, is vital to set up your business for both tax and legal planning.

QuickBooks will now walk you through a series of questions designed to help you set up your file correctly the first time. You'll be asked what type of business you are in; this will help QuickBooks choose the correct chart of accounts for your business type.

One question most people answer incorrectly is the first month of their company's fiscal year. The first month of your fiscal year is not always the month when you started doing business. Many small businesses use a calendar year for their business so their fiscal year is normally January through December. If you are using C Corporation taxation and a non-calendar year, talk to your tax advisor first to make sure you've got the right dates.

The QuickBooks interview will then save your company information, and set up the file on your computer. Now you'll be asked a series of questions designed to tell QuickBooks how your company runs. You will be asked if you sell services, products, or both. Do you sell on-line, charge sales tax, create estimates or have employees? How you answer each of these questions will determine how QuickBooks tailors itself for you. These settings are not set in stone; you can always go into the preferences later and turn on or off features as your business grows and you get more familiar with QuickBooks.

The main key to using QuickBooks or any accounting system is to consistently, accurately, and routinely maintain your information.

Every new business owner begins with an idea or dream and a set of skills that will allow that idea to thrive. Remember, you do not have to be an expert in all areas of business to make your dream come to life. Get the training you need to handle areas of running a business you are not familiar with, especially your accounting system. Or, you can work with a bookkeeper or your CPA to get your QuickBooks file set up properly.

Good accounting is a foundation to build your business on. It shouldn't be overlooked. Don't be afraid to ask questions if you don't understand something. It is better to learn how to properly do something now, than to pay to fix a problem later. That is something many business owners will tell you that they've learned the hard way. Enjoy the journey, but don't neglect the processes that make the journey worthwhile.

Action Steps

Action Step 1: If you don't yet have an accounting program, determine and discuss what you or your bookkeeper will use.

Action Step 2: Set up the dates for financial statements. Will you review them monthly? Quarterly? Annually? Schedule times for this now.

Resources

Come to our website, www.MySmarterBusiness.com to find links to Cyndi's webinars and other information for business owners.

Smart Business, Stupid Business: Section 4: Financial Statements Made Easy (and What You Can Do With That Knowledge).

www.intuit.com: Intuit, the makers of the QuickBooks suite of software applications, have many resources, tutorials and other training methods on their website.

Chapter 12:
You Can't Keep Good Books without Good Records

Keeping good records allows you much more control over your business operations. If you know where your business stands financially at any given point, you're in a much better position to take advantage of a great deal that you spot coming your way. You'll also learn more about how to read financial statements so that you can see the story in other people's financial statements immediately.

Here are three reasons why good records and accurate bookkeeping are vital to your business:

They keep the IRS happy

If you have a business and good records, you'll pay less tax than you would as an employee. Being a business owner is considered a higher risk than being an employee, and the government rewards those willing to take the risk with more tax breaks. That's the distinction: entrepreneur versus employee. It's not rich versus poor. It just happens that those tax breaks, plus the ability to control your financial future, tend to make entrepreneurs wealthier on the whole. Consider it the government's carrot.

If good recordkeeping keeps the IRS happy, why don't all business owners do it?

Contrary to popular belief, the IRS isn't an enemy, hell-bent on taking everything away that you've worked hard to earn. The folks in charge at the IRS understand that businesses, and the people who run them, keep the economy in this country going, just like business does in most other countries around the globe. But the IRS (or any other country's taxing authority) does have a mandate to make sure that businesses stay accountable and don't try to take advantage of a good thing. Forcing business owners to keep records under threat of losing business deductions and paying higher taxes, as a result, is the stick.

If the IRS comes to your business with a question on a deduction, whether in person, or (more likely) by letter, the way you answer will tell them a lot. If you have business records that clearly show how and why a deduction was taken, you're also sending a message that "we keep a tight ship – nothing out of line here." On the other hand, if you send some handwritten notes, illegible photocopies of receipts, or worse yet, you have no documentation to substantiate a deduction at all, you're sending a different message. One that says, "Audit here!"

What does the quality of your record-keeping say about your business?

Good records make for good financial statements

Have you ever read something on the internet that makes you wonder if the writer should be forcibly restrained from using a keyboard? You've all learned that the inability to clearly express yourself verbally or in writing will hold you back and cause you to lose out on opportunities. The business world is no different. A properly-prepared set of financial statements can tell you everything you need to know about a business, good or bad.

On the other hand, a confusing set of financial statements can do the opposite. It can tell you that the business owners don't have the knowledge or expertise to run a venture properly. It can throw up false numbers, making things look better or worse than they truly are. And it can tell other people the same thing about your business. You know the saying, "Garbage in, garbage out." That's especially relevant to financial statements. Unless you have solid, accurate information going in, you cannot pull accurate financial statements out.

Learning how to read a financial statement may be one of the single smartest things you can achieve. Every financial statement tells a story. Learn to read the financial statements of your business, and you'll pick up a valuable business skill, along with clear knowledge on what you need to do to improve your business.

Every financial statement tells a story. What does yours say?

Learn how to read the financial statements of other businesses, and things will get better. Now you have a great skill that will lead to new business opportunities.

Reading Someone Else's Financial Statements

One of Diane's tax clients turned his ability of keeping good records for his business into a huge business opportunity.

He had been a successful business owner who transitioned into buying large, commercial real estate properties. These were the type of large properties that were sold strictly based on the numbers. Most of the buyers for properties like this never even look at the physical properties. They are just looking at the return that they will receive on their money. For them, it's all about the finances.

He developed a computer program that could quickly sort through the financial statements for commercial properties, and he looked for anything that was not average. In fact, he even looked for properties that had expenses that were too high. You see, properties like those usually had a purchase price that was significantly greater than what the income of the property was(e.g., the purchase price was equal to two times the income, etc.). If the expenses were high, the profit was low. And, that meant that the price would be low.

One day, Diane's client came up with a property where the expenses just seemed too high. Interested, he started investigating, and he found that the seller had made a big mistake on their financial statements. In fact, they had overstated their property taxes by $50,000. The building was selling for a multiple of 10 times the earnings (in real estate terms, this is called the capitalization rate). He bought the property, waited six months, and corrected the financial statements. The new, corrected financial statements meant that his profit was increased by $50,000. With a multiple of 10 ($50,000 times 10), he pocketed $500,000 after just six months of ownership, and all that was due to simply understanding how to read a financial statement.

Here, the opportunity wasn't in the property. The real value came from being able to read the story of financial reports. That might be one of the biggest hidden benefits of having your own business. You get the job training for how to be a fantastic investor. How many opportunities are just out there waiting for you to discover?

We'll cover more about this in Section 4. It all starts with your record-keeping.

Good records are necessary to get financing

Want to grow your business with other people's money? You'll need good records to show where the profit and potential is.

The first thing a bank or investor will want to see is the financial records of your business. Having current and complete financial statements can allow a bank or other investor to evaluate how you operate your business and what kind of a risk you and your business are. The better your records, the more accurate a picture they present, and this frequently makes the difference between getting a loan or not.

What records should you keep?

According to the IRS, a business is responsible for keeping "proper records in order to prepare and support its annual tax return." There's a reason for using such a broad definition, and it's partially to allow the IRS a lot of room to review business records to make sure things are complete and in order.

Most bookkeeping and business records are made up of things like receipts, bills, invoices, bank statements, check stubs, deposit slips, purchase orders, Sales and Use Tax reports, Payroll reports, credit memos, lease agreements and loan documents. In the language of accountants and bookkeepers, these documents are all known collectively as "source documents."

These are the documents that back-up your expenses and deductions. One of the first things that you need to do is to set up a filing system to track, record, and store the source documents of your business.

In general, there are two types of files. These are temporary files and permanent files. The temporary files are created each year, and then, at year end, they can be packed away until it's safe to destroy them.

You'll stay better organized if you set aside a file drawer or file box for the current year. If you have enough room, keep two or three years open and available. But, remember to keep them sorted by year. So that the 2010 files are separate from the 2009 files, although you may have much of the same type of files for income and expense.

Let's start off with the temporary files and list the type of things that you should keep.

Income

Keep paperwork on sales. This could include invoices, receipts, cash register tapes, and end of the day internet sales totals from companies like Authorize.net, Paypal, or QuickBooks Merchant Accounts. You'll need to be able to track details on the sales, such as sales price, shipping, and the amount of sales tax collected.

Also keep records for any deposits that are made into your business accounts. You may need to be able to prove where deposits came from. Think of it this way. Let's say an auditor from your state sales tax division is looking through your business bank statements. He will question every deposit, and he will make you prove it was from a buyer outside your state. If you can't prove it, that sale is going to be treated as taxable by the state. You could get a huge, unexpected, and totally unnecessary tax bill.

Depending on the volume, you may want to keep a file per month for deposits or just one file for the entire year. Each deposit into the account should have some kind of detail so that you can prove what's income and what's not.

And, depending on your business, you may want to file your sales information by customer, alphabetically, or by month.

Expenses

In a perfect world, every penny that you spend on behalf of your business would come with a receipt. As with your invoices, all of your expense receipts should also have the date of purchase, amount of purchase, item description, any applicable taxes and shipping charges, terms of payment, and the name of the person or company you purchased the item from. If your purchase receipts don't have this information, add it in yourself.

Every business receipt should stand-alone. Add detail as needed so you have proof if the IRS asks.

There are several forms that a purchase receipt could take. Credit card or debit card statements, cancelled checks, cash register receipts, copies of accounts and bills that you've paid, supplier invoices and account statements are all great examples of purchase receipts.

Inventory Purchases

Inventory is an asset of your company. We'll talk more about why that is important later in Part 4. For now, though, let's clear up a common misconception about business.

If you spend money for something and it's not immediately disposable, then you have an asset. That means that you don't get an immediate deduction for the expense. For example, if you buy a ream of paper to run in your printer, you have an expense. However, the purchase of the printer itself is an asset, not an expense. Expenses are immediately deductible whereas the assets may not be.

Inventory is NOT a deductible expense.

Every time you buy something you are planning to resell, you are making an inventory purchase. These purchases could also include the cost of parts and raw materials for manufactured products or things that you buy to add to your existing products (like batteries or cables).

Your inventory purchases are typically backed up with the same type of source documents you receive for your expenses purchases. And that's to be expected. After all, they're basically purchases. You just don't get the same tax treatment.

Reimbursing Yourself

Until you get your business credit going, you are probably going to need to use your personal credit card to pay for business purchases. As soon as possible, get your business its own card. Until then, follow these six steps:

- Keep copies of receipts whenever the personal card is used for business purposes.
- When you receive your monthly statement, or print it out from a website, highlight the business expenses.

- Submit an expense report to your business from you, as an employee and/or owner.
- Attach a copy of the statement with the business expenses attached as well as the store receipts.
- Total the reimbursement amount.
- Business writes you a check for this, as a reimbursement of expenses.

Keep a very clear audit trail any time that you combine personal and business expenses. And, as soon as possible, stop the practice. This could seriously jeopardize your asset protection plan down the road.

Permanent Files

So far, we've been talking about temporary files that you create anew each year. Now let's talk about the records you will want to keep in permanent files. These are records that you don't close off and put into storage at the end of each year.

Your permanent files are the ones that have asset purchase information and any long-term liabilities, such as bank loans, car loans, and other debts that will take longer than one year to repay. Another example of a permanent records file would be your company's Minute Book, which will have the Annual Minutes of your business, Annual Reports, and founding corporate documents, such as the Articles of Incorporation, Bylaws, and Shareholder Register. If you are setting up a limited liability company, this would be your Articles of Organization and Operating Agreement.

As a rule of thumb, if the source document relates to something that will be a part of your business for more than one year (insurance policy, lease, mortgage, etc.), keep it in your permanent files. Once you sell an asset that you have been maintaining in your permanent records, you can move that information to your temporary files for the year that asset was sold.

Asset Purchases

The assets that your business purchases will also need to be carefully documented. That's because these items are subject to depreciation (a great tax-reducing write-off!).

To make sure that your assets are properly documented, keep track of the usual points (date of purchase, goods purchased, purchase price, tax and shipping charges, warranty charges, name of seller, and any terms of payment.) You will also need to track any costs to upgrade or maintain your assets. That way, if you have your computer overhauled and new components put in, you have a record of what was done, when, by whom, and for how much.

If your business is buying a vehicle, large pieces of equipment, or real estate, you may also receive things like a closing statement or mortgage documents. Take especially good care of these records!

How long should you keep the records for your business? We recommend to our clients that temporary files be kept for at least five years after the tax return for that year has been filed.

Follow the 5-year rule with business records. Wait at least 5 years before destroying back-up documentation.

The IRS has some additional requirements that we've set out below:

If you...	*Then you must keep records for ...*
• File a claim for refund or credit after the original return has been filed	• 3 years or 2 years after tax was paid
• File a claim for a loss from a bad debt or worthless securities	• 7 years
• Owe additional tax, and the next three situations set out below do not apply	• 3 years
• Have not reported income that you should have reported and that income is greater than 25 percent of the gross income you set out on the return	• 6 years
• File a fraudulent return	• An unlimited period
• Haven't filed a return for one or more years	• An unlimited period

Electronic Data and Federal Privacy Regulations

If you are only keeping records in electronic form, make sure that you back your data up regularly. Think about the critical impact that a lost, stolen or crashed hard drive could have on your business.

And, thanks to new federal privacy rules that went into effect in 2009, you have a whole new thing to worry about: security for sensitive client/customer data.

The Red Flag Rule, implemented by the Federal Trade Commission (FTC) on May 1, 2009, requires all financial institutions and creditors, to design a policy to keep confidential information secure and safe from ID thieves. A creditor is defined as any business that does work for clients and extends credit. If your business does work and then bills for it, you're a creditor. If your business operates on a subscription basis, you're a creditor. If you receive and store financial and personal data for your clients, you're also subject to these rules.

Under FTC guidelines, you need to create a system to keep client data confidential and to make sure that it's followed. In a business that accepts credit card orders by fax (like ours), we have a few rules.

Clients are required to send in a photocopy of the credit card they are using, along with a photocopy of their driver's license. That helps to establish that the right person is using the credit card. Our accounting records are held on a secure server that is encrypted and firewalled. We don't allow clients to send documents with personal information through unsecured email. Anything coming through email must be password protected, or even better, we have a secure file server where that information can be uploaded. We don't use third-party fax solutions that intercept a fax, convert it to a PDF, and email the fax as an attachment.

Penalties for breaking Red Flag Rules are steep. If data is stolen from your business, your clients suffer identity theft as a result, and you can't prove you had a good Red Flag Rules policy in place (and that it is being followed), you can be fined thousands of dollars per client.

The problem with entering the Information Age is that there is too much information and not enough protection.

To start preparing your Red Flag Rule policy, go to our website, www.MySmarterBusiness.com and register your book. Once you've done that you'll have access to information on figuring out what goes into a Red Flag Rule policy, and a sample that you can adopt (and adapt) for your business.

Action Steps

Action Step 1: Review your current record-keeping system. Do you have this system in writing?

Action Step 2: Review anti-Red Flag Regulations. Are you subject to these regulations?

Action Step 3: What action steps do you need to take?

Resources

The official US Federal Trade Commission's website contains information and additional resources on designing a Red Flag policy for your business. Visit http://bit.ly/128ajm to learn more.

Visit our website, www.MySmarterBusiness.com, to download a sample Red Flag policy.

Chapter 13:
The Best Business Structure for
Your First Business

Hopefully, you're operating in a formal business structure from day one. If not, making the change to a formal business structure needs to go to the top of your to-do list.

A formal business structure is one that you create by filing documents with your Secretary of State. Corporations, Limited Liability Companies (LLCs), and Limited Partnerships are all examples of formal business structures. Trade names, sole proprietorships, general partnerships, and Schedule Cs are all examples of informal businesses.

Informal businesses are cheaper to run. You don't need to keep separate records, or a separate bank account. The business income and expenses are reported on your personal tax return, so the business doesn't need its own tax return. The only problem with these businesses is liability. The liability is unlimited, and it's all falling on you. Your business can't pay its bills? No problem. You can. Your business gets sued? You get sued, too. Don't have the money to pay? No problem. Your creditors will settle for your house, car, savings account, and so on.

Unincorporated Businesses: All of the Risk. None of the Reward.

Informal businesses are bad from a tax angle, too. You lose all kinds of tax reduction opportunities, including the ability to stream income. That alone can cause you to pay thousands of extra dollars in tax.

But it can get worse. You could go into an informal business with one or more partners. Now you have all of the negatives we've already mentioned, multiplied by the number of other people you're in business with. This type of informal business is called a general partnership, and it's probably the worst choice of all. It only takes one partner to bind a business. So your partner(s) can put you on the hook and risk your personal assets without you knowing anything about it. Until, the lawsuits start flying.

If you really want to have an unincorporated, informal business, then there are only two times we would recommend it;

    (1) If there is very little risk from the business, or

    (2) You don't have anything to lose.

Formal Business Structures

Let's be clear here, though. We want you to have a formal business structure for your business. The number one reason is liability protection. We call this wall a corporate veil. If you obey all of the rules and regulations set out by state law and the IRS, you are, by law, protected. Those acts and debts stay with the business. If your business can't pay its debts, you are safe from its creditors (unless you have personally guaranteed the debt). If your business is sued by a client or third party, you can't be sued personally as the operator of the business, at least in most cases. Where you've done something criminally wrong, different rules apply. There are also different rules for professionals like doctors, lawyers, engineers, accountants, and the like. If a client makes a complaint against you to your professional association, you could be found personally liable, depending on the circumstances of the complaint, and it could affect your malpractice insurance coverage.

However, when you don't follow the rules and regulations, you can easily lose the protection of the corporate veil. Some of the things that can trip you up are:

    (1) Your records are incomplete,

    (2) You mix up business funds with personal funds,

    (3) You underfund the business (in other words, you don't invest a reasonable amount into the business at the beginning, or keep enough money on hand for your business to operate independently),

    (4) You don't file annual reports or keep proper corporate records,

    (5) You allow your business structure to be dissolved by the state for failing to keep up with state filing requirements

Do one of these things and you may as well be operating as an informal business, because that's how you're going to be treated by the legal system. We call this situation "piercing the corporate veil."

The corporate veil protects you from your business.

There are two main types of formal business structures: corporations and limited liability companies. Corporations can be broken down into C Corporations and S Corporations. They are similar from a construction and legal standpoint, but they are very different in how they are treated for tax.

Corporation history goes back for hundreds of years, and the same basic format is used throughout the world. There are probably more active corporations in the U.S. than any other formal business type. Limited liability companies are a hybrid of a corporation and a limited partnership. LLCs have been around in the U.S. since the 1970s. They started in Wyoming, and they are now available in all 50 states. Some states have even adopted a Series LLC, which is a regular LLC that can have an unlimited amount of subsidiaries. You can operate each subsidiary independently of the parent LLC. You can have different owners, elect different tax status, and otherwise treat each subsidiary as a separate business. And, as long as you follow the Series LLC rules, each subsidiary will be considered legally separate from the others, meaning no cross-liability. What happens in one subsidiary can't necessarily affect the others.

LLCs are more flexible than corporations. In fact, we prefer the LLC model over all others.

To make an informed decision about your best business structure choice, you need information.

The Corporation

The C Corporation is the traditional business structure. It has three elements: owners (called shareholders), operators (called officers), and shareholder representatives (called directors). The first two are pretty straightforward. Shareholders own the company, and officers run the company.

Shareholders are passive in a corporation. Unless you are also an officer or director, you can't participate in the active daily business operations.

That limits what you can do. However, it also limits how much you can lose. As a shareholder, you aren't responsible for what the officers, directors or the company does. If the corporation can't pay its bills, you aren't on the hook for its debts. If the corporation engages in criminal activities, you aren't going to jail. And if the corporation goes under entirely, you can only lose what you invested in the corporation to buy your shares.

Officers are the positions of president, vice-presidents, chairmen, CEOs, secretary-treasurers, etc. These are the individuals who carry out the daily functions of the business. These are the people who sign the checks, negotiate and execute contracts, buy and sell equipment on behalf of the corporation, and so on. You don't need to be a shareholder to be an officer of a corporation.

Directors act as representatives for the shareholders. As a director, you don't carry out business operations directly, but you do oversee business operations and the officers. Again, you don't have to be a shareholder to be a director.

Directors are elected by the shareholders, each year, at the corporation's annual meeting. Being a director gives you great power and limited power at the same time. As a director, you're also the one who appoints the corporation's officers each year. From that perspective, directors have great power. Yet, if you are only a director, you can't become involved in the daily operations of a corporation. You can't sign checks or enter into agreements on behalf of the corporation.

On the other hand, if you are creating a small corporation where you are the shareholder and the officer and the director, it's a moot point. This distinction really comes into play when the business is much larger and far more people are involved.

The Role of a Resident Agent

Your corporation must also appoint and keep a resident agent in the state where you incorporate and each additional state you register the business into. A registered agent is an individual or a service provider that acts as your corporation's legal face in that state. Legal documents are served on the resident agent instead of the corporation directly. A corporation cannot act as its own resident agent, but a shareholder, officer, director, or anyone else for that matter, may act in that role.

Can you act as the resident agent for your business? You can, but most businesses use a third party service provider for this service. It's easier to pay for the service rather than have to put your home address on the record for all to see. If you prefer to keep a low profile, that is hard to do with your name splashed on the public record.

Service provider rates vary from a few hundred dollars each year to more than $100 per month, so it pays to shop around. Look for an established provider that has been in business for some time. Remember, part of your corporation's existence is tied to this position. All corporations must have a current resident agent at all times. If your agent resigns, you forget to appoint a new one, or you don't realize your agent has resigned, your corporation could be dissolved by the state.

C Corporations and S Corporations

The structure for C and S Corporations is the same so far. When you get into the sub-sets, differences begin to emerge:

- **Shareholders.** Your C Corporation can have an unlimited amount of shareholders. Shareholders can be people, other business structures or trusts, and they can be located anywhere in the world. Your S Corporation, though, can have only shareholders. All of those shareholders must be people, or certain trusts, held by people. And, you must also make sure all of the shareholders in your S Corporation live in the U.S. or file U.S. tax returns.

- **Taxation.** Your C Corporation will file its own tax return each year. It will pay income tax at the corporation rate, which is on a different scale than personal income tax. You can distribute after-tax profits to the shareholders, or you can choose to leave the money in the C Corporation. If you decide to take out the after-tax profit (called a dividend), you'll have to declare it on your personal tax return and pay dividend tax on it. The dividend is not tax deductible for the C Corporation. In effect, both you and the corporation will have to personally pay tax on the same money. That's why you hear the expression "double taxation" with C Corporations.

  Your S Corporation also files its own tax return each year, but it doesn't pay taxes, at least at the federal level. Some states do require S Corporations to pay some state tax.

The S Corporation return reports the income, expenses, and gross profit. The profit is then transferred to you and the other shareholders, according to everyone's ownership percentage. If you're a 50% owner, you get 50% of the before tax profits, and so on. You must report the profit on your personal tax return and pay taxes on that profit at your own personal tax rate. In the early days of your business, you'll typically get better tax treatment with an S Corporation. Once your total personal income starts to top $300,000, though, it's time to make some changes.

- **Retained Earnings**. C Corporations can hang onto after-tax profits. S Corporations can't. The IRS considers all S Corporation income to be distributed each year. That can lead to phantom income.

- **Phantom Income**. Phantom income describes money your S Corporation should have distributed but didn't. For example, you had net profits of $50,000, but you needed the money to grow the business. The IRS sees the $50,000 net profit and assumes that you have the money. You get a tax bill for that $50,000, even if none of it hit your personal account. That's why it's called phantom income. To get around this, most S Corporations distribute at least enough money to pay the taxes.

- **Losses**. This is where S Corporations shine. Because of the way the IRS characterizes S Corporation income, a loss can be used against your other income. So, if you have a job where you made $100,000 and a S Corporation business that lost $10,000, you can reduce your taxable income from your job by offsetting it with that $10,000 loss. In a C Corporation, losses can't be pushed out to shareholders. In a C Corporation, losses are "suspended" until the business turns a profit. Once it turns a profit, it can use the losses to offset profit until the loss is used up.

- **Fringe Benefits**. The C Corporation wins, hands-down, when it comes to fringe benefits. It is the only formal structure that allows you to create a special medical reimbursement plan to pick up where your other medical coverage left off. Plus, medical insurance is fully deductible. And you can set up corporate plans to pay for physical fitness facilities, educational plans, and day care facilities.

Phantom income is money that you pay taxes on, but you DON'T personally receive.

You form a corporation by filing Articles of Incorporation with your local secretary of state. The articles are typically one page, and they provide a few pieces of key information:

- Resident agent (a person or business in the state that acts as the legal face of your corporation and accepts the service of legal and government documents)
- Share capital (how many shares your corporation is allowed to issue)
- Names of the officers and directors (at least in most states)

Your corporation will also need to prepare a set of bylaws, which is a document that sets out how the corporation operates. It covers how directors and officers are elected and removed, when meetings are called, who can call meetings, and so on.

Depending on where you live, your corporation will also be required to file an annual report. This report generally confirms the resident agent and makes any required changes to the directors and officers.

State law also requires your corporation to hold a yearly annual meeting. It's a pretty informal procedure unless you have a publicly-traded company. If that's the case, the procedure is set out in state and federal securities regulations. It's best if you keep a written record of the meeting. A written record, called minutes, is recommended for all of your corporation meetings, although not specifically required. When they are properly signed and kept in your corporate records binder, minutes are great evidence that your business is acting like a real business. This can be very important in situations where someone is trying to sue you, and they are claiming your business is a really an empty shell in which you are hiding.

The Limited Liability Company (LLC)

LLCs are very flexible. You can set up your LLC as either a single layer structure or a two-layer structure. Owners are called members, and they can be individuals, trusts, or other business structures. You don't have to be a U.S. resident to own an LLC, but you will pay extra taxes if you aren't.

LLCs are tax chameleons. They can take on any of the four available tax classifications.

In a single-layer LLC, called a member-managed LLC, the owners are also the operators. Everyone gets a vote, and everyone can act on behalf of the LLC. If you are operating a member-managed LLC with two other partners, any one of you has the authority to bind the business. It's like a general partnership except that in an LLC, you and the other owners are only liable for what you've invested into the business. So you can lose what you put in. But, unless you have personally guaranteed any of the LLC's debts, that's as far as it goes.

In a two-layer LLC, you have the option of creating a second layer that provides all of the management duties. This type of LLC is called manager-managed LLC. The people in the management layer are akin to officers in a corporation. As a Manager, you can sign checks, enter into agreements on behalf of the LLC, buy and sell assets on behalf of the LLC, and so on. Managers may be members of the LLC, but they don't have to be. When your LLC adopts manager-managed status, the members become passive owners, the same way that shareholders are passive. Unless you are also a manager, you don't participate in the daily business activities at all.

To create an LLC, you will file Articles of Organization with the secretary of state's office in the state where the LLC is formed.

Like corporation Articles of Incorporation, LLC Articles are quite short. You'll name a resident agent, just as you do with a corporation. The LLC Articles specify whether the LLC has elected to be managed by all of its members or by managers. If you've set up a member-managed LLC, you need to list all of the members. If you've set up a manager-managed LLC, you will need to list all of the names of the managers, and most state laws also require you to name the majority members (20%+ owners).

The LLC version of bylaws is called an Operating Agreement. It also sets out how your LLC operates, how you elect or remove managers, how you can buy into or sell your way out of the LLC, when meetings are called, who can call meetings, and so on. You aren't required by law to have an Operating Agreement, but we would never recommend you operate without one. Failure to have an Operating Agreement means you must follow state laws when disputes arise. Those laws often don't cover the problem, leading to expensive litigation, or they do cover the problem, but not in the way that you would like.

Depending on the state in which your LLC is formed, you may have to file a yearly report confirming that you still have a resident agent and listing the current names and addresses of managers and members.

LLCs are not required to hold meetings or to keep minutes. But, we recommend that you do, for all of the same reasons we recommend to corporation owners. One big area of litigation for LLCs is the "alter ego" argument. That says you aren't really using your LLC for business. It's just something you're hiding behind and operating directly. Good records, including separate bank accounts, financial statements, and written minutes, properly signed and kept in your LLC's corporate records binder, are great evidence to counter any such claim.

Why an LLC is a Great Choice for You

There are two major reasons to prefer an LLC over either a C or an S Corporation:

(1) Better Asset Protection, and

(2) Flexibility for Tax Elections.

The corporate veil gives you good personal protection from your business. But with corporations, it's a one-way street. If you do something wrong in your personal life, it can have an impact on your corporation. For example, you have too much to drink and cause a car accident where someone is injured. Your insurance doesn't cover the damage claim, and you lose the court case. When the other side comes looking for assets to pay out the claim, your shares in the corporation are considered an asset that can be seized. Once a creditor has control of your ownership, they can force the corporation to liquidate assets. This is especially true if you are the only shareholder or you hold a 50% + ownership. The creditor simply votes the shares in a liquidation proceeding.

With LLCs, things are different. State LLC laws clearly state that your ownership in an LLC is not an asset that can be seized, nor may a creditor reach into your LLC to force liquidation or attach a claim to the LLC's assets. A creditor may only place a Charging Order (which amounts to a lien) over your assets. That means that any net profit that would normally be paid to you will be paid to the creditor until your debt is satisfied. And, even though a creditor may control the profit from your LLC member interests, that creditor may not vote those interests. This allows you to retain control over the actions of your LLC.

An LLC gives you unparalleled tax flexibility and solid asset protection. It's the best of both worlds.

The second advantage an LLC has over a corporation is unparalleled flexibility in taxation. An LLC, unlike any other formal business structure, can decide how it wants to be treated for taxes. If C Corporation taxation is beneficial, an LLC can be taxed like a C Corporation. It would become an "LLC-C". If S Corporation taxation is a better deal, then an LLC can make that election instead, and become an "LLC-S". If other tax classifications are better, like the passive income elections, for example, an LLC can also make those elections and become taxed as a partnership or as a sole proprietorship. So you'll effectively receive all of the benefits of a corporation, along with the extra asset protection LLCs offer over corporations. It's this double-shot that makes the LLC your business structure of choice. You may even find that an LLC-S is the ideal business structure choice for most of your new business ventures.

Getting Your Business Structure Formed

Costs to form a business structure can range from less than $100 to more than $1000. There are plenty of services out there that help you to form a corporation or an LLC for less than $100. And, if you've got considerable experience forming and structuring businesses, that might make sense. There are also resources that we do recommend, like our *Operations Guide* series (available at www.USATaxAid.com) that go through all of this in great detail, provide comprehensive documents, and completion instructions.

On the other hand, if you don't know what you're doing, it's very easy to get things wrong. After 20+ years in the legal field, Megan could write a book on the horror stories masquerading as corporate records binders that she has seen. The problem with having things done incorrectly is that you often only find out about the problem when it's too late to have it fixed.

The most common mistake business owners make with their corporate records is not completing them in the first place. Many of the cheap incorporation providers give you a package of pre-printed documents and let you complete them on your own. The problem here is that the forms are either too general to be used safely, or are too confusing to complete on your own. So the package joins your incomplete accounting data and waits for an emergency to make itself known. Typically, this shows up in one of these ways:

(1) You lose out on a business opportunity or funding because the records are in bad shape, and you can't produce a needed document.

(2) You find out you don't even have a business because it was dissolved by the state when you failed to maintain a current resident agent.

(3) You lose out on valuable tax deductions or benefits because the IRS audits your records and finds no evidence that your business is acting like a true business.

(4) Your business becomes the subject of a lawsuit, and your incomplete business records make you a ripe target for a corporate veil-piercing argument by the other side.

Keep It Simple

In the early years of your business operations, there is no reason to have a complex business structure. You'll find some service providers will attempt to sell you multi-layered, complex structures that feature two or three business entities, perhaps an offshore trust, and a few other things, all to operate a simple web business. Honestly, in the early years, it's very unlikely you need any of these things unless you are running multiple businesses and already have a significant amount of assets.

In particular, resist the urge (and the sales pitches) that involve using out-of-state companies, like Nevada, Wyoming, and Delaware. There are times when this can be an effective and appropriate strategy, but the early years of your business isn't that time. In most cases, the claims (Nevada has no tax! You can set up Nevada residency with a bank account, virtual office, and local phone number!) are misleading at best, or outright lies, at worst.

Don't Have Enough Money to Pay For a Business Structure? Then You Probably Don't Have Enough Money to Start a Business.

A woman came to one of Diane's events and spoke to her at one of the breaks. She had started a business, but she didn't have enough money to spare to also create a formal business structure to operate through. Diane repeated her caution that without the business structure, the woman was exposing herself to unnecessary liability.

About 6 weeks later, the woman contacted Diane's office. Things were not going well with the business. In fact, someone was threatening her with a lawsuit. She wanted to know if Diane could put her in touch with someone who formed business structures.

But it was too late. Once there's a threat of a lawsuit – even if it's just a threat – the damage is done. It's what is in place at the time the cause of action arises that counts. And, in this place, there was nothing more than a trade name. The woman was going to be on the hook for any damages assessed against her business.

We don't want to sound like alarmists, but this is the United States of America, perhaps *the* most litigious country on the planet. If you're in business in the U.S. and have anything worth keeping, protect yourself. The bigger your business gets, the more likely it is that someone, some day, will try to take a run at you in court.

Action Steps

Action Step 1: Set up or, better yet, have a full-service provider set up, your business structure.

Action Step 2: Make sure initial paperwork, agreements, and minutes are in the permanent files of your business.

Action Step 3: Review corporation formation documents to make sure you have everything in place.

Action Step 4: Review your corporate binder at least once a year, about one month before the anniversary of the formation of your business. Make sure you renew your resident agent service and any annual reports are filed.

Resources

Operation Guide for your Corporation, available at: www.USTaxAid.com

Operation Guide for your LLC or LP, available at: www.ustaxaid.com.

Kennedy, Diane. 2004. *Loopholes of the Rich*. Wiley, revised edition.

www.legalshelfcompany.com. Visit this website to learn about how and when to use a pre-formed shelf company.

Chapter 14:
Avoiding the 3 Biggest Mistakes with Payroll

T here's more to payroll then just writing a check every few weeks to your employees. And this is where a lot of small businesses make their most fatal mistake.

The Mistake That Puts a Small Business Out of Business

Take a minute and imagine this. You have a small, local store, stocked with merchandise. In this case, it's a health food store/metaphysical bookstore. (Okay, maybe a bit of a stretch, but stay with us.)

You have a bookkeeper who takes care of paying your bills and doing the payroll for you, your spouse, and your two other employees. You go to a local strip mall-type franchise, tax return preparer to get your taxes done each year.

You make a little money, and you love what you do.

Then, early one morning, you're just opening the store, and you see big SUVs pull up and block the path to your door. You still have the door locked because it's a little early. A group of guys storm out of the SUVs and grab a battering ram to slam in your front door.

They storm through the door with guns drawn and order you against a wall.

And that all happened because your bookkeeper ignored a notice from the IRS.

But it wasn't an income tax penalty, which would have required a whole series of notices, a notice of attempt to lien, and then "merely" a lien or freeze on your bank account. Nope.

Miss this notice and you have a pseudo-SWAT team taking down your business. The local news picked up the story (which happened in Reno, Nevada) and showed pictures of the little shop after the raid. It looked like a bomb had gone off inside it.

So what was the tax notice that the bookkeeper hadn't handled? It was payroll taxes.

Payroll tax penalties and notice of non-payment are taken much more seriously then any other type of tax due. ALWAYS pay attention to those notices. You may not get your door broken down, but you still want to make sure these are handled right. Otherwise, the IRS may just put you out of business fast.

Don't make these three mistakes with payroll:

Payroll Mistake #1: Not paying yourself and/or your spouse.

Hopefully, you've taken the smart business path, and you are operating your business as either an LLC-S or as an S Corporation. Income from your LLC-S is going to all be taxable to you either as salary or a distribution. Your salary is subject to payroll tax, and the distribution is not. Guess which one the IRS is going to try to make you claim?

Your strategy should be to pay the minimum amount of payroll that you legally need to. In this case, the IRS is looking for a reasonable salary. In other words, how much would you pay someone else to do what you're doing? If you've been successful at working your way out of the day-to-day, you may actually work very few hours. That's great news for your payroll tax. That's because you wouldn't pay someone as much to work the hours you do now. Therefore, out of the income you make, a smaller amount goes to salary, and the bulk of the income comes to you as a distribution. That means less payroll tax.

On the other hand, if you're working day and night, you might find that the salary you'd have to pay someone else to do what you're doing is more than your business is even making. In that case, the IRS has allowed companies to dramatically reduce the salary for owners. They have recognized that, in the beginning, a responsible business owner pays himself last. That means that you don't need to pay yourself as much in the beginning, and that means lower payroll taxes.

Finally, there is the case of the somewhat stable business that still requires a lot of your time. Here, as a general rule of thumb, the argument that one-third to one-half of your income flowing to you in the form of salary would be appropriate. Try to go any lower, and you may raise eyebrows at the IRS. Go higher, and you could be paying extra tax unnecessarily.

The big thing to avoid is owning an LLC-S or an S Corporation with significant income but with no salary being paid to you. Try that, and you're painting a big "audit me" across your business tax return. In that audit, the IRS will claim that all of the income should be subject to payroll tax. Even if you settle somewhere in the middle, you're still now looking at a substantial tax, penalty, and interest bills, all courtesy of the IRS.

So is there any easy way to figure out how much you should pay yourself? Like so many things in the tax world, the right answer is, "It depends." You'll need to look at:

- Total income of the business,
- What you'd pay someone else to do what you do, and
- Salary as a percentage of total business income.

A good CPA or financial advisor will be a great resource here to crunch numbers and to help you find the number that's right for your business.

Payroll Mistake #2: Payroll tax payment and reporting is not in compliance.

Filing payroll reports is a big pain. There is no easy way to do it. And, if you miss a filing date, you could be looking at big penalties and maybe even a closed down business. Considering how cheap it can be to get an outside service to calculate payroll and make necessary filings, this is one area where you might want to immediately outsource.

Some of the services that our clients have successfully used include:

- QuickBooks° payroll service
- Bank of America payroll service
- Wells Fargo payroll service
- Peachtree payroll service

You can get direct links to some of our favorites at our website.

Here are some of the forms and procedures you'll need to follow for your small business payroll.

Upon Hiring: Have your employee fill out a current Form W-4 and an I-9. These forms should be kept in your permanent business files and then moved to the temporary files for the current year when the employee leaves.

On Pay Day: You may need to withhold, at a minimum, federal income tax, employee's portion of Social Security, Medicare tax , state income tax, and city income tax.

These withheld amounts need to then be paid to the state (or depository, per their instructions) and to your bank along with a Form 8109 Federal Tax Deposit Coupon which tells the IRS which company is making its deposit, the amount and the pay period the payment is for. Depending on the size of your business payroll, the deposit periods range from once a week to once a year. Most small businesses fall into the monthly depositor category, and file on the 15th of each month. If you live in a state that also collects payroll taxes you'll need to make these withholdings and deposits as well.

And, the age of electronics is catching up with the traditional payroll tax deposit methods. It's likely that at some point in the near future you won't be able to deposit payroll tax checks at your bank manually any longer. You will need to use the IRS's electronic filing system (EFPTS) or your bank's electronic payroll filing system, if they offer one.

When you're calculating the total amount of payroll tax to be paid, remember, that your business must match the Social Security and Medicare taxes that are withheld from the employee's paycheck. The total amount is then deposited.

Quarterly: Each quarter, you need to prepare and file state and federal payroll returns. The required state payroll returns to file will depend on your home state. For the IRS, you'll need to file Form 941 (reports the total amounts of Social Security, Medicare, and withheld federal income tax). Depending on the size of your payroll, you could also have to make an estimated payment for federal unemployment premiums.

Annually: You need to furnish employees with their Form W-2, Wage and Tax Statement by January 31st of the next year. You need to then file a copy of all of your W-2s, along with a Form W-3 cover sheet with the IRS by February 28th.

Finally, you will need to file a Form 940 Employer's Annual Federal Unemployment (FUTA) Tax Return by January 31st, the final quarter Form 941 TITLE, and any required state forms.

Payroll Mistake #3: Not reconciling your business tax returns with your payroll reports.

This is such a simple mistake, but it can get you into so much trouble. Make sure you or your tax preparer reconciles what you've told the IRS through the Forms W-2, 941, and 940 for wages to what you report on your personal tax return. The IRS instituted a matching program a couple of years back. If what you report on the business return doesn't equal what you and any other employees report on your personal returns, you're going to get a letter.

And make sure you or your tax preparer correctly breaks out the officer salaries from everyone else's payroll on the front page of your federal income tax return. Miss this step, and you're just asking for an audit.

Payroll is a tricky area. Don't forget about it. And, for sure, don't forget about depositing the withheld payroll taxes and timely filing your payroll reports.

If payroll reporting hurts your head, hire a bookkeeper who understands payroll taxes. You'll sleep better.

Action Steps

Action Step 1: Correctly and strategically pay salary to yourself in the right amount and at the right time.

Action Step 2: Verify that you have a system to ensure your payroll taxes are correctly and timely filed.

Action Step 3: If you are currently doing this yourself and want to stop, investigate good payroll providers.

Resources

Intuit, the company that makes QuickBooks, offers several payroll options. You can begin at http://payroll.intuit.com/ to learn which one will work best for your business.

PayrollTaxes.com has a comprehensive set of resources on their website to help you learn more. Visit http://www.payroll-taxes.com/

Chapter 15:
What State is Your Business In?

You might think that knowing what state your business is in would be a simple thing. Your business appears to be in the state where it operates. A doughnut shop in Philadelphia is clearly a Pennsylvania business. We call that having nexus. Because there's a physical location in Philadelphia, there is a clear link to where the income is earned.

Nexus is both a tax issue and a legal issue. When you make a sale of a product (or provide a service in some states), there is income tax and possibly sales tax to be collected. The problem you might run into is that more than one state will want to collect tax. And, to properly protect your business (and yourself) from liability, you may need to register your business to operate in more than one state.

As far as taxes go, states are fighting right and left over the right to tax you and your sales. In the case of the Philadelphia doughnut shop, it's clear. The business has a physical location from which all sales are made. Pennsylvania gets the tax. If your business had a location across the water in New Jersey, you would then have nexus in two states. You would now have to register your business in New Jersey and make sure you track income and expenses from that location separately.

You will collect and pay New Jersey sales tax on sales made at that shop, and you will pay New Jersey income tax on the company's profits.

Even if you don't have a location in New Jersey, you can still have a nexus issue if you cross state lines to provide a service to clients or deliver your products to customers. Most states take the position that when you cross the line and work on their turf, you create an obligation to pay tax on the income you earn there.

Over 95% of all businesses have underestimated their tax obligations to other states.

Some states provide more leeway than others, and they permit you to go into the state for up to 30 days without creating a problem. Other states have a lower threshold, of around 14-16 days. Other states have no threshold at all. Hawaii and Texas both claim nexus after just a single day within state borders. Texas law provides that if you attend a trade show and do nothing more than offer free information you have established nexus for tax purposes.

In a recent case, a seminar promoter got hit with a $1 million+ sales tax bill for seminars that he'd given in other states.

Nexus and Internet-Based Businesses

When you take your business to the web, things really change. You may be sitting in your basement in Los Angeles, creating a website design for someone in Cincinnati, using software that resides on a server in Nevada. You would prefer nexus to be in Nevada for lower taxes. California, on the other hand, will insist that because you own the business, worked on the design personally, and live in California, nexus is in that state.

Concerned about the IRS? That's probably the least of your worries. States have even less money, and you are their only resource.

Let's take it a step further. Let's say your internet business has affiliates. You sit in your office in Arizona, and your servers are in Arizona. So far, so good. You have Arizona nexus. That means the only time you'll have to collect sales tax is if you make a sale to someone in Arizona. Right? Wrong!

You may have brought another state into your nexus mix without even knowing it because of your affiliates. An affiliate is someone who advertises for your business on the internet and sends people over to your site. Your affiliate gets paid every time one of his referrals buys something from you.

The problem is that some states have taken the position that if you have an affiliate in their state you've also created nexus for your business. And that means you need to also collect sales tax in that state.

Is this fair? Well, up until recently, the retailer would have won that argument. However, hungry governments in several states are rushing to enact laws that say nexus (and the corresponding obligation to collect and remit sales tax) is where the sale occurs.

In other words, New York says that it was your website that caused the sale, and as you live in New York, nexus is there. This is the so-called "Amazon" law, currently making waves through the internet. Right now, the problem states are Minnesota, New York, North Carolina, and Rhode Island. These states have all passed laws expanding their nexus definition. California and Hawaii both vetoed legislation in 2009, but there is no guarantee that the issue won't arise again.

Overlapping Tax Laws = Extra Sales Tax on Consumers

Let's say your internet business is based in Washington and you have an affiliate in New York (one of the problem states). You make a sale to someone who lives in Washington through your New York affiliate. Washington still claims it has nexus for sales tax, and now, so does New York. Who do you pay? The sad answer is "both!" Try explaining to your customer why you have to collect sales tax from him for a state he doesn't live in.

Where You Live May Put You Out of Business

Overlapping taxation laws can be dangerous to you as a business owner from another perspective, too. Let's say you have an affiliate marketing business. In other words, you find people who want to buy something and send them off to websites where they can find what they want. You get referral income every time someone buys. However, if you're located in Minnesota, New York, North Carolina, or Rhode Island, you've just created a problem for some of the businesses you sell for. By allowing you to market and drive people to their websites, they have now become responsible for collecting and paying sales tax from your referral customers. But that's okay. Most vendors with affiliate programs have chosen to simply drop their affiliates in problem states.

If you are an affiliate marketer and are based in NY, MN, NC, or RI, your home state tax laws might have just put you out of business.

Nationally Mandated Sales Tax

One possibility is that a project called the Streamlined Sales Tax Initiative, or the SST program (SSTP), may gain approval. While no one is 100% behind it, it does answer the question of how to handle overlapping state sales tax laws.

The SSTP would change nexus for online purchases to consumers. This is called "destination sourcing." Businesses would become responsible for collecting sales tax on every single sale. And that could be a lot of work for you. You would need to track sales tax requirements for all 50 states (and in some cases, additional municipalities), collect the tax, and get the tax to the right state at the proper time. That would create some massive challenges.

On the other hand, it could also create a massive opportunity for software programmers.

To become effective, the SSTP needs to be adopted by three quarters of the states, and then it needs to be enacted by way of a federal Constitutional Amendment. Many states need to make adjustments to their own state constitutions to allow for the change to a destination sourcing tax. States also need to make sure that all municipality-based taxing is in order. This is proving to be harder than it looks, as municipalities aren't happy about giving up revenue. States are also having trouble reaching an agreement on what is and what isn't taxable. The SSTP has strong support in some states, lukewarm support in some states, and no support in others. It's certainly something to be aware of, although it will not likely become effective for several years, if at all.

Nexus for Your Other Business Taxes

You might have a nexus issue with other states for more than just sales tax. If your business has nexus that puts you in line for that state's income tax, you could have more tax issues than you realize.

For purposes of this section, we'll say state income tax, but the fact is that's not even that simple. For example, Texas doesn't have a state income tax. Instead Texas has a gross margin tax. That means that the total gross is subject to the tax, with very few deductions. Or, in the case of Hawaii businesses, there is a gross receipts tax. New Mexico has the same thing. So be careful about where your business may be building nexus. We call that the nexus footprint.

The more nexus footprints you leave, the more tax you're liable to pay.

Nexus Triggers

Employees and independent contractor relationships can create nexus. All states take the position that having an employee located in a state will create nexus for your business in that state. So, if you have a virtual assistant working from his home in California, and your business is located and operated in Arizona, guess what! You've got a nexus issue and an obligation to register and pay tax in California.

Many states now take the same approach to independent contractors.

If your head is spinning, you aren't alone. A recent study conducted by the tax-compliance organization, Sabrix, Inc., indicated that 95% of businesses surveyed had a nexus issue they were unaware of. It's not something you can put your head in the sand and ignore, either. States are becoming extremely aggressive in the quest for tax dollars.

California recently passed legislation claiming that out-of-state businesses that receive 25% or more of their income from California customers have a nexus obligation in California. Massachusetts attempted to pass a law forcing New Hampshire retailers to collect and remit sales tax from Massachusetts customers. This prompted New Hampshire to pass a law protecting its retailers from the effects of the Massachusetts law. Expect this kind of over-reaching to continue unless the federal government or the U.S. Supreme Court steps in to moderate the issue.

Nexus from a Legal Perspective

Don't forget to look at the legal perspective of nexus as well. If you are operating in multiple states you want adequate legal protection in all of those states. You'll want to be able to chase down and perhaps sue people who don't pay their bills. Plus, you'll want to be able to protect yourself from an angry or injured client. If you are operating in a state without being registered you are putting your business at risk for no real benefit.

If you do find you have a nexus obligation in more than one state, registration is relatively simple. It's typically a two-part process: once with the secretary of state's office, for the business structure, and once with the Department of Taxation, to take care of sales and income tax obligations. When registering your business into another state remember that all of the same types of obligations will now apply in that state, too. You will need to have a resident agent and file annual reports in that state, as well as in your home state.

Remember, you'll need to track your income and expenses by each extra state as well. Come tax time, you'll need to file a tax return for each state in which you have nexus. Talk to your bookkeeper about the best way to track those based on the software program you are using.

Determining Your Business Nexus

When it comes to determining the nexus of your business, start by answering these questions:

    (1) Where do you live? If the business has multiple owners, where do they live?

    (2) Where is the work being done?

    (3) Where is your business inventory stored?

    (4) Where does your business inventory ship from?

    (5) Where are your website servers located?

    (6) Where do your customers or clients live?

    (7) Where are your employees or independent contractors located?

    (8) Where are sales people (including affiliates) located?

    (9) Where do you give presentations or hold live events?

Keep it simple. If you are located in Connecticut and you operate a service-based business, form your business in Connecticut. It doesn't matter how you deliver the service to the client (unless you work on-site at the client's location in another state). You're going to be considered a Connecticut business by state tax authorities.

If your business has multiple owners, look at their involvement in business operations. A passive money partner, who doesn't perform a service or do anything in the business doesn't always create nexus. Depending on the laws of their home state, they may be considered simply an investor.

Finally, don't get caught up in the Nevada/Delaware/Wyoming incorporation game. The old strategies of attempting to create Nevada nexus simply by establishing a mailing address, virtual office, bank account, etc., are just that: old, and no longer valid solutions. Unless you have a specific business purpose in the state, you won't gain anything by setting up a business structure there, particularly when it's clear that your business has nexus somewhere else.

Action Steps

Action Step 1: Take the business nexus test you'll find at our website, www.MySmarterBusiness.com. Do you have a possible nexus footprint in another state?

Action Step 2: Discuss your nexus status with your tax strategist. Do you need to collect sales tax in another state?

Action Step 3: Are you subject to tax in another state? What strategy can you do to minimize the tax consequences?

Action Step 4: Do you have the right home state for your business?

Action Step 5: Do you need a nexus expert on your team or do you have the resources you need?

Resources

www.sabrix.com: Sabrix provides transaction management and nexus guidance for companies of all sizes. You'll find information, resources and more at their website.

www.ustaxaid.com: Diane's website provide discussion forums and other articles on nexus and how it impacts business owners in the United States.

Chapter 16:
20 Deductions to Put More Money in Your Pocket

In the first years of your business, it's easy to overlook all the tax deductions you can get. Don't make that rookie mistake!

Here are twenty deductions that are designed to put more money in your pocket.

Deduction #1: Cost of Goods. The cost of goods sold (COGS) is the total of direct costs that are related to your income.

For example, if you are in the business of providing services with a consulting firm, your COGS would be the salary and independent contractor fees paid to people who provide services along with the payroll taxes and benefits paid to them or on their behalf. It could also include informational materials that you provide to your consulting clients. In general, though, you won't have as much in the way of COGS as a product seller.

Now let's say that you have an e-commerce business where you sell products through eBay*, Bonanzle*, Craigslist*, and Amazon*. The products that you sell will have a cost associated with them. Typically, these are items that you sell out of your inventory. So, the normal accounting process is to first put them into inventory (an asset account) and then take them out of inventory to create a tax deductible expense, such as a COGS.

Deduction #2: Home Office. Don't be afraid to take this deduction! There are two requirements to legally taking the deduction:

(1) The space for your home office must be exclusively used for business.

(2) You must regularly use the space for your business.

You don't need to see clients in your home office to qualify. You don't need a separate door. All you need is to meet those two requirements.

If you can meet those requirements, follow these five steps to legally and safely take the home office deduction:

(1) Measure the square footage of your home office. Compare this to the total square footage of your home. The percentage of the home office to the total is your business use percentage.

(2) Take a picture of your home office to ensure you've got proof in case you later move.

(3) Add up all of your home related costs such as mortgage interest, property tax, insurance, homeowner's association dues, utilities, maintenance, repair and the like. These are indirect costs. The business use percentage is applied to the total of indirect costs each year when you prepare your tax return.

(4) Add up all of the expenses directly related to your home office. These are expenses that you spent on that space alone and can include remodeling costs for your home office, paint, draperies, floor coverings, shelving and more. These are direct expenses that are allowed 100% against your income.

(5) Give these amounts to your tax preparer at year end for inclusion on your tax return.

Deduction #3: Inventory Space. Inventory space can be treated as separate space from your home office. What's nice about inventory is that it's a straight, two-dimensional space calculation that isn't based on a single-purpose use. So if you keep things in your garage you can take a deduction based on the square footage of space your inventory is using up, regardless of whether or not your garage is also holding your cars, camping supplies, fishing gear, and so on.

One of our clients asked whether it would be okay to write off his entire garage if he laid out all of his inventory boxes on the ground, instead of installing shelving along the walls. The answer is yes. While it's not the most practical use of space, it is a deductible one. Of course, you need to find a new place to park at night.

Deduction #4: Contributed Assets. When you first start your business, particularly if you're bootstrapping, chances are, you contributed a lot of things to your business. This probably included things like a desk, chair, cell phone, printer, computer, decorations, file cabinet, and even more.

Don't forget to take a deduction for these items. Here are the four steps to safely take that deduction:

(1) List all the personal items you have contributed to your business.

(2) Calculate the fair market value (FMV) for each contributed item. Check in at eBay or Craigslist for an estimated value.

(3) Make a note in your files of how you calculated the FMV. Better yet, print out a copy from a third party source that shows a representative value.

(4) Write yourself a check from the business for the total value. If the company doesn't have enough funds, loan the funds to the company. This is the best way to provide an audit trail.

Deduction #5: Telephone. The IRS hasn't really kept up with technology when it comes to telephone deductions. The rules are still pretty clear. In order to take a deduction for a regular phone via a land line, you need to have another phone into the house.

And, at least at this point, you aren't allowed to use a VOIP to qualify. A VOIP (Voice Over Internet Protocol) includes services such as Vonage˙, Skype˙, or Magic Jack˙.

If you have just one land line, even if it's used exclusively for business, you won't be able to take a deduction.

In the case of a cell phone, the IRS is getting tougher. You will need to be able to show a phone log to prove what calls are business and what are personal. Only the business portion will be deductible. If you have both personal and business usage and a flat rate plan, you will need to pro-rate the business deduction. In other words, it's not 100% deductible.

Deduction #6: Internet Service Provider (ISP). If you've got a home based business or even just a home office with a business office somewhere else, you've probably got an ISP. You will need to prove that you have business use for the ISP.

But, it's not quite that simple. For example, many ISPs now bundle in cable service for TVs, so you have a combination of personal and business use. Plus, what if your kids use the same ISP to access their MySpace˙ account?

At this moment, there isn't any formula or clear-cut rules on deducting your ISP. However, we can follow the lead that the IRS is using now with cell phones and say that you probably are safest using an allocation for the ISP cost.

Deduction #7: Equipment. The business equipment you buy such as computer, printers, fax machines and the like are considered assets. That means you don't get an immediate deduction for buying these items. They are instead capitalized and then depreciated or subject to Section 179 immediate expensing.

When you buy equipment, even if you're financing it, the cost of the equipment is fully subject to deprecation and/or Section 179.

Deduction #8: Travel. What's deductible for your business? The answer is "It depends!" An expense must be ordinary and necessary to the production of income in order to be a deduction.

If you have travel that helps your business or is otherwise necessary, you have a deduction.

Let's say that you need to see a vendor in Orlando, Florida. You take along your family and turn the trip into a family vacation. The cost of your trip there and back will be deductible. So will the associated cost for business days. The cost of going to Disney World isn't deductible unless it is somehow directly related to creating income for your business. And the cost for your family to travel is not deductible, unless your family members are also active in the business and the trip has a business purpose for them as well.

Remember that the cost of your annual meeting (required for corporations) will be deductible. So, if you choose to have your annual meeting outside of your home town, you probably have at least a partial deduction.

If your trip is outside the US, there will be further limitations on how much is deductible. For example, you will need to pro-rate the airfare based on how many business days you have compared to total days on your trip.

Deduction #9: Software. Don't forget the deduction for software you buy to help you with your business. This can add up fast and the program costs are fully deductible.

Deduction #10: Meals. The cost of meals is deductible as long as there is a business purpose. If you and your spouse work together in your business, you might end up with a bit of too much of a good thing when it comes to deductibility. Generally couples who work together spend a lot of mealtimes talking about the business. In normal circumstances, a business discussion over a meal is going to mean a deduction. But what if every single meal has an element of a business deduction?

Technically, you probably could get away with taking a deduction for each meal. Practically, it's probably not a good idea to get aggressive with family meals as a deduction. Take some as a deduction, but not all.

Make sure you keep a receipt from the meals and make a note as to:
- Who it was with,
- Where it was,
- When it was, and
- Why this qualifies as a business deduction.

If you use a paper calendar system like a Day Timer, just clip the receipt to the date of the meal. This can be a great way to keep track of your receipts.

This strategy will get you a deduction of 50% of the cost of your meals. But if you're the kind of person who wants even more, you're going to love this next part on how you can deduct 100% of your meals.

If you have to eat at your place of employment for the sake of your employer, you have a 100% deduction. This could mean that picking up a latte and a bagel in the morning to eat at your desk as you check your business email accounts will get you a 100% deduction. Or, if you have lunch brought in for a mid-day meeting for your staff, then you have a 100% deduction.

When is a meal 100% deductible? When you eat at your desk "for the benefit of your business."

Deduction #11: Labor. If you pay someone for something they do for your business, you have a deduction.

But, it's not quite that simple. You need to also decide if they are paid as casual labor (temporary work), employees (with payroll considerations), or independent contractors.

If you hire your kids to work in your business, it's especially important to be able to prove that they legitimately do work and are paid a reasonable wage. Here are the three things we recommend for our clients who pay dependents:

(1) Have a written job description,

(2) Keep track of hours worked, and

(3) Pay a reasonable wage for the work done.

Deduction #12: Insurance. Don't forget about the cost of insurance such as E & O (error & omissions) and health and disability insurance, provided your plans are in compliance with federal and state regulations requiring you to provide equal insurance to all of your full-time employees (in other words you can't create a gold-plated medical plan that's only available to you, and isn't available to your 6 full-time staff members. That's discriminatory, and it can get you into all kinds of trouble).

Deduction #13: Education. One of the truly amazing things about having your business is that you get paid to learn. Well, you're not exactly going to get a paycheck from the government, but you are going to get a tax deduction if the expense is something that helps your business. The education can't prepare you for another career. It can only be used to enhance your current business.

If you're an employee, the cost of your education is probably not deductible. If you're a business owner, it probably is!

Deduction #14: Advisors. Remember back in Chapter 4, when we talked about the 9 Factors that the IRS wants to see in order to prove that you have a business? One of those was that if your business has a loss, you need to be able to prove that you are taking steps to try and make your business profitable. One of the ways to demonstrate that is to hire advisors who have more business experience than you do.

Not only does the IRS let you take a deduction for that expense, they actually use it as a requirement if your business is running at a loss!

Deduction #15: Auto. If you use your auto for business purposes, you have a lot of choices in how you can take the deduction.

The business does not have to own the car, but you do have to carefully document the expenses. There are two ways to take expenses:

actual expenses or a mileage allowance. With actual expenses, you need to track expenses, such as:

- Gas and oil
- Tires
- Repairs
- License and registration
- Lease payments
- Garage costs (if you rent space to store your vehicle)
- Insurance
- Depreciation

You may take a pro-rata portion of these expenses based on the amount of business miles the vehicle was used. So, if you use your vehicle 50 percent of the time on business, then 50 percent of these items would become deductible!

The second alternative is to track your business-related mileage and take a straight deduction of that amount. The mileage rate changes every year, so make sure you're using the most current number.

To take this deduction safely, keep a small notebook in your car and record your mileage for at least a 1-3 month period. That will give you a baseline of average mileage that you can extrapolate from there. This is one area the IRS loves to challenge, so make sure you've got some kind of proof for this deduction.

Here's a little tip combining a couple of the deduction strategies. The IRS does not allow you to deduct miles spent commuting to and from your work. However, if you have a home office, your commute may be as simple as walking down the hall! That means that every time you leave your house on business-related purposes, the mileage becomes deductible. And that includes the drive to your outside office!

This is one of my favorite deductions. I love driving and tend to use my car for most of my travels, including the 1200+ mile round trip to meet with Diane. To my everlasting disappointment, I have learned that, unlike gas, oil, repairs and insurance, the tickets I get while speeding through the desert are not tax deductible.

-- Megan

One other thing to bear in mind here is that once you have selected a deduction method you have to stay with it. The IRS won't let you use the percentage method for a couple of years and then switch to the mileage deduction method.

Deduction #16: Websites. The cost of websites and internet marketing is all deductible for your business. Here's a tip: If you have a new business, get it started first and then incur your programming costs. That way you have current expenses and don't need to amortize them as start-up costs.

Timing is everything. Get your business IN business fast to create deductions. Otherwise, you have start-up expenses that you have to amortize.

Deduction #17: Promotion. If you have a business in today's world, there is one thing you need to do and that's marketing. So, whether you're doing PR, advertising, marketing, or promotion, make sure you track all those expenses.

Some of the things are unbelievably cheap these days. For example, you can buy pens with your website name printed on them for not much more than the cost of regular pens. Why not get some and hand them out freely? Someone is always looking for a pen.

This is a great way to promote your business and get a tax deduction as well.

Deduction #18: Office supplies. The little things can really add up for your business. That includes the cost of office supplies. It's amazing how many people forget about all the quick little runs to the local office supply store. Remember the cost of supplies is deductible.

Deduction #19: Interest. Have you used your credit cards to fund your business? Then your business is responsible both for paying you back for that and for a reasonable interest rate for the loan. That's also true if you've made an outright loan of cash to your business or contributed items that you haven't been paid back for. Your business needs to pay you back, plus pay a reasonable interest rate.

Deduction #20: The Finer Things. This is probably the tax deduction everyone wants to have. What is it that you really love to do and that you're currently buying with after tax dollars? If you have a business purpose for it, you probably have a deduction.

At our live seminars, Diane frequently asks attendees for a list of the items they want to learn how to write-off. Then, as a group, they figure out ways that they could possibly be deductible.

Here's a recent list, with some ideas of who might get the deduction:

- Movie tickets. If you are a screenwriter, video producer or otherwise involved in the film industry, you probably have a deduction here.
- iTunes cards. If you're involved in the music industry in some way, you've got a deduction. Or, if you're like me, you need the music for a live event. Make sure you get appropriate permission before you use music commercially. Or maybe you want to use the music for your office ambience.
- Wine. Okay, we had to throw this one in there. If you have a party for your clients, vendors, prospects, staff, or just about anyone that you can prove has a legitimate business purpose, you've got a deduction.
- Tips. This is a tough one. If you travel for business a lot, chances are, you know there is a lot of money that you end up having to spend in cash. At the end of the trip, it's hard to account for it all. Wherever possible, get receipts. If that's not possible, match up cash withdrawals from your bank account with a list of the expenses that you've had to pay in cash.

The final point to make with deductions is this: pigs get fat, hogs get slaughtered. So when it comes to tax deduction, it's okay to be a little piggy, but don't go whole hog. Not everything is going to be deductible.

Action Steps

Action Step 1: Review the 20 possible deductions. Are there any deductions that you're not currently taking that you could?

Action Step 2: Remember, a business deduction needs to be ordinary and necessary to the production of income. What do you spend money on that could be a legal business deduction?

Resources

www.MySmarterBusiness.com: When you register your book at our website you'll receive access to all kinds of extras, including our self-test, "Where Does Your Money Go?" which features a list of almost 1,000 potential business deductions.

www.USATaxAid.com: Will it deduct? Come to Diane's website, join our free Forum, and post your question.
Kamoroff, Bernard B. 2008. *422 Tax Deductions for Businesses and Self Employed Individuals.* Bell Springs Publishing; 7 edition.

Chapter 17:
Don't Make These Eight Mistakes When You File Your First Tax Return

If you've already filed your first tax return for your new business, it may be too late for you. However, it's a good idea to go back and take a look at the decisions you might have inadvertently made. Is there anything you need to fix now?

Here are the eight tax mistakes Diane sees most commonly in her tax business:

Mistake #1: Selecting the wrong business type for your business. Each type of business return (Schedule C for Sole Proprietorship, Form 1065 for partnership, Form 1120-S for S Corporation and Form 1120 for C Corporation) requires you to select the type of business you have.

This may be the last thing you think of as you're filing your return. In fact, you might have even had a tax preparer who didn't even understand your business make the decision for you. That can be a very costly mistake.

Mistake #2: Selecting the wrong NAICS code for your business. The IRS keeps statistics on business expenses based on the type of business. They assign a specific number to each kind of business. But, if you use the wrong code when you file, that can confuse things. For example, if you have a restaurant, the IRS expects to see an average of cost based on your income. If you report under a restaurant code when you really have a restaurant consulting business, your expenses are going to be skewed, and you're just asking for an audit.

Mistake #3: Failing to elect to amortize your start-up costs. Your business, just like every other business that ever started, has start-up costs. These are the costs that you incurred before you started your business. The IRS expects these expenses to be written off over a period of time, i.e., amortized. The mistake most businesses make is either (1) not counting them at all or (2) lumping the costs into regular operating expenses.

If your first year return is audited and you have lumped your start-up costs into operating costs, they will be disallowed. And you may not be allowed to switch them over to be amortized instead. They may simply be disallowed forever.

Mistake #4: Not selecting the correct accounting method. You might already have an idea on whether you are a cash-basis or accrual-basis taxpayer. There is actually a third one that you might know about, called a hybrid-basis taxpayer.

A cash-basis taxpayer means you have income when you get paid, and you have a deduction when you pay it out.

An accrual-basis taxpayer has income when work is done, regardless of whether the money has been received or not. And, on the other hand, expenses are deductions, whether or not they've been paid.

The hybrid-basis is somewhere between the two. If you have a retail business, you have inventory. That inventory is considered an asset of your business. It's not an expense. You need to sell the item to get the deduction, and even then, it's called a cost of goods sold (COGS), rather than an expense.

So, you're not quite a cash-basis taxpayer because you can't take the deduction right away for paying for the inventory. But you're also not an accrual-basis taxpayer, because you don't have to take into account income or expenses that haven't had a cash transaction yet.

If this describes your business, make sure that your CPA understands and prepares the right kind of return.

If you're a hybrid-basis taxpayer, make sure YOU understand the difference, too! I had a momentary panic attack once when I thought I owed an extra $70,000 in taxes. Then I learned how to change my QuickBooks settings to display my true financial picture.

-- Megan

Mistake #5: Not taking the full amount of loss in the start-up year. In the first few years of your business, you're likely to experience a loss. Don't make the common mistake of figuring that if you have a loss, there isn't any point in finding the rest of your expenses.

A loss can be carried forward to offset future years. That can mean money in your pocket down the road. Report all of your legitimate business expenses even if they don't make any difference on your current return. Those expenses can make a huge difference down the road.

Mistake #6: Not reporting inventory for a retail business. We've talked about this one a few times already. It's one of the biggest mistakes that retail operations make. If you don't report a number of inventories, you're asking for an audit!

Mistake #7: Making a mistake with your salary. There are two big mistakes that you can make with the salary you take from your business (outside of fraud or failing to pay or report your payroll taxes). Those two mistakes are:

(1) Paying yourself a salary, or
(2) Not paying yourself a salary.

When to NOT Pay Yourself a Salary

Let's start off with the times when you wouldn't want to pay yourself a salary. If you have a loss in your company in its early years, the IRS is not going to require you to pay yourself a salary. (That is unless you are taking some benefits from your company. If that describes your situation, make sure you pay yourself a small salary). The IRS does acknowledge the fact that owners don't always get to pay themselves in the early years. When there's not much income, other things take priority.

The other time you don't want to pay yourself a salary is when you are operating as a sole proprietor or you're a partner in a partnership. The IRS doesn't permit you to take a salary in either case.

For sole proprietorships, all of the net income of the business IS your salary. It's all subject to self-employment tax, which takes the place of payroll tax. You'll show that on the Schedule C of your business, which will be attached to your personal return.

In the case of a partnership, you receive a guaranteed payment, not a salary. You'll see that income on the Form K-1 that you'll get when the partnership prepares its return. You'll then report that income on your personal income tax return. An LLC that is being taxed as a partnership would have the same exact rules. Don't pay yourself a salary if you're in that spot!

When TO Pay Yourself a Salary

If you have a profitable S Corporation the IRS is going to want to see that you took a salary. They want to make sure that you didn't try to avoid payroll taxes by taking all of your income out as a profit distribution (which is only subject to income tax).

If your S Corporation or LLC-S made a profit, make sure you pay yourself a reasonable salary. If you submit a return with no salary reported, you can almost guarantee an audit.

Mistake #8: Not setting up an audit defense. The IRS is increasing its audit force, and that means that there are a lot more audits coming your way. Protect yourself!

Here are some strategies to reduce your audit risk:

- Watch the percentage of expenses. A business with $1 million in sales can have a meals expense of $2,000, but a business with $2,000 in sales might have a really hard time justifying that amount of expense.

- Determine your audit risk. What positions have you taken with your tax return that might make you at risk for an audit? This could include the industry you're in or being on the IRS Dirty Dozen[7]. It doesn't mean you're doing something wrong, just that you're more likely to get an IRS audit.

- File an extension. IRS auditors have a certain number of audits that they must do every year. The later you file your return, the further down the list you are. That means you're less likely to get an audit.

- Disclose any grey areas. If you and your CPA are taking a position on your tax return that is not exactly clear-cut, disclose the details in the footnotes to your return. You will start the statute of limitations running for your return.

- Prepare to win.

---

7   Come to our website, www.MySmarterBusiness.com to receive a list of the current IRS "Dirty Dozen" list of suspicious businesses and business activities.

Getting an audit notice is not the end of the world. Here are some strategies to give yourself the best chance of success:

(1) Have your CPA or attorney respond within the IRS deadline. You'll need to sign a POA (power of attorney) to give the auditor the opportunity to talk to him first. The IRS trains their auditors to get you to talk, don't make the mistake of talking to them on that first call.

(2) Get your records organized. When your professional shows up with neatly organized files with ready proof, audits seem to go much faster and better.

(3) Review your risk first and be ready with a pre-emptive strike. If you're concerned that they are going to challenge your travel, then be ready with lots of third party proof that verifies the purpose of your trips and how this went on to help your business.

Your tax returns are an important part of your overall tax strategy. Make sure they're filed correctly so you can take advantage of all the deductions you've got coming.

Want to have Diane's company do a FREE CPA Tax Review of your past year's returns? Drop an email to Richard@USTaxAid.com to find out how you can get a confidential review.

Action Steps

Action Step 1: Review the tax return mistakes in this chapter. Are there any items you need to discuss with your tax preparer?

Action Step 2: Talk to your CPA/Tax Strategist about reducing audit risk on your return. Get a copy of their audit risk assessment and reduction program. If they don't have one, ask them to prepare one for you.

Action Step 3: Get your own FREE CPA review of your past return by calling Richard at 888.592.4769 or dropping him an email at: Richard@USTaxAid.com.

Resources

www.ustaxaidservices.com: Diane's tax practice has an advisor for business owners in all stages. Work with someone who truly understands you and what you're trying to accomplish.

www.census.gov/epcd/www/drnaics.htm: At the "Ask Dr. Naics" website (an offshoot of the U.S. Census Bureau), you can find resources, articles and more on helping you properly classify your business.

Chapter 18:
Survive or Thrive: Your Early Year Checklists

Your first year in business is a whirlwind. You're establishing a company, brand, identity, finding customers, getting known, making sales, and hoping for the day when there is enough money at the end of all the bills to pay yourself a salary.

There is one more thing that you need to think about. Or rather, there are a lot of things you need to think about, all under that heading of "doing business." Here's a handy checklist to help keep yourself up to speed on what you need to get done.

Don't spend too much time thinking over the decisions contained within this chapter. Having a business doesn't mean just owning a corporation or an LLC. By having your own business, it means that you are following through on all aspects of the set-up and maintenance of your business. You don't necessarily have to do the work yourself, but you are ultimately the one responsible for the work getting done.

Action Item	Notes	Date Completed	Responsible Party
Business Structure • **Entity Type** • **Formation State** • **Resident Agent** • **Incorporation Date** • **Renewal Date**			

Action Item	Notes	Date Completed	Responsible Party
Federal Tax Classification • **EIN Obtained** • **EIN Number** • **Tax Classification** • **Form 8832 filed (if applicable)** • **Form 2553 filed (if applicable)** • **IRS acceptance received** • **IRS exception letter received** • **IRS exception letter resolved** • **Tax Classification at State Level (if applicable)**			
City/State License Requirements • **Obtained state license (if required)** • **Obtained county license (if required)** • **Obtained city license (if required)** • **Trade name application filed (if required)** • **HOA approval sought/received (if required)** • **Registered for state Sales/Use tax collection**			

Action Item	Notes	Date Completed	Responsible Party
Banking • Bank and branch location • Checking account #1 opened • Checking A/C Number • Checking account #2 opened • Checking A/C #2 number • Savings account opened • Savings A/C Number • Merchant account opened • Merchant account provider • Merchant account number • Check signer names • Overdraft protection established • Merchant account connected to checking account #1 or #2			

Action Item	Notes	Date Completed	Responsible Party
Bookkeeping • Software used • Payroll module • Bookkeeper name • Relationship (1099, W-2, etc.) • Frequency of bookkeeping updates (daily, weekly, etc.) • Frequency of A/P payments • Frequency of A/R report • Frequency of A/R follow-up • Procedure for collecting delinquent A/R • Name of CPA • Frequency of CPA review sessions • Next CPA review session date			
Record-Keeping • Permanent files created • Temporary files created • Red Flag Policy • Who is responsible for tracking and filing receipts and records? • Frequency of filing?			

Action Item	Notes	Date Completed	Responsible Party
Payroll • **Payroll preparer** • **Payroll frequency** • **Who is responsible for making payroll tax deposits?** • **Frequency of payroll tax deposits** • **Date registered for electronic payroll tax payment system (EFPTS)** • **Location of password details for EFPTS system**			
Monthly Financial Processes • **Deadline to provide previous month's financial records to bookkeeper** • **Date bank statement received** • **Date bank reconciliation prepared** • **State sales tax deposits made** • **Payroll tax deposits made**			

Action Item	Notes	Date Completed	Responsible Party
Quarterly Financial Processes			
• **Payroll tax report filings made with IRS**	_____	_____	_____
• **Payroll tax report filings made with local government**	_____	_____	_____
• **Sales tax report(s) prepared and filed**	_____	_____	_____
• **Use tax report prepared and filed**	_____	_____	_____
• **State unemployment returns prepared/ filed**	_____	_____	_____
• **Estimated income tax payments (business) made**	_____	_____	_____
• **Estimated income tax payments (personal) made**	_____	_____	_____
• **Financial statements prepared**	_____	_____	_____
• **Financial statements reviewed**	_____	_____	_____
• **CPA check-in**			

Action Item	Notes	Date Completed	Responsible Party
Calendar Year-End • Cut-off date to provide financial data to bookkeeper	_____	_____	_____
• FUTA report prepared and filed	_____	_____	_____
• State workers compensation paid	_____	_____	_____
• State unemployment reports prepared and filed	_____	_____	_____
• Payroll forms prepared and issued (W-2, 1099)	_____	_____	_____
• Payroll form report issued and filed (W-3)	_____	_____	_____
• State tax reports prepared and filed	_____	_____	_____
• Federal income tax return prepared and filed	_____	_____	_____
• State income tax return prepared and filed	_____	_____	_____

Action Item	Notes	Date Completed	Responsible Party
Fiscal Year-End (if not calendar) • **Cut-off date to provide financial data to bookkeeper** • **Federal income tax return prepared and filed** • **State income tax return prepared and filed** • **Deadline to file extension for business taxes noted** • **Deadline to file extension for personal taxes noted**	_____ _____ _____ _____ _____	_____ _____ _____ _____ _____	_____ _____ _____ _____ _____
Business Anniversary • **Resident agent service renewed** • **Annual report filed at state level** • **Annual meeting held** • **Annual minutes prepared** • **Temporary records files from previous year packed** • **Temporary records for next fiscal year begun**	_____ _____ _____ _____ _____ _____	_____ _____ _____ _____ _____ _____	_____ _____ _____ _____ _____ _____

Action Steps

Action Step 1: Complete the checklist.

Resources

Come to www.MySmarterBusiness.com, to get your free, downloadable copy of the Early Years Business Checklist.

Section Four: Financial Statements Made Easy (and What You Can Do with that Knowledge)

Chapter 19:
Live or Die by the Cash Flow Cycle

C ash flow is the lifeblood of your business. Without cash flow, nothing else matters. You can't pay your bills, build you company, pay employees, or do anything. Make it, borrow it, or sell off your assets. Whatever you do, it's got to be about the cash flow.

Cash flow is actually two words: cash and flow. You need cash, and you need to understand the flow. Cash is always flowing. In this case, you need to make sure it's flowing toward you and not always away from you.

Understanding the Cash Flow Cycle

Your business needs to have three financial statements prepared on a regular basis so that you truly understand how your business is going. These should be done at least every quarter, but preferably every month.

Everything starts with the profit and loss statement (also called your income statement). It shows the income and expenses of your business over a period of time. It's like a movie picture with a timeline. The top number of the profit and loss statement is gross income. Income to your company comes through at that line. Subtract from that the cost of goods sold (COGS) to get gross profit. From gross profit, subtract general and administrative costs (G & A), and you have net income.

The next financial statement that you've probably heard of is the balance sheet. If the profit & loss statement is the movie of your company, the balance sheet is a snapshot. It shows assets (things you own) and liabilities (things you owe) as of a certain date. So you might have a profit and loss statement for the year from January 1, 2010, to December 31, 2010, and a balance sheet as of December 31, 2010.

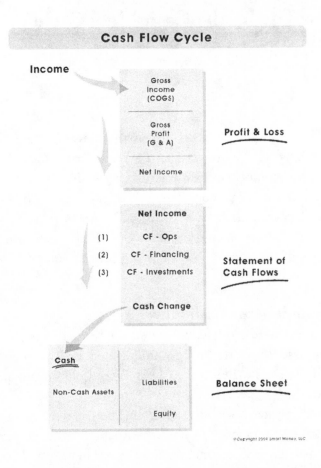

The third financial statement is the statement of cash flow. It's the translator between the profit and loss statement and the balance sheet. It's probably the one you'll have the most trouble learning to read. It's also the most important statement your business produces, because it deciphers the cash flow for you.

Following the Cash Flow Cycle

The cash flow cycle begins at the top of the profit and loss statement in the form of income. From the gross income, you subtract the expenses, until you get net income. But net income does not equal cash. It first needs to go through the cash flow statement.

Follow through on the Cash Flow Cycle Diagram. It starts where the profit and loss statement ends. Then there are three adjustments made.

"Statement of Cash Flows: Net Income"

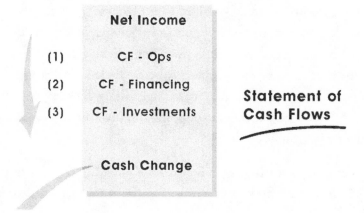

First, the cash is adjusted by the cash flow that is received by or spent in operations. These are adjustments that affect net income, but do not affect cash flow. For example, depreciation is a deduction for net income, but it does not cost any cash flow. Depreciation doesn't require you to write a check. Because depreciation doesn't impact cash flow, the depreciation expense is added back to net income. An increase in inventory doesn't change net income, but it does impact the cash flow of your business. . You've got to write the check to buy the inventory. So an increase in inventory would be subtracted from net income to get to cash flow. A decrease in inventory would be added to net income to get to cash flow. That represents money you are no longer spending on inventory.

If the cash flow changes are making your head spin a little, that's okay. It may take you awhile to understand it all, but don't give up. It's vital that you understand how cash flow works.

All aspects of the operation of your business (accounts receivable, accounts payable, deferred income, accrued expenses, and others like this) are accounted for in the cash flow from/to operations.

Net income does not equal cash flow.
Your business needs both to survive.

Next up is the category of financing. There are two primary sources of cash flow changes due to financing. Your cash flow increases when you take out a loan and your cash flow decreases when you pay back a loan. Neither of those, loans or repayments, is reported as part of the net income of your business. So loans have to be added to net income to get to cash flow, and repaid loans are subtracted from net income to get to cash flow.

Continuing cash flow from financing can be a danger sign for your business. It means your business is being fueled by loans and not by operations. In the beginning, that might make sense as your business is brand new and you're bootstrapping it. However, if it continues, you could be in trouble.

The early warning signs for trouble ahead in regards to your business cash flow can be found in the statement of cash flow.

The third adjustment is cash flow from investments. If you increase your investments you've used cash flow to do so. In other words, you've tied up cash by making those investments. You have decreased the cash flow of your business. But it doesn't correspond to your net income numbers. Making investments doesn't mean a decrease in the net income of your business. So, you need to subtract the amount used for investments from net income to arrive at cash flow.

It's a little different when your business sells off an investment. There may be an impact on net income to the extent that there is reportable gain or a loss. The sale of the principal, or the original investment, will not be reflected in net income. But it will affect cash flow.

Just like with cash flow from financing, cash flow from investing could be a sign of trouble. Your business may have cash in the bank, but it came from selling off assets.

The statement of cash flow shows how well your business is at turning profit into cash. How are you doing?

As you look at your statement of cash flow, and consider: Which way is the cash flowing for each of the categories? Temporary changes in cash flow, either way, aren't necessarily a sign that you've got a problem, but they could be warning signs if there is a persistent pattern.

At the end of the statement of cash flow is the cash change. This affects the cash line item on the asset portion of the balance sheet.

Statement of Cash Flows: Cash Change

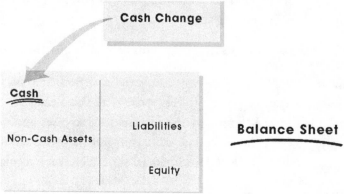

Five Myths about the Cash Flow Cycle

Cash flow is the lifeblood of your business. It's also the most misunderstood part of business by many small business owners. Here are five common myths regarding the Cash Flow Cycle.

Cash Flow Myth #1: If there's cash in the bank, everything is fine.

Use your statement of cash flow to find out why there is cash in the bank. If the cash is all from financing or selling off assets, that could be a warning sign of trouble ahead.

Cash Flow Myth #2: There is no money in the bank, so we must not owe taxes.

Net income does not equal cash flow. The money could have all been spent on items that are not tax-deductible. Make sure your tax planning is measured by more than how much is in the bank.

Cash Flow Myth #3: Building inventory is a good thing.

When you build inventory, you turn a highly liquid asset (cash) into a less liquid asset. That's part of the theory behind the business management theory of "just in time inventory." Don't build inventory at the sake of your cash.

Cash Flow Myth #4: As long as you're growing, things are going to turn out great!

If your business is growing fast, you'll need to build up your inventory and staffing; and your G & A expenses are going to climb, too. Those are expenses that take your cash right now, even though you may have to wait to get paid. You'll see that in your statement of cash flow. Your business is growing, you have net income, but your operations will be sucking cash.

Not enough or too much in sales can kill your cash flow.

Cash Flow Myth #5: When cash is tight, concentrate on sales and forget about reporting; your gut response is all you need.

Calculating cash flow, and the reasons for increases and decreases, is simply too complicated to just trust your gut. If you're serious about business, watch all three of your financial statements on a regular basis.

Learn All Three Financial Statements

The best way to learn to read the story of your financial statements is with practice. Review all three of your financial statements with your bookkeeper or accountant on a regular basis. As you master your own financial statements, you'll soon be able to read the real story of other people's financial statements.

Action Steps

Action Step 1: If you aren't already regularly getting all three financial statements, set up a schedule to receive those.

Action Step 2: With your current most current financial statements in hand, review your cash flow. Where does it come from? Where is it used? If you don't have current financial statements, please download a sample from our web site at www.MySmarterBusiness.com. You can learn the skill now and then apply it when your financial statements are regularly being prepared.

Action Step 3: What are the most critical points for the next 90 days regarding your business cash flow?

Resources

Understanding Financial Statements Home Study Course (found at Diane's website, www.USATaxAid.com)

Kiyosaki, Robert and Lechter, Sharon. 2000. *Cashflow Quadrant: Rich Dad's Guide to Financial Freedom*. Business Plus.

Ittelson, Thomas R. 2009. *Financial Statements: A Step-by-Step Guide to Understanding and Creating Financial Reports*. Career Press; Rev Exp edition.

Chapter 20:
Financial Statement Basics

F inancial statements are made up of three main pieces:
- Balance sheet (the snapshot)
- Income statement (the movie)
- Cash flow statement (the bridge between the two)

Each statement is important on its own, but it's better when read together. You need all three to see the entire picture.

Remember the Accounting Equation

Assets = Liabilities + Equity

Accounting is all about balance. If you survived basic algebra, then you know that everything on either side of the equal sign needs to balance. Your liabilities and equity must add up together to be the same amount as your total assets. If not, something is improperly recorded or missing.

Assets are things your business owns. Liabilities represent money your business owes. Equity is the difference between the two and represents either net worth or loss. A healthy business should have more assets than liabilities. A balance sheet going the other way can be a sign that your business is in trouble.

Breaking Down the Balance Sheet

Assets: Assets are anything that your business owns. You'll typically find them broken down into two categories: current and fixed.

Current assets are cash and anything else that will either be used up or converted into cash within one year. Inventory is a great example of a current asset. It's an asset because your business owns it, and it's current because you are trying to turn it over as quickly as possible. Another example is accounts receivable. This is money your business is owed when the work or product has been done or provided. If you are prepaid for products or services, then that money is really a liability. Until you do the work or deliver the product, it's a debt you owe your customer.

If you are prepaid for services or products, then that's a liability. It's a debt you owe to your clients.

Fixed assets are those with a longer lifespan, and they are usually tangible things such as equipment, vehicles, buildings and real estate, and machinery.

Assets will show up on the balance sheet based on their historic cost. In other words, if you paid $500,000 for an office building years ago and it's now worth a million, it'll still show up as $500,000 as an asset. And if you've built up an asset out of little or nothing, the new value won't show either. For example, if you have an amazing system that is patented, the only value showing up will be the cost that it took to create the patent. It won't show what the patent is really worth.

This one little idiosyncrasy of generally accepted accounting standards wreaks havocs on businesses that hold or build appreciating assets. Companies often include notes to the financial statements when they present them to others. True, fair market value is generally shown in these financial statements.

Liabilities: Liabilities are debts your business owes. Like assets, they are also broken down into current and long-term categories. A current liability is something you'll repay within a year. This would include the taxes you pay each year and your monthly expenses. Long-term liabilities are debts that are repaid over a longer period of time. Mortgages, car loans, and leases would all fit into this category.

Equity: Equity (sometimes also called owner's equity) is the difference between the dollar value of the assets of your business and its liabilities. Another name for it would be the net worth of your business. That belongs to you, as the owner, rather than to the business, which is why it's not called business equity.

If your business has more assets than liabilities, this number will be positive. But if your business owes more than it owns, this number will be negative. Remember, the accounting equation must balance. Having a negative equity doesn't always mean the worst, especially in the early days, but it's certainly something you want to keep a close eye on.

Breaking Down the Income Statement

The income statement is probably the statement that you are most used to seeing and the first one you'll take a look at each month for your business. This piece of the financial statement picture shows the income of your business, expenses and profit (or loss) for the period of time it reports. Another common name for this is the profit and loss statement.

A balance sheet shows you your overall assets, debts, and equity at a specific date. An income statement shows you a summary of the income and expenses of your business over a period of time. But the income statement still isn't a clear picture. It doesn't show you how the income and expenses relate to other aspects of your business.

For example, say you had a huge, one-time sale in June. If you looked at your income statement for that month, it would reflect that sale. That will make your business picture look pretty rosy. Likewise, a large expense could make your business appear to be less profitable than it really is. To get a real picture you need to widen your scope, and look at each month compared to other months, other years, and against your year to date numbers.

Income Statement Basics:
Gross Income – Cost of Goods Sold = Gross Profit
Gross Profit – G & A = Net Income

Gross Income: Income is classified into two sections: sales income and service income. Sales income comes from products sold, and service income comes from services your business provides. You want to separate the two so that you can properly match up expenses. That will help you to track the areas of your business that are working and those that need work.

Cost of Goods Sold (COGS): The cost to provide a service or sell a product is the cost of goods sold of your business.. If you travel to provide services, then all of your costs associated with that travel (air fare, hotel, meals, car rental, gas, etc.) would be included in your cost of goods sold. For product sales, you need to include the costs associated with selling that product (packaging materials and postage). You will also need to include your costs for creating or buying the product. So, if you buy products for resale and keep an inventory, the cost of the inventory purchase, including shipping and taxes, is also included in your cost of goods sold.

Be careful with inventory. Things are not as straightforward as they seem on the surface. You may only expense inventory against your gross income as it is sold. If you buy $1000 worth of inventory, it's considered an asset. If you sell $100 worth of that inventory, only the $100 represents your COGS.

Inventory starts as an asset and becomes an expense. Make sure you get your timing right!

Gross Profit or Gross Income: Gross income minus the cost of goods sold equals gross profit. Cost of goods sold is also sometimes called your direct costs. Gross profit is an important measure of how profitable your product or service is. Generally speaking, service industries have a much higher margin (in other words, the gross profit is higher) then product sellers.

If your gross profit is a gross loss, you've got a serious problem. That means you're selling your product or service for less than the cost of delivery. In the beginning, that might be necessary so that you can establish prototypes and markets, but after a short time, you should have gross profit.

G & A (Expenses): Your general and administrative costs are the expenses of your business. They represent the debts your business owes after those debts have been paid. Before payment, those debts are liabilities. So, when your bookkeeper calculates payroll, he will deduct the appropriate income and payroll taxes from the checks. Until the money is sent to the government, it is a payroll liability. Once the payroll taxes are sent in to the IRS, the amount is reclassified as an expense.

Net Income or Loss: The difference between gross profit and G & A is your net income or loss. If you have more income than expenses, you have a profit. If it's the other way around, then you've got a loss. This amount flows back through the books to become part of your equity.

After breaking it down, your expanded profit equation now looks like this:

Net Income = Gross Income – Cost of Goods Sold – G & A

Breaking Down the Statement of Cash Flow

The last financial statement is the statement of cash flow. It begins with the net income of your business and deducts items that impact cash but don't impact net income. Examples of that are increases or decreases in inventory or accounts receivable. An increase in inventory will not change your net income, but it certainly will impact your cash. The statement of cash flow also adds back items that impact your net income but don't cost you any cash. The best example of that is depreciation. Depreciation is also called a phantom expense because, while it hits the books as an expense, it doesn't impact your cash.

The statement of cash flow also breaks down other types of income, such as income from investments your business has made and income it receives from financing, and it deducts the direct costs from those other income sources as well. If you had a line of credit, for example, the statement of cash flows would show all deductions you made for repayments, interest, insurance, and any other costs to service that debt.

Confused? You're not alone. It's the hardest financial statement to explain. That's why many accountants don't prepare them for clients. Don't let this happen to you. Make sure you insist on having a statement of cash flows prepared each time your financial statements are done. It's too important to leave out. The statement of cash flows is the best indicator of the strength of a business. A business could have plenty of income and still fail.

Success Almost Kills Business

Joanna's customized aromatherapy business was a huge hit and she was having trouble keeping up with the demand for her products. She hired staff to help with the work. She also significantly increased her inventory of essential oils.

Both expenses concerned her. But when she mentioned this to her CPA, he told Joanna not to worry. Her business was making a lot of money. He showed her an income statement that showed the huge revenues pouring in.

Joanna didn't have a lot of down time, and she trusted her CPA's advice. But then her cash flow turned upside down. She had a huge tax bill due on the profits and no cash to cover it.

Joanna didn't understand. If the business was so profitable, and she'd made so much money, where was it? She brought her financial statements to us for review.

The news she received shocked her. The huge inventory of oils that she had purchased had eaten up her cash flow. But because only a few drops of oil went into each product she created, all that inventory cost wasn't showing up as an expense. Only a fraction of the inventory cost had been included in her COGS so far.

By not looking at the whole picture, Joanna had assumed that the huge profit was hers to spend. But the true picture showed her business was asset rich and cash poor.

We showed Joanna a statement of cash flows and helped her to understand what it meant. She realized that if she had seen one six months prior, she could have made different business decisions. But what was done was done, and now Joanna needed to focus on saving her business. She took out a second mortgage on her home to fund the business through its next year, and we took over as her tax advisors. Fortunately, her product's popularity continued and Joanna's business is still going today.

Lack of cash is the #1 reason businesses fail.

Your new business will chew up cash while it's getting established, during slow times and also during times of rapid growth. That cash needs to come from somewhere. You will succeed if you plan for it, but you've got to make those plans ahead of time. To make those plans, you've got to have the vital information that only properly-prepared financial statements can provide.

Action Steps

Action Step 1: Review your financial statements income points: gross income, gross profit, and net profit.

Action Step 2: Look at your balance sheet. Is your equity increasing? Do you have "off balance sheet" assets that aren't recorded at fair market value? If so, what will you do to take those assets into account in your overall assessment?

Resources

Understanding Financial Statements Home Study Course at
    www.USTaxAid.com

www.MySmarterBusiness.com: You'll find sample financial statements
    on our website.

Gerber, Michael E. 1995. *The E-Myth Revisited: Why Most Small Businesses Don't Work and What to Do About It*. HarperCollins.

Chapter 21:
Analyzing Your Business Financial Statements

Once you've got your arms wrapped around the different ways that financial information is presented, you can begin to analyze it. By understanding and tracking the relationship between your business's assets, liabilities, income, and expenses, you'll be able to identify successful trends and potential problems.

One of the easiest ways to analyze the financial status of your business is by ratio analysis. If that sounds intimidating, it isn't. Why? Because we analyze ratios everyday. We think about miles per hour, calories per day, and cooking measurements without much conscious thought.

Here are some common financial statement ratios:

Current Ratio (Current Assets to Current Debt)

You'll find the current ratio of your business by dividing is current total assets (found on your balance sheet) by its current total liabilities.

A 1:1 current ratio means your business has $1.00 in current assets to cover each $1.00 in current liabilities. You're looking to keep your current ratio above 1:1 and as close to 2:1 (or higher) as possible.

"Current" is defined as three months. So, assets that are currently cash or that will be cash within three months are considered current. Liabilities that are due now or within the next three months are considered current.

Debt Ratio (Debt to Equity)

You'll find your business's debt ratio by dividing your current liabilities by the equity, or net worth, of the business.

The higher the ratio, the greater the risk will be to a present or future creditor. You'll want to shoot for a debt to equity ratio in the range of 1:1 to 4:1. This is especially important if you're looking for credit. Most lenders use strict credit guidelines and limits based on the debt to equity ratio. You'll find that a 2:1 ratio is commonly used for small businesses. On the other hand, not using debt can mean a company that is not growing with any leverage.

Gross Margin or Profit Margin (Gross Profit by Sales)

This ratio measures the ability of your business to make a profit. You'll find it by dividing the gross profit of your business by its gross sales figures.

Return on Sales (Net Profit to Gross Sales)

This one is similar to your profit margin. You'll find this ratio by dividing the net profit of your business by its gross sales.

The value of this ratio is that it shows you how much profit comes from every dollar of sales. Looking at this over time, can help you to spot trends, and whether or not you are managing your operating and overhead costs.

Accounts Payable Turnover (COGS to Average Accounts Payable)

To learn the accounts payable turnover of your business, take your cost of goods sold and divide it by your average accounts payable balance each month.

The higher your rate of turnover the shorter the time between buying raw material or inventory and paying for those purchases. The lower the turnover, the longer the time between buying inventory or raw materials and getting those bills paid. This could be a great early indicator that your business is heading for a cash shortage to pay the bills. A low turnover may indicate a shortage of cash to pay your bills or some other reason for a delay in payment.

Investment Turnover (Gross Sales to Long-Term Assets)

This ratio is created by dividing the amount of the gross sales of your business by the value of its long-term assets.

This ratio is a volume indicator that can be used to measure efficiency of your business from year to year. If your business isn't creating enough income to buy long-term assets, why? You may be pulling the extra income for another purpose, or you may need to take a look at where the money is going.

Return on Investment (Net Profit to Equity)

You will find this ratio by dividing the net profit of your business by its equity.

This is a ratio you'll become very familiar with over your business and investing life. It represents what you put into a business versus what you get back out. You'll use this ratio over and over again.

Financial statements are a window into your business, and they show the truth of how your business is really performing. Learn what each element of a financial statement shows you, and how to interpret those results. You'll wind up learning a powerful tool that you can use to evaluate your business and that of your competitors. It will also help you to tell the difference between good business opportunities and bad ones.

In the next chapter, Chapter 22, Your Financial Scorecard at a Glance, we will go over a few of these common ratios in more detail and introduce a few more to you.

Action Steps

Action Step 1: Get used to looking at ratios. Grab your financial statements or download some sample ones from our web site, and practice calculating some ratios.

Action Step 2: Check out your industry standards. Are your ratios close to what the industry is?

Action 3: What ratios are most valuable to you?

Resources

Public companies in the United States are required to make their financial statements public and file them with the Securities & Exchange Commission on a quarterly basis. You can look up a company's entire public filing record here: http://www.sec.gov/edgar/searchedgar/companysearch. html. Many companies also make their financial statements available through their websites (look under investor relations).

There's also plenty of information available at the US Government Census Bureau (http://www.census.gov/econ/). You can get statistics from across the country, broken down into industry-specifics, regions, and more.

Chapter 22:
Your Financial Scorecard at a Glance

I n school, you received a report card. It showed some numbers or letters that supposedly said how much you were applying yourself in school and how good you were at taking tests. Based on those report cards, you received accolades, scholarships, or labels that haunted you for years. Yet when school was over, no-one really cared about your report card.

In business, the report card has been replaced with your financial scorecard. Some companies are judging their companies based on the impact they are making to the world and/or environment, in addition to the financial numbers.

Those are great to add in at a later time, or maybe even right now. But for the focus of this chapter, we want to help you create a graphical representation of what you need to keep track of your business. It's not a substitution for a full blown set of financial statements, and it's not meant to be.

This is the financial statement that you can look at quickly and tell, at a glance, the financial health of your company now and spot trends.

Do you have trouble getting the numbers of your financial statement to talk to you? Use the Business Financial Scorecard!

Your Business Financial Scorecard
The Business Financial Scorecard is used at Diane's mastermind event for her private clients as a way for them to access where they are.

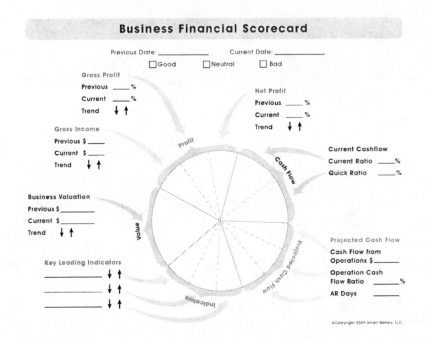

You can download your own copy of the Business Financial Scorecard and all of the other forms at: www.MySmarterBusiness.com.

Getting Started with Your Own Scorecard

Start off with noting the time period you will be comparing. You may want to look at this monthly or quarterly. Doing the review annually is a good start, but ultimately, you will want to watch it more closely than that.

Write down the two time periods you are comparing. For example, if you're looking at the quarter that ended March 31, 2010, and the quarter that ended June 30, 2010, then March 30, 2010, should be written under previous date and June 30, 2010 should be written under current date.

Part of the fun of the scorecard is that you get to make your own visual representation. Pick three colors to represent good, neutral, and bad. For example, good might be green, neutral might be yellow, and bad might be red. Color the squares with the corresponding color. That will be your legend as you work.

The Trend is Your Friend

There is a saying in stock investing that the trend is your friend. The same is true for your business. Your business numbers might look phenomenal right now, but if they used to be super phenomenal, you're on a downward trend that could be a serious problem.

Contrast that with numbers that don't look great. In fact, you are barely making a profit. Is your company in trouble? It's hard to say without knowing what the trend is. If it's just your first year in business and the first two quarters showed big losses, it looks like you're recovering quickly.

The trend is your friend when it comes to business. What does your Business Financial Scorecard say?

Watch the trend. It's the foreteller of what's going on.

Profit from Your Business

Cash flow may be your business lifeblood, but without profit it will eventually run dry. Profit will sustain your business. In the beginning, it might take you awhile to find your path, and so you will likely have some losses. But, if your sales and marketing is working, you'll see upward trends on your gross income.

Let's go through the three elements of profit that are reported on the Business Financial Scorecard.

Gross Income

First up is gross income. Make a note of your past period total sales at "previous" and your current total sales at "current." Remember that you need to compare apples to apples. For example, if you report three months worth of sales at previous, you will want to compare that to three months worth of sales currently.

Additionally, some businesses are seasonal, so a comparison for subsequent quarters won't make sense. A ski lodge won't have the same kind of gross income

Gross Income

Previous $ _____

Current $ _____

Trend ↓ ↑

for the period from April through June that it does for the period from January through March.

The gross income comparisons are based on total dollars received for sales. Is your business trending up or down? Circle the correct arrow, and then color the associated pie segment in the center of the scorecard below as good, neutral, or bad.

Take it one step further and consider how you can either turn the trend around or make something good even better.

- What worked in this past period that you can expand on?
- How can you do that?
- What additional products or services do your customers need?
- How can more people hear about your products or services?
- How can you sell more to the customers you already have?
- How can you focus your company even more?
- How can you expand the focus of your company?

If you have a networking group that you work with, this can be a great exercise to do as a group. Have each business owner quickly share their personal circumstances (without using numbers unless they really want to), posing the questions and getting responses. After everyone gets a turn to ask, take eight minutes so each person can process the information and come up with three to five action steps for the next 90 days.

Discuss the action steps, make a commitment, and find an accountability partner in the group, or use the group for accountability as well. An accountability partner is someone that you check in with who simply holds you accountable. Did you do what you said you'd do? If not, when will you? If you did, celebrate!

Gross Profit

Next up is gross profit. Gross profit is expressed as a percentage of your business sales.

If your total gross income from sales was $100,000 and your total gross profit after the cost of goods sold was $70,000, you have a gross profit percentage of 70%. ($70,000 divided by $100,000).

Gross Profit

Previous _____ %

Current _____ %

Trend   ↓ ↑

Now let's say your next period shows $150,000 in sales. Your sales are trending up. Your gross profit after deducting cost of goods sold has also increased, and it is now $75,000. Based on dollars alone, you've seen an increase. You went from $70,000 to $75,000 ($150,000 - $75,000). But, what happened to your gross profit percentage? It's now 50%. ($75,000 divided by $150,000).

	Before	After	
Gross Income	$100,000	$150,000	↑
Gross Profit	$70,000	$75,000	↑
Gross Profit Margin	70%	50%	↓

If these were your numbers, what would you do? Is the increase in sales worth the decrease in your gross profit margin?

There could be a lot of reasons why this happened. For example, you might have reduced the price and that brought a lot more sales, but it caused your gross profit margin to go down as well. The next part of the equation, net profit, will tell you whether that is a good idea or not. For example, you might have reduced your costs to the point where you are running at a loss.

Or you might have launched a new product line that is wildly successful, but you haven't quite got the cost of fulfillment dialed in yet. The next batch will be cheaper, and so you know the issue is just temporary.

Calculate your own gross profit percentages. Is the trend up or down? Circle the correct arrow, and then color the associated pie segment in the center of the scorecard below as good, neutral, or bad.

Some questions to consider in your networking group:

- How does your gross profit margin compare to other companies in your industry?
- What can you do to add more value to your products or services without increasing the COGS?

- How can you make your process quicker, better, smarter?
- What happens if you raise your prices?
- What happens if you lower your prices?

As before, take time for each person in your mastermind group to briefly outline their business and ask their questions. The point here isn't necessarily to do all the things (raise your prices AND lower your prices) but rather to explore possibilities. When you stretch your creative business mind in this way, you'll find some unexpected answers. Keep to the same time limits that you established in the beginning. Otherwise, you'll find that some people may end up taking more than an equal share of time, and others will feel slighted.

Net Profit

The final profit item is net profit. Net profit is the amount after the general and administrative costs have been deducted. This is shown as a percentage of sales.

You now know that for every dollar of sales you make, you will keep a certain percentage of it as gross profit and another amount as net profit.

Net Profit

Previous _____ %

Current _____ %

Trend ↓ ↑

Those numbers – total gross income, gross profit percentage, and net profit percentage – predict the future of your business. Without profit, your business can't last.

As you look at your net profit percentage compared to the last period's, is it trending up or down? Circle the correct arrow, and then color the associated pie segment in the center of the scorecard below as good, neutral, or bad. You now have the profit quarter of your scorecard completed. When you complete the entire circle, you'll have a good idea of where your company is, at a glance.

Here are some things to consider regarding the net profit percentage:

- If you've seen a big change in this percentage, it will have been due to one or all of the three significant factors. Your total sales in dollars have gone up or down, your cost to fulfill have gone up or down, or your G & A costs have gone up or down.

- Business owners are often too quick to ramp up administrative expenses in an upturn and too slow to pull them back in a downturn.

Beware of Long Term Contracts!

Over the past year, two separate clients fought us tooth and nail about their justification to expand their administrative space. Well, that's probably an exaggeration because, of course, you can choose whatever course of action you want. We just want to make sure you've got all the facts so that you make an informed decision.

In this case, both clients had a slight uptick in business. It was just one month, but the growth was tremendous. The clients were in related industries so it wasn't that coincidental after all. But the problem was that each of them had then extrapolated that increase into the rest of the year.

"If every month increases like this one did, I'll need four times the space!" one of them insisted.

And that additional space would have meant more equipment, furniture, and just general cost to maintain. Plus, it would have meant long-term rental agreements and probably a loan or two to cover the cost of all the equipment and furniture.

In the end, it turned out that the increase was just a one-month blip. It wasn't a long-term trend. And both are very happy they didn't get caught in long-term contracts.

Some questions to consider in your networking group:
- What is most influencing your net profit percentage?
- What three changes can you make to improve the bottom-line number that will have the highest degree of leverage and give the biggest impact?
- In which of the three areas do you want to concentrate over the next 90 days?
- What are three action steps you can commit to over the next 90 days?

Your Business Financial Scorecard should include three profit points: total gross income, gross profit percentage, and net profit percentage.

Current Cash Flow from Your Business

Now let's look at the current cash flow from your business. By current, we mean right now. Can you pay your bills today? Can you pay your bills over the next 30 days?

You will track two ratios for current cash flow. Note that these definitions might be a little different than the standard. These are the ones we use with our clients.

Current Cashflow

Current Ratio _____%

Quick Ratio _____%

Quick Ratio: The quick ratio is the total of ready cash divided by total of liabilities due in the next 3 months.

Current Ratio: The current ratio is the total of cash plus other money you will collect in the next 3 months divided by the total of liabilities due in the next 3 months.

You may need to refer to past periods to make an assessment of whether those numbers are sufficient to meet your liabilities. It will tell you whether your cash reserves are enough to carry you through the current liabilities if something happens to your business.

Both the quick ratio and the current ratio assume that you won't make any sales and that you won't incur any more expenses. In other words, if you have enough cash to meet your obligations for the next 3 months, that's a good feeling if some kind of catastrophe hits. But it also means that you have to stop all expenses immediately. And there will be no money to pay you either.

Most business owners ramp up too quickly and ramp down too slowly.

Color in the corresponding pie-shaped pieces in your scorecard with the good, neutral, or bad color. Your scorecard is taking shape!

Here are some questions to consider for your networking group:

- There is a fine line between having enough cash to do what you need to do and having so much cash that your ROI (return on investment) sucks. Your cash is stagnant. What are some considerations for your type of business and industry? Which is more important?

- What are ways to improve your business cash security without parking cash and no return?
- How can you maximize your ROI and keep your business safe?
- What are three action steps that you need to take in this regard?

Projected Cash Flow from Your Business

Cash Flow from Operations: Go to your statement of cash flows and note the total showing as "Cash Flow from Operations".

Which direction is the cash flowing?

- To your business or from your business?
- And is that a good thing or a bad thing?

The answer isn't always clear cut. You could show a lot of cash flow coming from your operations. That could mean

Projected Cash Flow

Cash Flow from Operations $_____

Operation Cash Flow Ratio _____%

AR Days _____

that you have a profitable business model, and it's paying off big time. Or it could mean that you're shrinking your inventory and getting ready for a big "Going Out of Business" sale. Or it could mean that you're shrinking your inventory, and thank goodness for that. You were carrying way too much inventory.

You could show cash flow going into your operations. In other words, there is no cash flow coming from them. This could be a portent of the end. Or it could mean that you're building a business, and you have a temporary need to feed the business. Or it could mean that you've just started a massive marketing plan that will take six months or more to pay you back. Or it could mean that you've just put a great tax savings plan in place, and your financial statements are showing the taxable income, which is dramatically reduced. In the case of the last possibility, make a note of how much of the expenses are more discretionary. In other words, these are expenses and benefits that you've added to the company. They are legitimate and legal, but are more beneficial to the owners.

This is the step that takes some art, and it's not your coloring ability. Color the segment that references the Cash Flow from Operations.

Is this good, neutral or bad? There isn't a bright line definition for these categories. You need to be able to identify and decipher the story behind the numbers.

Operating Cash Flow Ratio

Next, calculate your operating cash flow ratio. This is the amount of your operating cash flow divided by your current liabilities. Make sure the period amounts match. In other words, if you're using the operating cash flow for one year, then use the current liabilities for one year. If you have a negative operating cash flow, then you know right off the bat that you're going to have to do something about getting cash to keep going.

Again, color in the segment: Is it good, neutral, or bad?

Accounts Receivable Days

Finally, let's look at accounts receivable (A/R). These are the amounts that your clients, customers, or patients owe you. If you have a business that is strictly cash basis, you may want to substitute inventory days for this calculation.

Accounts receivable days is calculated as 365 times A/R with the total divided by gross income for the year.

$$(365 * A/R) / (\text{Annual Gross Income})$$

If you want to use a shorter period for the gross income, then change the days as well. For example, let's say you want to use your gross income for the past quarter. In this case, you'd use 91 days (365 / 4). The formula would be:

$$(91 * A/R) / (\text{Quarterly Gross Income})$$

Is this a good number, bad number, or neutral? Color the segment as appropriate.

Congratulations! You're 3/5 of the way through creating your Business Financial Scorecard. Your pie graph in the middle is starting to look very colorful. Up until now, the process might have seemed rather daunting. There is a learning curve. Keep on it, and you'll soon have a very valuable tool right at your fingertips.

You might have also discovered that you can probably have your bookkeeper do a lot of the work for you. There will be judgment calls that you won't be able to delegate such as when it comes to determining whether the trend is good or bad and what action steps you need to take.

So far, you've determined some action steps to improve the profitability of your business and assessed how your current cash flow is looking.

Here are some questions to consider for your networking group:
- What are the biggest barriers of your business to creating massive cash flow into your business?
- What one thing can you do in your business that would bring in cash flow quick? (You may want to go refresh your memory with the bootstrapping and other techniques in Chapter 6: Funding Your Business)
- What three action steps are you prepared to take over the next 90 days?

Your Business Leading Indicators

There are two purposes for the Business Financial Scorecard: To assess the past and to predict the future.

The more frequently you come back to look at your statistics, the easier this process will become. Soon you'll get to the point where you can look at other people's financial statements and know at a glance whether they are in trouble now or soon will be.

Key Leading Indicators

The best skill of all, though, is knowing how to predict what is going to happen with your business. This is a skill, but it's also partially intuitive.

A forecast is the end result of a continuous process aimed at predicting the future. You can't consistently predict the future with complete certainty. But you can refine your skills. This process has a feedback step built into the process to allow you to reconsider the projections and the leading indicators you have selected.

When it comes to forecasts, though, it's clearly garbage in, garbage out. You need the best information about your market and identify those indicators that specifically relate to your business. The better your forecasts are, the better you can prepare. And, your forecasting should be continuous and ongoing. It's not a static item.

There is no hard and fast forecasting process, but the following nine steps are generally applicable to most forecasting efforts:

(1) Take some time and list out all the basic facts about past trends and forecasts.

(2) What have you noticed about changes in past actual demand? Why did it increase? Why did it decrease?

(3) Analyze the cause of deviations between what you forecasted in the past and in what actually happened.

(4) Determine factors that are likely to affect future demand.

(5) Based only on info available to you before the period, generate a forecast for a past period. Then measure your accuracy and reliability against the known results. NOTE: This is an important step. It's testing how reliable the leading indicator you've selected is. However, if the leading indicator is something that you would internally track about your business, it could be that you don't have this data available for the past. For example, we might want to track how many visitors come to a particular website. If we didn't have a statistics program running in the past, we wouldn't have that information. If that's the case, look for at least one leading indicator that is available.

(6) Make any necessary changes to your process until it is an acceptable predictor of the actual results of the past period. This allows you, via a trial run approach, to construct a proven effective process on known data.

(7) Create a forecast for the future using your revised and tested indicators.

(8) Monitor the performance of the forecast against actual outcomes and determine the causes of variation from forecast.

(9) Revise the forecast when new data or obvious errors appear.

Some of the things you might want to consider tracking, if they are applicable for your business:

- GNP
- Personal income stats
- Retail sales
- Employment

You may also want to consider these questions for your product or service:

- What particular age group purchases your products/services?
- Do your clients come primarily from a specific ethnic group?
- Is your product purchased more frequently by either gender?
- Is the product/service geographically restricted?
- Are the products/services purchased by someone from a particular income level?
- Are sales of the product/services tied to sales of other products?
- Are sales related to any one industry or job?
- What is the educational level of purchasers of the product?
- Now consider what data is available regarding your specific niche?

Write the new calculations and color the pie shaped corresponding section on your Business Financial Scorecard.

You may be a few months, maybe even years, away from having the best predictive indicators dialed in for your business. That's okay. Every step forward in the right direction is positive action.

In the beginning, you might want to color each of the three segments of the indicator portion with neutral. As you begin to have confidence in your leading indicators, watch your predictions.

It is possible that the leading indicators cause you to forecast a tough time for your business. And you'll need to signify that by coloring the appropriate segment with the bad color. But, if there are bad times coming, wouldn't you rather know about it now?

You might also find that some of your indicators show that there will be an uptick, just when other indicators show there will be a downtick.

And that's life. The more information you have, and that you take action on, the better your business will be.

Before you have identified the best key leading indicators:

- Review the questions regarding your business products/services and answers with your mastermind group.
- What published stats could I use to forecast for my business?

After you have identified the indicators and have some confidence in your forecasts:

- What can I do to position best for the forecast for my business?

- What will be my biggest risk with this forecast?
- Where is my biggest potential reward?

And, of course, come up with three action steps you can take in the next 90 days.

The Value of Your Business

Finally, take a look at the value of your business. Again, compare it to a prior period. In this case, you may want to review the value at a less frequent rate than you do profit, cash flow, and leading indicators. If that's the case, it's okay to just make a note on how often that is done.

Business Valuation

Previous $ _____

Current $ _____

Trend   ↓ ↑

You will probably want to jump ahead to review Chapter 31: Increasing Your Business Value first to determine the method you're going to use to value your business.

Calculate the new value and determine the trend. Is it up, down, or staying the same? An up trend probably gets you a good color on the rating scale, a down is your bad color, and staying the same means using the neutral color.

Write down the new calculated value, and color the pie shaped corresponding section.

Your Business Financial Scorecard

Your Business Financial Scorecard is the easiest way for you to keep track of how your business is doing. Over time, the trends will be the most important part of determining just how successful your business will be.

Action Steps

Action Step 1: Unless the Business Financial Scorecard ratios are completely wrong for your business (and we don't think they will be), please use it, as is, a few times before you substitute your own rations. It's good to learn a system before you change it.

Action Step 2: Set up a schedule for completion of the Business Financial Scorecard. How often will you review your business?

Resources

Come to www.MySmarterBusiness.com to print off your own artist's copies of the Business Financial Scorecard. Thank you to Eva Brunette of Apex Design!

Smart Business, Stupid Business: Chapter 31: Increasing Your Business
    Value

Section Five: Advanced Tax & Asset Protection Strategies

Chapter 23:
Multi-Layered Structures: The New
Millionaire's Favorite Planning Tool

Remember back in Chapter 13 when we talked about keeping things simple for your business structure? That's fine for the early days, but as your business grows (along with your income) there is going to come a time when you will literally outgrow the structure you started with. At that point, it's time to take a look at how a multi-layered structure can help you.

We see multi-layered structures most commonly in four areas:

(1) Upstreaming income,

(2) Avoiding alternative minimum tax (AMT),

(3) Multiple owners with different wants and needs, and

(4) Additional asset protection.

Upstreaming Income

One of the hundreds of tax saving strategies we use with our clients involves upstreaming. Upstreaming simply means to move income from one taxpaying entity to another. It could be a person, a pension plan, or, in this case, a C Corporation or an LLC-C. An LLC-C is a limited liability company (LLC) that has elected to be taxed as a C Corporation. An LLC-S is an LLC that has elected to be taxed as an S Corporation.

The C Corporation/LLC-C is used to pull off the excess income from the S Corporations and LLC-S entities, where it can be parked or used for other investments.

Before you jump into a C Corporation, though, make sure you look at Chapter 24: Tricks and Traps of C Corporations to discover all the potential traps such as double taxation and controlled group issues.

Upstreaming Strategy Step by Step

Let's say that your income is solidly at the highest tax rate and you're currently operating through an S Corporation or an LLC-S. Each extra dollar your company makes is taxed at the highest possible personal income tax.

If you can take that highest layer taxed at, say, 39.6% and move it to the C Corporation tax rate of 15% for the first $50,000, you will have saved approximately $12,500. Sure, there are some costs involved in setting up and running a C Corporation. But if you use this strategy correctly, and avoid the traps of a C Corporation, you'll save $12,500 year after year. That's not a bad deal.

Before you jump into a complicated upstreaming C Corporation strategy without the help of a tax strategist, though, remember that you have to have a legitimate reason for upstreaming the income. You can't simply use tax savings as a reason to start a new company. Actually, the IRS has some very specific laws and penalties against doing that. Get some professional advice here. This is definitely not a strategy to try on your own.

As your personal income tax rates climb and corporate tax rates decrease, the gap between the personal and C Corporations will widen even further. There is also talk of payroll tax rates increasing, including a removal of the cap on Social Security payments. All of these factors point towards a C Corporation becoming an important part of your tax planning.

How Couples Save Taxes by Upstreaming

Often we see couples with successful businesses operating through flow-through entities. This works until the couple reaches the point where their income is so high they are paying taxes at the highest personal tax bracket and also losing out on many deductions because their income is now too high to qualify for itemization.

It's important that both spouses provide some kind of service to the business, either directly or indirectly. There are no sham businesses or transactions here!

One idea might be to separate the functions of the two spouses. One continues to work through the S Corporation, with the flow-through tax treatment. The other owns the C Corporation and receives other income.

The C Corporation can be maximized to provide all possible benefits, including a self-directed pension plan and a MERP.

The ownership of the two companies needs to be completely separate, and the non-owner spouse cannot be an officer or director of the company or receive a salary. Otherwise, any benefits would need to be offered to all employees of both companies.

The C Corporation spouse is paid a salary through this business, and an aggressive self-directed pension plan can be set up. At the same time, income will continue to build in the C Corporation. This money can be used to invest as well.

We've safely and legally saved hundreds of clients tens of thousands of dollars using variations of this strategy.

Many clients save $30,000 or more each year using just this one technique. But remember, both spouses need to be providing a real service to the business. The IRS will permit upstreaming only where there is "economic substance" to the transaction. In other words, we need to have a reason for making the change that isn't simply "to save taxes."

Avoiding Alternative Minimum Tax (AMT)

AMT is a flat-level tax that was created by the government years ago as a method to stop high-income taxpayers from arranging their finances in such a way that they paid no tax at all. Unfortunately, it didn't quite turn out the way it was planned. Because it was created with rigid tax brackets and no legal way for the government to move them around over time, we have come to our current situation: where AMT affects far more middle-class earners than was ever intended. Depending on the kind and amount of income you earn, you could find yourself paying AMT with an income somewhere in the $40,000's.

AMT is a parallel tax system. If you fall under the AMT guidelines (typically because you have high income, a lot of deductions, real estate or capital gains), you are required to calculate your yearly income tax burden under both the traditional method and the AMT method. You then pay whichever tax is higher. To add to your pain, you lose many of the deductions you could otherwise take under the traditional tax system. The net result is your taxable income increasing, along with your tax bill.

When it was made law, AMT applied to individuals and businesses. But exemptions and loopholes introduced over the years have resulted in most businesses now escaping AMT. In fact, if you're paying AMT as an individual, one of the best things you can do for yourself is to begin a business. You may find that you can get back all those deductions you lost under AMT and more, including being exempted from AMT altogether.

Owners with Different Wants and Needs

If you have a partner in your business and have ever had a conversation about saving taxes, you've probably already discovered that no one ever wants the exact same thing when it comes to fringe benefits. Some owners have young families, and they want all the medical coverage they can get. Other owners want a huge pension plan. Someone always wants a hot car or maybe even an airplane. A multi-layered structure is ideal in this situation, because it can be set up to give everyone what they want. (Well, anything you want, as long as it's legal and tax deductible.)

The cornerstone to a multi-layered structure in this strategy is a pass-through structure that is tax-neutral. We typically use an LLC that is taxed as a partnership. Each of the owners creates the business structure that best works for them, and they hold their ownership in the business through their respective structure. All of the income flows right through the LLC and into the underlying business structures. It is then taxed at the secondary level. What follows, is a real-life example of this strategy in action.

The Two Doctors

Multi-layered structure

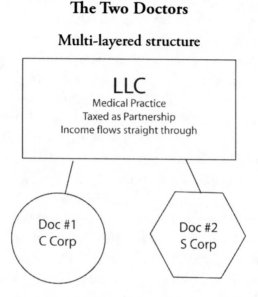

In this case, we had two doctors in different stages of life, with different needs. Doctor #1 had other income streams from investments, and he didn't need all of his medical income to live on each month. He was single, and he was heavily involved in real estate investing on the side. Doctor #2 had a young family and a husband still in school finishing up his psychology doctorate. She needed everything she made to support her family.

Rather than use a single structure that gave each of them something but neither of them everything, we developed a two-tier structure to do it all. By creating the medical practice as an LLC, with default partnership taxation, we were able to flow all of the net profits before tax through to the doctors. The staff was employed through the LLC, which offered a pension plan option and other benefits. Then, instead of having the profits flow through to the doctors individually, we created tailored structures to maximize their tax savings.

For Doctor #1, the C Corporation was a better structure. He had some other activities within the business that allowed him to escape Personal Service Corporation. He could draw a salary through the C Corporation and leave the remainder of the income in the business as retained earnings, which could be dipped into for his real estate investments as he needed.

For Doctor #2, we used an S Corporation, allowing her to take a reasonable salary and flow the remainder through as her profit distribution, free of payroll taxes or self-employment tax.

Both doctors were also able to establish Solo 401(k) plans with Roth add-on components in their individual corporations. This option would not have been available to them if we had used the single-layer structure. A Solo 401(k) plan is only available to businesses owned by one person, or by a married couple who file jointly, and may not be used where the business has full-time employees. Neither doctor would qualify for a separate Roth IRA because their incomes were too high. But the Solo 401(k) plan with Roth add-on is available to business owners, regardless of their income.

This same strategy can be applied to any form of business relationship with multiple owners. It's often the quickest and the easiest way to keep everyone happy, maximizing their respective tax savings opportunities and giving each owner the flexibility to arrange their personal finances.

Additional Asset Protection

Multi-layered structures also provide you with a second level of asset protection, but not necessarily in the way that you'd expect. In this case, the multi-layering protects each of the owners of the business from the others.

There are some businesses where you can't completely insulate yourself from personal liability. Doctors, lawyers, engineers, accountants, and generally anyone required to carry malpractice insurance, is a likely example. In these professions, you can insulate yourself from the person who slips and falls in the office parking lot and sues your office. That type of claim doesn't touch your malpractice insurance. That is a claim that any other business owner could face, and as the business owner, you aren't liable for the actions of the business (i.e., the walkway was covered in ice, and it was dangerous).

But the person who was misdiagnosed by your partner, during the course of treatment, is a different story. This person can sue your partner, the company, and all of the owners. You can be named in this suit, and if the malpractice insurance doesn't cover the total cost of the damage award, the plaintiff will have the right to come after all of the owners. In this case, having your ownership held through a second business structure can help to shield you from personal liability. The lawsuit would be directed against your secondary business structure as the practice owner and not you.

The same idea applies to fights between business owners. You may have all gotten along great at the beginning of the business, but five or six years down the road, things aren't so good. Your business partner is now threatening to sue you for some reason. By having a secondary business structure holding your ownership in the main business, it means that he will have a much harder job trying to reach your personal assets. You, on the other hand, have the ability to weigh your options and decide how to manage a lawsuit in the way that suits you best. You aren't forced into any defensive reactions simply as a way to try and protect yourself and your family.

It would be great to say that this kind of thing is rare, but it isn't. A multi-layered structure can help you not only make that million (or two, or twenty), but it can also help you hang onto it.

Action Steps

Action Step 1: Have you outgrown your current business structure?

Action Step 2: Do you need to re-address your asset protection?

Resources

Business Structures for 2009 & Beyond (you can find this product at www.USATaxAid.com). It expands on the ideas set out here and provides you with additional resources to design your asset protection plan.

Adkisson, Jay and Riser, Chris. 2004. *Asset Protection: Concepts and Strategies for Protecting Your Wealth*. McGraw-Hill.

Chapter 24:
Tricks & Traps of C Corporation

W e've been through some of the tricks of the C Corporation: upstreaming income, providing additional medical benefits, retaining earnings, etc. Now we'd like to tell you about some of the traps.

Professional and Licensed Businesses
Depending on the type of business that you have, the IRS can tag you with some additional designators, like professional, qualified personal service, and personal holding. Each of these designations can impact how your corporation is taxed, and can be important factors in influencing when to use a C Corporation over an S Corporation and vice-versa.

Professional Corporations
As a rule, professional status for corporations is reserved for businesses where all of the owners are required to hold the same professional license. Depending on your state, you may be able to use any of the three incorporated structures (C Corporation, S Corporation or LLC) as professional businesses. The rules aren't the same for all states, so check ahead of time before you file any paperwork to start the business.

Not everyone can participate in a professional corporation or LLC. Ownership in these structures is often restricted only to those professionals who are properly licensed. For example, if you use a professional corporation to form a law firm, each shareholder of the corporation may need to be a licensed attorney. The reason why we say may, is that it's not always the case. There are a number of states that permit non-licensed spouses to also hold stock or interests in a professional entity.

Because they are specialized structures, you don't need to use them for other, non-related businesses. If you got a group of doctors together to invest in a real estate project like a shopping center, your group wouldn't need a professional LLC. The LLC isn't going to provide medical services, so a plain LLC would do fine. This would also allow doctors to hold ownership jointly with spouses or children, which they couldn't do otherwise unless their spouses or children were also doctors.

In many states, forming a professional corporation means you'll need the pre-approval of your state licensing board before your corporation's paperwork will be filed. In other states, you are required to first incorporate your business structure with the secretary of state's office, and then register it again with your local state licensing board.

You'll also need to make sure you can use the structure you want. You might want to use an LLC-S or an LLC-C for the additional flexibility and asset protection it provides, but your state only permits professional organizations to run as corporations. So, one of the first steps for you is to first determine: (a) whether or not you need to operate through a professional entity, and (b) whether you can use a professional corporation or a professional LLC.

Unfortunately, states are inconsistent on whether or not a professional business can be a corporation or an LLC. The best way to find out if you need to operate through a professional corporation is to contact your licensing board and ask them what their local requirements are.

States are also inconsistent on the list of professionals required to incorporate as a professional corporation. Generally speaking, if your profession requires you to be licensed and you need to belong to a state or federal regulatory body, you may need to operate through a professional corporation.

Here are some of the most common occupations that must be operated through professional corporations. Again, contact your local licensing board if you have any questions about your own profession.

- Accountants
- Engineers
- Health care professionals, such as audiologists, dentists, nurses, opticians, optometrists, pharmacists, physical therapists, physicians, and speech pathologists

- Lawyers
- Psychologists
- Social workers
- Veterinarians

Taxing a Professional Corporation

Even if you don't have a choice about your professional status, you do have a choice in how your business is taxed. Whether you use a corporation or an LLC, you can elect either C Corporation taxation or S Corporation taxation. That classification does not matter to your state licensing board. But there are still some tax issues to consider, particularly if your business is also considered to be a qualified personal service corporation.

Qualified Personal Service Corporation

The IRS defines a qualified personal service corporation (sometimes called a QPS or a PSC) as a specific type of business where the owner-shareholder provides his or her own services for the corporation.

The IRS considers most professional corporations to also be personal service corporations. Some recent additions to the list may surprise you. Actuaries, performing artists, and consulting companies are all now considered to be personal service corporations, even though they have no corresponding professional corporation requirements.

A qualified personal service corporation is subject to a flat tax of 35 percent, and it has a lower threshold for accumulated earnings tax than a regular C Corporation does. That means the traditional lower C Corporation rates no longer apply, which means you'll pay a higher tax bill.

A qualified personal service corporation is also required to have a December 31st fiscal year-end, eliminating any tax-timing benefits normally available to C Corporations with staggered year-ends.

If you think your business might be considered a qualified personal service corporation, you have two options. You can:

- Operate as an S Corporation, or
- Try to fail the IRS qualified personal service company test

There are two ways to fail the test. One way is to show that less than 95 percent of your employees' time is spent in personal service company activities. For example, if you're a veterinarian, you may also offer animal boarding and care. As long as your practice can show that its employees are spending at least five percent of their time caring for boarded pets, your practice can operate as a C Corporation without being tagged as a qualified personal service corporation. That lets you enjoy all of the standard C Corporation benefits.

Another example is optometrists. Have you ever visited your eye specialist and been able to buy your glasses, frames, and contact lenses on site as well? How about a chiropractor who also sells relaxation materials, a doctor's office that sells vitamin supplements, and so on? The same theory is at work here. By offering services that are not directly related to the professional side, you can fail the personal service company test.

The second way to fail the test is to make sure that at least five percent of the ownership of your business is held by people who aren't personally providing the professional service. If you're lucky enough to be in a state that permits non-licensed spouses to also hold ownership in a professional corporation or professional LLC, this is easy. Make sure someone else owns five percent or more.

Strategies to Avoid PSC Penalties

- 5% or more of the company owned by a non-professional, and/or
- 5% or more of total employee time is spent on non-professional activities.

Personal Holding Company (PHC)

A personal holding company is a corporation that has been established for the main purpose of collecting dividends, interest, and other solely passive investment income. It's defined as a C Corporation that is owned by one to five individuals, who together control 50 percent or more of its ownership, and earns 60 percent or more of its earnings through passive income.

The problem with the PHC classification is the extra taxes that go along with it. Personal holding companies are taxed on their retained earnings on top of the regular corporate income taxes. From 2003 to 2008, that extra tax was lowered to 15 percent through the Jobs and Growth Tax Relief Reconciliation Act of 2003. But that provision has now expired, and the tax rate on retained earnings has returned to its former rate of 35 percent. LLCs with default tax treatment are not subject to this tax, which is one more reason why an LLC is such an attractive structure to hold passive investments. S Corporations are also not subject to this tax, but they don't offer the same high level of asset protection as the LLC.

Strategies to Avoid PHC Issues

The best (and probably only) way to avoid a PHC penalty is to hold assets in the right entity. And that's not a C Corporation.

Accumulated Earnings (or Retained Earnings) Tax

When a C Corporation goes over the $250,000 accumulated retained earnings cap set by the IRS, that money may become subject to something called the "retained earnings tax." This is a tax the federal government set up to make sure that C Corporations distribute profits from time to time. The Feds saw it like this: the more retained earnings that a company has, the more attractive it becomes to investors. The more attractive the investment, the longer an investor will want to hang onto it. And, the longer an investment is static, the lower the tax revenue. Remember, the government doesn't get paid until a dividend is declared or until the stock gets sold.

The government determined that by installing a tax on retained earnings, sooner or later, a C Corporation would likely put the onus on paying this tax onto its investors instead. And that meant declaring a dividend. And that meant that the government could collect tax on the dividends paid.

A great example of this is Microsoft. In July of 2004, Microsoft had retained earnings of approximately $60 billion and was paying dividends of around $0.16 per share each year. Investors were wondering if they would ever get some serious money out of the business, short of selling their shares. Well, in the July 2004 announcement, Microsoft stated that in December 2004, it would make a one-time dividend payout to its shareholders of about $32 billion, along with doubling its annual dividend rate to $0.32 per share.

Why had Microsoft held out so long? There are many reasons, but one of the most commonly-cited ones was that Bill Gates had held up the dividend payout because of the impact it would have on his taxes. Because of his position as a major shareholder, Mr. Gates had the clout to persuade the directors to hold off on paying out distributions. When they were paid out, Bill Gates received some $3.6 billion and donated the entire amount to charity, offsetting the tax hit he would otherwise have faced on such a huge windfall.

So what happens if your C Corporation is accumulating retained earnings? There is a strategy that you can use to accumulate the money, as long as you are doing it the right way.

The accumulated earnings tax is a much-litigated portion of tax law. The simple definition, from the tax code and regulations, states that accumulated earnings are the previously taxed income in the corporation reduced by any net capital gains. In other words, they are the retained earnings held by the corporation without any capital gains reflected.

There has been significant case law supporting the Bardahl formula, which basically says that accumulated earnings are the working capital of the company. The working capital, or Bardahl formula, approach defines working capital as the amount necessary to run your company.

The necessary working capital for your business can be used to reduce the accumulated earnings. For example, if you discover you have a total of $350,000 in accumulated earnings in your company for a potential 35 percent tax on $100,000 (the excess over $250,000), you may also find that your company has working capital needs of $100,000. You're fine this year. But next year, as your company makes more money and accumulates more earnings, your risk of this excess tax will also increase.

Besides the working capital, your company can also withhold a certain amount for projected growth and investment in the business and can take an accumulated earnings deduction for life insurance paid on the lives of key officers of the company.

You do not actually report the calculation of working capital needs. If the retained earnings on your corporate return show an amount over $250,000, your corporation may get a letter from the IRS that asks about the accumulated earnings. You will be a long way ahead of the game if you can immediately offer copies of your working capital calculation, additional forecasted needs for the company, and corporate minutes that substantiate all of it.

Strategies for the Avoiding Accumulated Earnings Penalty

• Calculate the necessary working capital for your business and make it part of your business minutes.

Appreciating Assets

In general, you never want to have appreciating assets such as real estate held within a C Corporation. To demonstrate why, let's go through an example of holding property inside an LLC (limited liability company) versus a C Corporation.

Let's say that you and your partner buy a property for $600,000. Over time, the property appreciates to $2,000,000, and you sell the property.

• In an LLC: You have gain of $1,400,000 that is split between you and your partner. The $700,000 each is taxed as long-term capital gains. Assuming you are paying at the top long-term capital gains rate of 20%, the tax per partner would be: $140,000

• In a C Corporation: You have a gain of $1,400,000 that is taxed at the top C Corporate tax rate of 35%. The tax per partner would be: $245,000

But it doesn't stop there. All the money is still held within the C Corporation. How are you going to get it out? If you take it out as dividends, it'll be taxed again.

NEVER put appreciating assets inside a C Corp. (And we're not that crazy about you doing it in an S Corp either)

Controlled Group

If you control multiple corporations, you probably have a controlled group issue. It's possible to have a controlled group issue when it comes to nondiscriminatory benefit plans, as we'll discuss in Chapter 25: Benefits That Benefit You.

In this case, we're talking about multiple C Corporations with controlled group status. When a controlled group issue occurs, the corporations are collapsed into just one corporation for tax purposes. There is only one tax rate table. The benefits of multiple corporations go away.

The IRS caught on pretty quickly to the trick of using multiple corporations to take advantage of the graduated tax rates for each corporation. The trick would have been (if it worked) to keep $50,000 of income in each C Corporation so that you never pay more than 15 percent in tax. The IRS said no, and that's why it came up with the concept of controlled groups. In essence, if one or more of the same people maintain control of a group of corporations, they are considered to be just one corporation. This has become a significant problem for many people when they simply buy a corporation setup plan without the overview of their entire plan.

The key to avoiding controlled group status is to avoid having control with any small group of people. One way to do that is to have unrelated persons (unrelated by blood or marriage) own a portion of the corporation. If you follow this strategy, make sure you have a buy-sell agreement so that you can buy back the stock in case something goes awry.

Avoid Controlled Group Status

If you have multiple C Corporations, talk to an experienced Tax Strategist. Don't try to plan this one by yourself. It's tricky.

Avoid a C Corporation if:
(1) Your business has losses. Any C Corporation losses will stay within the structure and won't give you any tax benefits.
(2) Your business has high income. The C Corporation will need to distribute most of the income out to you in the form of salary. That means you'll pay high payroll taxes. If you instead use an S Corporation for the business you will be able to flow some of the income through to you in the form of a distribution.
(3) Your business is a qualified personal service corporation.
(4) Your business is a personal holding company
(5) You want a very simple structure. A C Corporation will require better and more diligent bookkeeping.

Action Steps

Action Step 1: After reading this chapter, consider: is a C Corporation for you?

Action Step 2: If so, review possible issues. What can you do to prevent problems down the road?

Resources

Your tax advisor! Talk it over, get clear on your professional status, or any of the other C Corporation traps, and lay the groundwork for growth and development.

Fishman, Stephen. 2009. *Tax Deductions for Professionals*. Nolo

Chapter 25:
Benefits That Benefit You

Y ou're in business for a lot of reasons, and, one of the biggest ones is so that you can make money for yourself and your family.

There are five primary ways that you can take money out of your company:

(1) Salary you draw

(2) Loans from the company to you personally

(3) Distributions/dividends

(4) Investments funded through the business

(5) Benefits

Plus, of course, there is the value of the business itself. For now let's talk about the money you get while the business is operating.

There are tax consequences for each of these:

Benefit	Tax Consequence/Treatment
Salary	Deductible for the business; taxable income for you
Loans	Neither deduction nor income for the business or for you, but could create an issue when using a C Corporation or where you fail to repay the loans
Distributions/ Dividends	Not a deductible expense to the business; taxable income for you.
Investments	Taxation consequences vary, based on strategy
Benefits	Deductible for the business; not taxable to you (in most cases).

When you're looking for how you can draw money from your business, first consider the benefits you can receive. Benefits are the best of both worlds. Your company gets a deduction, and you get a benefit, without paying taxes.

There are 5 different ways to take money out of your company. Of these, tax-free benefits are the best!

Let's look at some of the common benefits that your company can have. Some of them are nondiscriminatory. That means that if you take the deduction, you're going to have to offer the same deduction to all full-time employees. With all of them, you will need to be an employee as well.

Medical Benefits

Medical Insurance: Medical insurance premiums are a deduction. The amount of the deduction, and where it is taken, depends on the type of business structure that you have.

If you have an S Corporation or an LLC-S and you are a greater than 2% shareholder, your deduction is reported separately on your personal return as a Schedule A - Itemized Deduction. That means it will not be fully deductible. It also means you will need to be an itemized filer to take the deduction.

At the other end of the scale, a C Corporation medical insurance premium is paid at the corporate level and is fully deductible by the corporation. That's one of the unique benefit advantages of a C Corporation – full deductibility for medical insurance premiums.

Medical insurance is a nondiscriminatory deduction. You must include all employees who work more than 1020 hours per year.

HSA (Health Savings Accounts), FSA (Flexible Savings Accounts): A health savings account (HSA) is a tax-advantaged medical savings account available to employees of a company that has adopted such a plan. The funds are deducted from paychecks before tax. Unused balances can roll over to the next year and accumulate.

A flexible spending account (FSA) is also tax-advantaged, but the funds must be used before year-end or they are lost.

Medical Expense Reimbursement Plan (MERP): The MERP is allowed for C Corporations, LLC-Cs, and in some cases, sole proprietorships. It is not allowed under partnerships, S Corporations, or the LLC-S.

A MERP is a reimbursement plan, meaning you can personally pay for the medical expense. It can be set up to have payment limits or to be limitless. How you craft the plan will depend on your business. If the business covers you and your family, limitless may be exactly what you want. If you have a half-dozen unrelated employees, an open checkbook plan could be expensive. A MERP is a nondiscriminatory plan; so whatever you give yourself, you must give to all of your full-time employees.

It's also possible to set up a MERP for your employees if you have a sole proprietorship. However, as the owner, you can't draw a salary. That means you aren't an employee, so the MERP doesn't apply to you. Your only way to receive MERP benefits here is by employing your spouse in the business and going through their coverage. If you're single, this won't work. And in any event, you are then facing all of the liability and excess tax issues that sole proprietorships bring with them.

Pension Benefits: The next big section of benefits to consider are all the different types of retirement plans. Most of these are nondiscriminatory which means you have to cover all of your employees as well. However, there is a way around that with a two-tiered system. The base level is open to all employees, and typically takes the form of a 401(k) plan. Remember, though, if you offer employer matching contributions to a 401(k) plan for yourself, you will need to offer the same employer match to all employees in the plan.

Now that you've offered a benefit to everyone, you are free to add a second plan. This one doesn't have to be open to everyone. It can be reserved for executives alone. This plan is structured differently from a typical 401(k), and it allows much higher contributions. In fact, by stacking plans like this you could find yourself being able to put away retirement deductions of $150,000 or more per year. These plan contributions would all be deductible from your personal income and a great way for you to invest tax-deferred or tax-free.

Pension Plan Primer

Defined Contribution versus Defined Benefit: In a defined contribution plan, what goes into the plan each year is based on a percentage of your salary. What comes out, depends on how your plan contributions were invested and grew. In a defined benefit plan, you receive a defined specific pension amount. Your contributions are calculated based on a guaranteed amount that you will receive upon retirement.

Most benefit plans these days are defined contribution plans. That's because you can calculate much more easily how much a pension plan will cost. Plus, your business won't bear any risk if the investments go down in value. Remember, a defined benefit plan guarantees the amount that is to be paid after retirement. If investments are bad and the value goes down, your business is responsible to put more money in. Defined benefit plans are the ones you've heard about – usually because they have failed spectacularly, leaving retirees with nothing.

Self-Directed Plans: You won't find the term 'self-directed' in the IRS Code. It simply means that you have greater control over your investment decisions. The level of control varies depending on the plan. Some plans allow you to self direct only from a list of supported investments. Others allow you wider access, and some allow you to invest in anything you want (except those things prohibited by law).

Not every plan can be self-directed. Most employer-sponsored plans that allow all employees to participate aren't fully self-directed. You'll be limited to whatever the plan custodian is offering for investment choices. If you've got a business with employees, this is where the two-tiered system can help you. The second, discriminatory plan can be set up as a self-directed plan.

Prohibited Transactions and Disqualified Persons: There are some things your pension plan can't invest in, and there are certain people your plan can't invest with. For example, pension money may not be used for the direct benefit of the owner and his or her lineal. Your pension can't buy you a house; you're the owner of the plan. It can't buy one for your parents or your children, either. They're lineal relatives. But other relatives are okay. So, feel free to buy your brother a house. Ask him to buy you one in return with his pension, and you'll both benefit.

Prohibited transactions include:

- Sale, exchange, or lease of any property between a plan and a disqualified person
- Furnishing goods, services, or facilities between a plan and a disqualified person
- Using any portion of the IRA as security for a loan by a disqualified person
- Use of income or assets of a plan by a disqualified person for his or her own benefit

---

Prohibited Investments: There's not much that you can't do with a truly self-directed plan. But here are some definite pension fund no-no's: art, rugs, antiques, precious metals, gems, stamp, coins, alcoholic beverages, other tangible personal property, and life insurance.

Tax-Deferred or Tax-Free?

Tax-deferred means tax later. Tax-free means tax never. A tax-deferred plan means you defer the tax due on income in the pension until a later date when you distribute the money out. The distribution will all be taxed at your regular income tax rate. A tax-free plan is funded with after-tax dollars. It grows within the plan tax-free, and all withdrawals are tax-free. A tax-free pension plan may be the ultimate in delayed gratification.

Examples of tax-deferred plans are:

Traditional IRA: The traditional IRA was created for individuals that don't participate in an employer-sponsored retirement plan. IRA plans have annual contribution limits that are established by the government and rise gradually with inflation; individuals age 50 and older can make slightly higher "catch-up" contributions.

SEP IRA: A SEP (Simplified Employee Pension) IRA has simpler compliance and reporting requirements than those for qualified plans such as 401(k) and 403(b) plans. For that reason, SEP IRAs are often used by small companies. Tax deductible contributions by the employer are made to IRAs because IRAs are the funding vehicle for SEPs. You can contribute up to 25% of your annual income, to a maximum of $49,000 each year (as of 2009).

Charitable IRA: An IRA that is sponsored or promoted by a non-profit or charitable institution. It's generally a traditional IRA, subject to regular IRA rules, with an administrator that supports this type of plan.

Spousal IRA: If your spouse doesn't work, a spousal IRA is one way to establish a plan for them. You must be married, file a joint tax return, and at least one of you must be working.

Beneficiary IRA: If you inherit an IRA, you are called a beneficiary. A beneficiary can be any person or entity that the owner chooses to receive the benefits of the IRA upon death. If you inherit an IRA from anyone other than your deceased spouse, you cannot treat the inherited IRA as your own. This means that you cannot make any contributions to the IRA. It also means that you cannot roll over any amounts into or out of the inherited IRA. Like the original owner, you generally will not owe tax on the assets in the IRA until you receive distributions from it.

Keogh Plans: Most are defined contribution, although you can have a defined benefit option. You can contribute up to 25% of your annual income, to a maximum of $49,000 each year (as of 2009). Keoghs can invest in all of the same types of securities as 401(k) plans and IRAs, including stocks, bonds, certificates of deposit and annuities. Keogh plan types include money-purchase plans (used by high-income earners), defined-benefit plans (which have high annual minimums), and profit-sharing plans (which offer annual flexibility based on profits).

401(k) and Solo 401(k): A qualified plan established by employers where participants contribute using pre-tax dollars. Employers offering a 401(k) plan may make matching or non-elective contributions to the plan on behalf of eligible employees and may also add a profit-sharing feature to the plan. Earnings accrue on a tax-deferred basis. You can contribute up to $16,500 from salary earnings into a 401(k) plan.

A Solo 401(k) plan is something relatively new. It's a tax-deferred plan designed for single-owner businesses, businesses owned by a married couple, or businesses with no employees, who work more than 1000 hours each year. The Solo 401(k) pretty much mirrors a standard 401(k) plan, but because of the restrictions on who can participate, it can easily be established as a true self-directed plan that invests in real estate, other businesses, and so on. You can put $49,000 or more into a Solo 401(k) plan. $16,500 of that amount can come from your salary, just like a regular 401(k) plan, and the remaining amount can come from profit sharing. The Solo 401(k) plan may be a business owner's best friend, for the flexibility and power of investment it offers. Please check with your tax advisor or our website at www.MySmarterBusiness.com for the most current limits on pension plan contributions and latest tax news.

Examples of Tax-Free Plans:

Roth IRA: A Roth IRA is funded with after-tax dollars. Because you've already paid tax once, before you put the money in, it isn't taxed again. It will grow in the plan tax-free, and when you take it out, it'll come out tax-free. This is one of the reasons Roth IRAs are such popular retirement vehicles. Like a regular IRA, there is a contribution limit. But unlike a traditional IRA, a Roth IRA also has an income limit.

Solo Roth 401(k): If you meet the criteria to establish a Solo 401(k) plan, then you can also add the optional Solo 401(k) Roth component to that plan. Now you have the option to take the $15,500 in salary contributions and put all or a portion of that money into the Roth side instead. You can only contribute salary to the Solo Roth 401(k); any profit sharing must be fed into the Solo 401(k) tax-deferred side instead. All contributions made to the Solo Roth 401(k) plan are made with after-tax dollars, meaning they also accrue tax-free and come out tax-free.

The Solo Roth 401(k) beats the Roth IRA hands down for five very important reasons.

(1) There are no income limitations! You can make a ton of money. and finally, for the first time, be able to use the fantastic tax strategies of the Roth.

(2) You can put away up to $15,500 per year into this plan, versus $5,000 into a Roth IRA. You'll need to have your own business, and you'll need to draw a salary at least equal to the amount of the contribution you make. If you're age 50 or older, you can put away an additional $5,000 per year. If you're married and both employed by the company, you both can put the maximum amount in the plan.

(3) The Solo Roth 401(k) can invest in S Corporation stock and life insurance policies, something that the traditional Roth IRA rules do not let you do.

(4) You can borrow up to $50,000 from your Solo Roth 401 (k) plan

(5) If you invest in real estate with leverage through your Solo Roth 401(k) plan, you will avoid the tax issues that come up with leverage in other types of IRA plans. You can learn more about the tricks and traps of leverage with your pension plan in my book, "The Insider's Guide to Tax-Free Real Estate Investments: Retire Rich Using Your IRA" (Kennedy & DeRoos, Wiley, 2006).

And, there's one more benefit. You can also invest your existing Roth and traditional IRAs, including SEP IRAs, right along with your new Solo 401(k) into the same or multiple properties.

Education (Coverdell) IRA: This plan is designed to pay for the qualified education expenses of a designated beneficiary. Unless the beneficiary is considered special needs, the designated beneficiary must be under age 18. Contributions are made with after-tax dollars, so withdrawals are tax-free, unless the funds are used for non-qualified expenses. If that happens the funds are taxed and possibly penalized. Qualified expenses include elementary and secondary education, and they cover tuition, fees, academic tutoring, special needs services, books, supplies, and other equipment which are incurred in connection to the beneficiary's enrollment at an eligible educational institution. Allowable expenses for K-12 also include room and board, uniforms, transportation, and supplementary items and services (including extended day programs), as well as computer technology or equipment.

Education Benefits: If you go to college, very little of the expense will be deductible. There are some interest deductions now and some ways to save for the future expense, but in general, education is not deductible.

That is, unless you have a business. Once you have a business, any education that helps you be a better business owner becomes a deductible expense.

The cost of this book is a deduction if you have a business. If you don't have a business, start one tonight! Otherwise, the cost of the book is coming out of your pocket.

But it doesn't just stop with books and courses. The cost of advisors, who teach you to be better business owners and make more money, is a deduction for your business.

When you think about it, until you make that first big step to own a business, the government isn't prepared to give you many tax breaks at all. But once you make a step forward, you can start keeping more of what you make as you learn on the government's nickel.

Trying to figure out how to pay for your kid's college education? Legitimately employ them and then take a deduction for any classes directly related to the work they do.

C Corporation Benefits
The best benefits of all come through owning a C Corporation. This alone shouldn't be your reason for determining what type of business structure to be, however.

Favorite C Corporation Benefits
We've already discussed the increased tax breaks for medical insurance and MERP with the C Corporation. There are a few more C Corporation-only tax deductible benefits for owners as well:
- Public transportation passes
- Term life insurance (up to $50,000 of term life insurance)
- Child care facility
- Physical Fitness facility

In general, the government has been cutting back on the allowed number of tax breaks for companies with employee/owner employee benefits. You can't often find discriminatory plans. Figure on having to include your other full time employees as well.

Providing Discriminatory Benefits through a Second Business
Many business owners want to find a way to provide some benefits to employees, and also provide more benefits to themselves. A simple approach would seem to be the creation of a second business, where the additional benefits are offered. It's a good idea, but it doesn't work. The same controlled group, status issues that come up when you own more than one C Corporation come up here, too. Only this time, it doesn't matter what type of business structures you've got. Employees in one business structure are entitled to the same benefits and perks as employees in all the other structures, too.

MD Discovers He Can't Exclude Employees

Dr. X had a very successful medical practice. He had staff who had been with him a very long time, and he paid them well. What he really wanted, though, was a defined benefit pension plan. That's because the defined benefit plan allowed him to put as much as $185,000 per year away, and it was completely deductible from his company.

The problem with the defined benefit plan, though, is that the calculation for contribution is based on the needed benefit for the future. So, the older the employee, the higher the deduction. And the more the employee was paid, the higher the deduction. Dr. X had highly compensated employees who were as old as he was. He would have to fund all of his employee's pension plans at the same level he had, if he wanted to take that benefit himself.

So, he decided to start a new company, and he'd be the only employee. Unfortunately, he did that without seeking the advice of an experienced tax advisor. You can count on that not ending well. And it didn't.

A few years into the plan, he got caught. And because he had the same ownership in both companies, he had to then fund all of his employee's plans.

It put him out of business.

Don't try to get sneaky with nondiscriminatory plans. There are very clear rules for what you can and cannot do.

If you want to put such a plan in place, you still may be able to, but you're going to need an experienced tax advisor to help you.

Don't forget the benefits as you're building your own tax strategy plan. There can be some tricks, but there can also be some huge rewards.

Action Steps

Action Step 1: Review the benefits possible in your business. What programs do you want to include in your business?

Action Step 2: What kind of pension will give you the biggest benefit?

Action Step 3: If you're going to use a self-directed pension plan, what do you want to invest in?

Resources

Kennedy, Diane and De Roos, Dolf. 2005. *The Insider's Guide to Tax-Free Real Estate: Retire Rich Using Your IRA*. Wiley.

Peterson, Nora. 2006. *Retire Rich With Your Self-Directed IRA: What Your Broker & Banker Don't Want You to Know About Managing Your Own Retirement Investments*. Atlantic Publishing Company.

www.pensco.com: Pensco Trust Company is one of the nation's leading websites for self-directed pension plans, including the Solo 401(k) and Solo Roth 401(k).

Section Six: Make More Money, Pay Less Tax

Chapter 26:
Increase Your Personal ROI

There comes a time where your business starts to work. The bills get paid, the customers get their products, happy clients get great service, and it all just works.

Unless you lead a charmed business life, you've gone through some unpleasant business moments to get here. There were probably times when you didn't know if you could make payroll or pay the bills. You had a key employee or partner let you down, and you were left holding the bag. Or you had a vampire client who sucked the life and energy out of all your staff in a never-ending quest to try to make him happy. Those are the moments that stick with you, unfortunately. And if you've ever had an employee who damaged your business and your reputation, you may want to keep close control of the business forever.

Welcome to the entrepreneurial dilemma. How do you give phenomenal service, create raving fans, and make outrageous sums of money by doing good in the world, if you're not involved in it every step of the way?

On the other hand, if you do everything yourself to make sure it's "done right," you've limited how much your business can grow, and you've tied yourself to it, every single day. You've created a bottleneck in your company. Everything in the business slows down to the speed of you.

How much are you worth? Most small business owners sell their time way too cheap.

Each year, Diane selects twenty-five business owners to work with personally. These private clients participate in a quarterly mastermind meeting with Diane and select experts. One of the exercises that Diane goes through is calculating personal ROI (Return on Investment).

Back in Chapter 22 we talked about ROI as it related to your business. It's the ratio between what you put in and what you get back out again. Sophisticated investors never invest on emotion. They invest based on ROI.

ROI is also applicable to your personal time as well. The only difference is that you express your personal ROI in terms of dollars. How much is your time worth? Or more importantly, what is the minimum that you will accept for your time.

Smart investors have a benchmark ROI for their money. Smart business owners have a benchmark ROI for their time.

You can go fishing and not get paid.

-- Diane

(This is one of Diane's favorite sayings when it comes to business and business owners who give away their time for free.)

There are two different ways you can get caught in the Entrepreneurial Time Trap:

Trap #1: Spend your time doing everything. Do you give away your time on something that someone else could probably do better anyway?

When you've bootstrapped your company and put your own money and hours of sleepless nights into it, it's hard to turn it over to someone else. This is where entrepreneurs get trapped.

Bookkeeping is a great example of an Entrepreneurial Time Trap. Are you a trained bookkeeper? If not, why try to be one in your business? It is almost certainly taking you longer than it would take someone with that knowledge, and chances are you're doing at least part of it wrong. Or, worse, you're letting it sit until you have time to get to it. Understanding how to review your financial records and monitor financial activity is one thing. Sitting in front of a computer puzzling over payroll tax reports is something else entirely.

An employee gets stuck because of fear. An entrepreneur gets trapped because of distrust.

Trap #2: If you sell knowledge, watch out for an even bigger Entrepreneurial Time Trap: The Free Giveaway. Think of it this way. Let's say you own a plumbing supply company. You have an inventory that you invested time and money into building. Someone comes in and says they need parts to hook up their new bathroom in their house. What would you do if they said they wanted to take the parts home and see how good they were? They wouldn't ever pay you for those parts. All you were doing is giving away inventory to someone you don't even know and hoping they liked your parts enough to come back and buy something else.

That's a ridiculous question. Right?

But, if you're a professional who is paid for expertise, then you do the same thing every time you give a free consultation. You've devalued your time and your expertise.

Do you give away your time in free consultations or answering "quick" questions that consume your day?

There are times when you will want to give away advice to establish that you are an expert. It's a great idea! But do it in a way that gives you leverage, such as with articles that you write, or through public forums where others get to take advantage of your knowledge as well. Why answer a question 100 times if you can find a way to answer it just once? And, at the same time, you receive exposure and acknowledgement.

Now, let's take a look at how much your personal ROI actually is.

Personal ROI Exercise

Step One: Find Your Biggest Check. Think back to the biggest check you ever received from the work you did. This could be a series of checks that equals one deal or it could be one solitary check. What was the relationship, deal, or event that provided the biggest amount of income at any point in your life. Think about how much you received and why you were paid.

Go to our web site, www.MySmarterBusiness.com and download the 4-page worksheet called "My Biggest Check." On the worksheet, list out all you can remember about the deal that got you the biggest check. How did you feel? What did you do really well? Why did it work? What made it an amazing deal? What problem did you solve for someone else?

Step Two: Complete the "My Biggest Check" below.

My Biggest Check

Time Period:

To:

ME!

Amount:

Relationship/Deal/Event:

Step Three: What were the total hours spent in putting the deal together and then executing?

Total Hours Spent

Step Four: Divide the amount in your "Biggest Check" by the total hours you spent making it happen.

This will give you your Personal ROI on this deal.

You may find that your hourly rate is fantastic, or at least acceptable. If that's the case, move on to Step Five.

On the other hand, you may find that your Personal ROI wasn't that good on your biggest check after all. That's because

Current Personal ROI

it took a tremendous amount of hours, either putting the deal together or your time spent working on the project.

If your ROI isn't what you thought it should have been, go back and look at your biggest check. If it took that much time, was it really such a good deal? If there was a steep learning curve that you don't need to repeat, go back through the exercise using the estimated number of hours as if you didn't have to repeat the learning curve. Estimate the hours you'd spend if you were doing that deal today. What would your personal ROI have been if there was no learning curve?

Or, if you find that it just took a tremendous amount of time and really wasn't such a good deal after all, start over with your next biggest check. Repeat all the steps.

The goal through this process is to find a deal that made you a lot of money and rewarded you for your time.

Step Five: Your Personal ROI Standard. The bell curve has long been used in business as the graph of choice. Most things happen in the middle, and the smaller and bigger trail off in equal measure. Up until now, your biggest check has been at the far right of the bell curve.

This next step is going to ask you to stretch that a bit. What if your personal ROI wasn't the best you could do but was instead the average that you did?

Stretching Your Personal ROI Standard

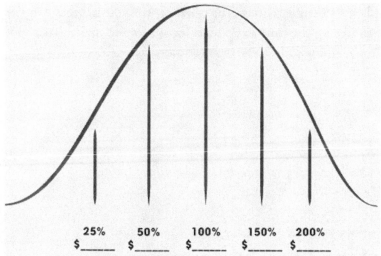

```
   25%      50%     100%     150%     200%
$_____  $_____  $_____  $_____  $_____
```

Write your personal ROI dollar amount at the line that says 100%. Now let's look at the smaller end of that. Take 50% of your personal ROI dollar amount and write it on the line below the percentage. Now take 25% of the personal ROI dollar amount and write it on the line below 25%. Those are your new "lows." It's very possible that those lows were just average for you merely 15 minutes ago. Things can change that fast when you change your mind first.

Now take 150% of your personal ROI number and write it in the appropriate spot. And finally take 200% of the amount and write it in the final blank.

> NOTE: Why copy pages out of this book when you can download the original, beautiful, artist-rendered worksheets from www.MySmarterBusiness.com? By signing up to register your book, you'll receive the worksheets, free updates to this book as tax law changes, and notification of free teleseminars regarding taxes and other important information for Smart Business owners.

So, how much is your time really worth? Remember, this calculation is with your current level of systems and business model. You'll learn later how to make your time more valuable.

For now, though, look at that number. That's how much you should make for every hour you spend working. Or at least for all the time you spend in focused activities. The question for you is, what can you do now to free up the time so you can focus more to make that happen?

You're going to love the next chapter.

Action Steps

Action Step 1: Do the PROI exercise.

Action Step 2: Think back on what you do on a daily, weekly, and monthly basis. What low level PROI activities are you ready to get rid of?

Action Step 3: What is your new standard for your PROI?

Resources

www.MySmarterBusiness.com. Download your personal return on investment guide.

Allen, David. 2002. *Getting Things Done: The Art of Stress-Free Productivity*. Penguin (non-classics).

Blanchard, Ken and Bowles, Sheldon. 1993. *Raving Fans: A Revolutionary Approach To Customer Service*. William Morrow.

Chapter 27:
Ultimate Systems, Infinite Income

You're going to roll up your sleeves again on a whole new set of exercises in this chapter. When you're done, you'll have a fully documented system that you can use to make more money today!

Why Have a System?

When your business is just you, there's little need for systems. Most of the time, you're making it up as you go along. In fact, you might even be an entrepreneur today because of the restrictions and bureaucracy of your past jobs. Systems stifled your creativity and the ability to do your best work. You wanted out and your own business seemed like the sure path to creative freedom.

No wonder entrepreneurs are so reluctant to have systems in the beginning. It seems anti-creative and against the reason you started the business in the beginning.

That all changes, as soon as the fun of having your own business wears off, and you realize that with your first employee came more questions then you ever thought possible. It's more work, not less, because you still have to do the work plus find the time to train the new employee. Inevitably, he gets something wrong, because your lack of a system led to confusion or worse. But you're the one who will be paying to fix the errors, explaining oversights to the client, and feeling the hit on your bottom line. Sooner or later, it hits you: systems don't constrict your creativity. They allow it.

Systems don't constrict creativity. They allow it.

A system will fundamentally change your business. But, it has to be the right system, broken down into manageable learning chunks, and then taught to capable and willing employees. With a system and trained employees in place, you now have a line to which you can hold them accountable. If they don't follow the system, you now have something to talk about. The chances are your employees will disappoint you a whole lot less with a system than without one.

If you've ever said:
"It's faster for me to just do it myself, rather than teach someone else."
"I can't count on my staff to do this as well as I would."
"I'm the only one I can count on to get this right."
Then: You need a system.

Stop Spending All Your Time Working IN Your Business

The minute you go from working in your business to on your business, you've started to move from being self-employed to having a business. A business can grow bigger, better, and take a whole lot less of your time.

If you work IN your business, you are:
- Doing the work
- Talking to each customer through every level of service
- Handling customer service issues
- Managing your team
- Tracking the cash
- Paying the bills
- Making the deposits
- Writing reports
- Selling
- Writing marketing materials
- Ordering inventory

If you work ON your business, you are:
- Planning for the future
- Hiring key team

- Leading the team
- Writing/building systems
- Coaching key employees
- Envisioning and focusing the vision
- Creating powerful joint venture relationships
- Monitoring daily, weekly and monthly key stats
- Identifying and expanding niches
- Creating sustainability
- Building a legacy

Hopefully, you're excited about the idea of having systems that work in your business (so you don't have to). Let's get to work creating some great systems to make that happen.

The Sticky Note Process™

You'll need a few supplies to get started on this. Get a few pads of sticky notes, a couple of pens, and a piece of heavy tagboard. Get a big piece. We like to use 3' x 2' tagboard for this process.

Step One: Identify a task you do in your business at least once a month and that is something that is significantly below your personal ROI threshold. For added measure, make sure the task is something you hate to do and you're not any good at. If you don't have something that meets all this criteria, just pick something that you'd love to get off your plate.

Step Two: Go through every separate function you do as part of this process. Write each separate step down on a separate sticky note. This works best if you can do this as fast as possible. Just make a note of what the step is, tear the sticky note off and slap it on the tagboard. Go on to the next step. It's okay if they're out of order and messy on the tagboard. For now, you're just doing a brain dump of every step you can think of for that process.

Wait until you've exhausted all the steps you can think of and then re-order the sticky notes on the tagboard. As you go through this, you'll likely think of more steps; add them in.

Step Three: Review each of the sticky notes. Are they all broken down in their most basic pieces? You don't want a sticky note that says something like "complete the project." That's not a step you can hand off to someone else.

If you need to expand the number of steps, add more sticky notes into the process.

Step Four: Now that you have all of the steps lined out in this job that you want to hand (at least partially) off, look at each step. Who could do that step? If you need to hire someone, make a note of the level of experience and education you would need. For example, if you want to hand off the record-keeping and bookkeeping, but are concerned that your new bookkeeper wouldn't do as good of a job, you may want to hang on to key steps. Initial what she would do, and then put your initials on what you would do.

A CPA Takes the First Step at Letting Go

I started off my first tax practice in a very traditional way. I saw clients, did the work mostly myself, worked long hours outside tax season, and unbearable hours during tax season. It's a common story for most professionals.

Gradually I brought on people who could do functions I didn't want to do or that were below my personal ROI. But there were still big chunks of work that I continued to do.

One of those was "tax return preparation." My highest level of expertise is tax strategy development. I love planning big pictures, lots of moving parts, converting active income into passive, discovering hidden business deductions, income splitting, all the fancy stuff that saves my clients an average of over $30,000 per year after just one phone call.

But here's the rest of the story. The best strategy in the world isn't worth a thing if the tax return isn't prepared correctly. Your preparer has to understand your strategy and fill out the forms correctly. Plus, he needs to create an audit defense strategy for how the information is presented: clear, honest, and with full disclosure of tax positions taken in the strategy. Otherwise, your strategy is worse than worthless. It could even be dangerous in the hands of a preparer who fills out the forms incorrectly.

So, even though preparation of a tax return isn't my highest and best use, I didn't think anyone could do it as well as I could.

Then, one long weekend, my husband and I went away to a bed & breakfast in Sedona, AZ. We took along a couple of pieces of tagboard and some sticky note pads. (Doesn't everybody take them on a romantic weekend out of town?)

I knew that my insistence on preparing tax returns was the bottleneck of my company. I had let go of the simpler ones and the straightforward Form 1040 Individual Income Tax Returns, but I still did all the business ones myself.

I made it my mission to figure out how to turn the tax strategy process, implementation, and tax return preparation into a system.

It took us three days of solid hard work to get through just the first pass. That's because along the way I discovered that there were actually a number of major phases to a successful tax strategy. And that was more than just one sticky note on a tag board.

In fact, as I thought through the process that I already had, and what it could be, it became pages and pages of tagboard (I had to keep recycling because I'd only brought two).

The next step was implementation.

The final phase is the compliance step. But that is more than just the preparation of a tax return. It means properly reporting the strategy to provide full audit defense. Compliance also meant doing all that is needed to keep the business structure and my clients' other assets safe.

I didn't finish the process in 3 days. But what I did do was transform my business life forever. I went on to write "Loopholes of the Rich," got invited on CNN, CNBC, New York One, became a fact checker for major print publishers, and built web sites that were one-of-a-kind in providing tax knowledge for small business owners and investors.

It all started with the Sticky Note System. I thought I was lining out a system. Instead I wound up building a brand new type of company.

You might find that the Sticky Note System process starts you thinking about what your business really is and how you can take each one of those integral parts and expand it.

None of it can happen without a system. The final step with the Sticky Note System is to list all the steps in one place.

You now have a system. Refine it. Hand off pieces and see if someone else can follow it with minimal supervision. If it works, teach it and put the new system in place to make sure systems are followed.

This is how smart businesses grow, step by step and system by system.

S	ave
Y	our
S	elf
T	ime
E	nergy
M	oney

Cooperative System Building

As your business grows, you will reach the point where your employees and independent contractors know more about certain aspects of your business than you do.

You could have them sit down with the Sticky Note System process as well, or you could try out the Cooperative System Building system we use when we bring multiple people into the system building.

Here's how it works:

Step One: Set up a private forum online. We have a link off of one of our web sites. It's not visible or published unless you have a username and know your password. Figure that it will cost a few hundred dollars to set up with a programmer.

Step Two: Give your key people access to the forum. Post notes, questions, and best of all, the beginning of systems on the forum. The interactive nature of the forum allows others to comment and the system gets built on the forum.

Step Three: Once a system has been refined and talked through, close that particular thread. Write up the final system and add it to your growing system manual.

Six Steps to Creating an Interactive System Building Powerhouse

(1) Set up a private forum on a password protected link. For example, www.Yourwebsite.com/private is a page you might use. Then, password protect it.

(2) Determine the forum categories and sub-categories. Keep it simple.

(3) Invite everyone who is part of the system including the people who will do the work.

(4) When you get a question about how to do something, ask your employee to post it on the forum.

(5) When someone has a complaint, have them come up with some ideas on how to fix it and post it.

(6) When someone wants a change, have them post it.

No matter how you grow your business, you're going to find that there will be a time when systems will set you free. Start documenting as soon as you can and begin the process to work less and make more money.

Action Steps

Action Step 1: What systems do you need now?

Action Step 2: What methods do you want to use to develop systems? Do you want to do them all yourself, have specific people instructed to do it, or build a forum and crowd source it?

Action Step 3: Write down your employee and contractor system for education about the systems.

Action Step 4: Institute the procedure for ensuring system compliance.

Resources

Abraham, Jay. 2009. *The Sticking Point Solution: 9 Ways to Move Your Business from Stagnation to Stunning Growth In Tough Economic Times.* Vanguard Press.

Carpenter, Sam. 2009. *Work the System: The Simple Mechanics of Making More and Working Less.* Greenleaf Book Group Press.

Chapter 28:
Multiple Streams of Passive Income

W ho doesn't love the idea of passive income? Make money while you sleep. Never get out of your pajamas. Live at the beach. It's the stuff late night infomercials are made of.

It's also the dream that a lot of people chase with real estate investing. In fact, a lot of business people look at real estate as the answer to the Entrepreneurial Time Trap. And it is one answer. For this chapter, though, we're going to look at other options that can make you more money, faster, easier, and safer than ever before.

Tax Definition of Passive Income

The term "passive income" gets thrown around a lot. From a tax perspective, there are three types of taxable income:
- Ordinary
- Portfolio
- Passive

Ordinary income is taxed at the ordinary tax rates. It includes earned income, which is also subject to payroll tax or self-employment tax. Ordinary income comes from a trade or business in which you are active.

Portfolio income is income that your money makes. It includes interest, dividends, and capital gains from the sale of assets. The distinction becomes important when you have an expense like an investment expense. This can only be used to offset investment income. The same is true with capital losses. These are limited to capital gains plus a little bit extra against ordinary income. This part of tax law is changing. Check back on current laws at www.USTaxAid.com.

Passive income is money your real estate or businesses make without you actively working. There is an important distinction here between what late night infomercial guys tell you is passive income and what the IRS says is passive. In this case, pay attention to what the IRS tells you; because if you have a business or real estate that is considered passive by them, you probably won't be able to write off any losses.

The IRS tells us that passive income is:

(1) Trade or business activities in which you do not materially participate in during the year.

(2) Rental activities, even if you do materially participate in them, unless you are a real estate professional.

Following that concise definition, the IRS then expands on the definition of material participation for a business. The assumption is that if you're not materially participating, then you have passive income.

Here's what they say: "A trade or business activity is not a passive activity if you materially participated in the activity."

And here's what that means in practical terms:

Material Participation Tests: You materially participated in a trade or business activity for a tax year if you satisfy any of the following tests:

- You participated in the activity for more than 500 hours.

- Your participation was substantially all the participation in the activity of all individuals for the tax year, including the participation of individuals who did not own any interest in the activity.

- You participated in the activity for more than 100 hours during the tax year, and you participated at least as much as any other individual (including individuals who did not own any interest in the activity) for the year.

- The activity is a significant participation activity, and you participated in all significant participation activities for more than 500 hours. A significant participation activity is any trade or business activity in which you participated for more than 100 hours during the year and in which you did not materially participate under any of the material participation tests, other than this test.

- You materially participated in the activity for any 5 (whether or not consecutive) of the 10 immediately preceding tax years.

- The activity is a personal service activity in which you materially participated for any 3 (whether or not consecutive) preceding tax years. An activity is a personal service activity if it involves the performance of personal services in the fields of health (including veterinary services), law, engineering, architecture, accounting, actuarial science, performing arts, consulting, or any other trade or business in which capital is not a material income-producing factor.

- Based on all the facts and circumstances, you participated in the activity on a regular, continuous, and substantial basis during the year.

You did not materially participate in the activity under test (7) if you participated in the activity for 100 hours or less during the year. Your participation in managing the activity does not count in determining whether you materially participated under this test if:

- Any person other than you received compensation for managing the activity, or
- Any individual spent more hours during the tax year managing the activity than you did (regardless of whether the individual was compensated for the management services).

Participation: In general, any work you do in connection with an activity in which you own an interest is treated as participation in the activity.

Work not usually performed by owners: You do not treat the work you do in connection with an activity as participation in the activity if both of the following are true.

- The work is not work that is customarily done by the owner of that type of activity.
- One of your main reasons for doing the work is to avoid the disallowance of any loss or credit from the activity under the passive activity rules.

Participation as an investor: You do not treat the work you do in your capacity as an investor in an activity as participation unless you are directly involved in the day-to-day management or operations of the activity. Work you do as an investor includes:

- Studying and reviewing financial statements or reports on operations of the activity,

- Preparing or compiling summaries or analyses of the finances or operations of the activity for your own use, and
- Monitoring the finances or operations of the activity in a non-managerial capacity.

Spouse's participation: Your participation in an activity includes your spouse's participation. This applies even if your spouse did not own any interest in the activity and you and your spouse do not file a joint return for the year.

Proof of participation: You can use any reasonable method to prove your participation in an activity for the year. You do not have to keep contemporaneous daily time reports, logs, or similar documents if you can establish your participation in some other way. For example, you can show the services you performed and the approximate number of hours spent by using an appointment book, calendar, or narrative summary."

Well, it might not be exactly concise, but at least it's long.

It's still a bit up in the air with how the IRS is going to handle businesses that are held in limited partnerships, or in LLCs that elect partnership taxation. If a limited partner is considered, by definition, to always be passive, that could be a great way to create some passive income to offset passive losses. For example, passive real estate losses are generally suspended and not currently allowed as a deduction against other forms of income.

But if your business has a loss, be careful that you don't run into the passive activity loss rules by stepping out of your company too much. It's a moot point if it's always showing a tax profit.

That's a lot about passive income from a tax perspective. Now let's look at what passive income can really mean for you: Freedom!

Passive Income: Money That Works So You Don't Have To

There are three primary ways you can use to create passive income from your business:

(1) Turn active income into leveraged and passive,

(2) Invest business profits into real estate or other businesses, and

(3) Turn under-utilized business assets into passive income.

Turn Active Income to Leveraged & Passive Income

In this section, we've talked about techniques to turn active income into leveraged income. You're still working, but you'll be a lot more effective with a higher PROI.

Now, how can you take the next step to start to turn it into passive income? If your business gets big enough, you may be able to turn your role into that of just an investor. In other words, you turn the business over to a CEO, CFO, and other initialed people to run.

The trick here is to build the company big enough with enough profit to replace yourself, hire the talent you want, and to figure it'll take a little bit of a profit hit as you add some necessary levels of bureaucracy. It's a great goal to work toward, and it provides an exit strategy as well. You never have to actually exit the business, you just collect the money.

Your Business Invests in Real Estate

If your business is currently renting a space from someone else, how about making yourself the landlord?

This can be a way to create some passive income from your business. But in this instance, you don't want the business to make the investment directly. It will be safer and more advantageous to you from a tax note if you take the money out of the business as a loan. Have your business loan money to a new LLC and have that LLC buy the building.

Once it's set up, your business begins paying rent to the new LLC. The rent is an expense for the business and income for the LLC. But, because the LLC is able to depreciate the real estate (and get a big deduction for it) you're almost always going to see cash flow. And the money isn't taxable, because of the depreciation offset.

Make sure the rent you pay is fair market value. Generally, you want the rent amount as high as possible, but, of course, it has to be an amount you can justify if the IRS ever asks. What would you pay for space in a similarly equipped building somewhere else?

Generate Passive Income From the Assets of Your Business

What assets does your business have? Your first thought might be to go look at your balance sheet or give your bookkeeper a call. That's how you will find out the hard assets that your business has. That would include equipment, furniture, machinery, and other items that your business has bought or you have contributed.

What hard assets do you have with excess capacity?

Take a minute and jot down the items in your business that spend part of the day sitting idle.

Success stories of converting hard assets into more income:

Success Story #1: One of our friends bought a commercial building with a small auditorium/meeting spot. Her own business occupied the entire space, except for the auditorium. She used it once or twice a year. She realized that she had a valuable asset just sitting around idle, so she advertised it as a place for meetings and mini-seminars.

The extra rental income covered the entire mortgage. Her other business just got a place for free! Plus, she made some great connections with the people who rented the space and came to the seminars.

Success Story #2: A serial entrepreneur, with years of experience in owning businesses, bought a struggling manufacturing company. He first looked at how busy, or rather, not busy each division was. One of the divisions was basically just sitting there with nothing to do. There was a lot of capital in the company and he knew there were two choices: (1) close it down or (2) get it busy. So, he looked at the sales department. The 'top' sales guy said he had not made an outbound phone call in 35 years. The VP of sales said that their reputation was everything. They didn't need to get sales, they just wrote down the orders.

He fired everybody and hired a whole new sales force. He took one of the sales people and put her full-time on the division with one mandate: pay for herself within 3 months. In 3 months, she'd booked over $1 mill in business for the once idle division. And this was in the middle of the worst recession our country has seen since the Great Depression.

Success Story #3: Actually, this idea didn't have an immediate cash pay-off, but it indirectly created a whole new client base! One of our clients, a financial planner, was looking for ways to attract new business. He had a great office space with a conference room. He realized that a lot of his connections worked virtually or in smaller offices. He offered his conference room for meetings for his clients and business associates.

His clients were happy and he got new referrals and prospects delivered right to his office!

Take a look at all of your hard assets. Here are some questions to consider yourself, or within your networking group.

- What assets are you currently underutilizing?
- What facilities do you control that could be used cooperatively?
- What do you own, rent or otherwise control that could be used to help others?
- How can you get a better return on the assets you currently have?

In addition to the hard assets, your business also has passive assets. These are the ones that don't generally show up on your balance sheet. They're called soft assets and include things like your expertise, unique capabilities of your business, your database, your prospect list, your systems and even your vendors and competition.

Step One: Take five minutes and pull out a pen and a blank page of paper to list all the soft assets of your business. As you're doing that, think back to one of the early-stage exercises you did back in Section One, where you asked your friends and colleagues to tell you the five things you're really good at. List those traits and abilities as part of your soft assets.

Step Two: Consider why your customers come to you. What need are you fulfilling? What pain do you take away? What hope do you give them?

Increase Your Return

If you have a networking group to work with, consider this topic to increase the value of assets you and your group already have.

If you don't have a networking group, grab your journal and start making notes!

Step Three: You already are fulfilling some client's needs and/or alleviating their pain on some front.

Consider other ways you can fulfill that need. Is there an information product that you can create and fulfill with your own automated web sites?

What about the people you can't help? Can you refer them to someone else for a referral fee?

What other things do your current clients need?

List out 10 things you could do with your underutilized assets, using your unique abilities to help your clients or prospects. Don't worry about how you can fulfill or whether it even makes sense. You're brainstorming, so don't self-edit. There are no wrong answers during this point.

Step Four: What ideas can you implement now? This is a great exercise to repeat every quarter or so.

Don't look for one way to make $10,000 per month in passive income. Look for 10 ways to make $1,000 a month instead. You'll find that it's always easier to create multiple streams of income. Plus you have added security. If one goes down, you're only out $1,000. You can't say that if all your eggs are in one basket instead.

Is Real Estate Really the Only Answer for Passive Income?

For years, I've been known as the real estate accountant. I've helped thousands of clients through complicated real estate transactions and have developed systems to help any real estate investor take advantage of the best tax breaks available.

And, during all those years, I've seen a growing number of business owners who actually step over piles of money to reach for a dime. They ignore huge passive income possibilities from leveraging their intellectual property and soft assets of their business to instead break out in a whole new area: real estate.

Can you make money in real estate? Of course. A lot of people have. But it's one more thing that you'll have to learn and manage. There will be a learning curve and it's going to take a lot of time for possibly just a small reward.

Passive Income for 2010 & Beyond

The years 2008–2009 saw a lot of changes in how businesses and investments work. Prior to that, real estate was in a crazy spiral. Good, semi-good, mediocre, and even some downright bad real estate investments made money. But few of them actually created long-term cash flow. Most were just appreciation, fix-n-flip, sell to the greater fool type of deals. As long as appreciation continued, it could cover a multitude of problems.

In the aftermath of the real estate bust, there are probably going to be some appreciation deals still. But they aren't as prevalent as they were a few years ago, when pretty much anything real estate related went up in value.

Today, people are looking for the cash flow. You might have been told that real estate is the best way (or maybe only way) to get that. In the right circumstances, it can work. If real estate investing is your path to passive income, you may discover that it will take hours and hours of time and thousands of dollars searching out a deal that will get you $200 per month in cash flow.

Passive Income Success Stories

Success Story #1: Affiliate Marketing. An affiliate marketer puts up web sites, buys, and/or gets traffic through strong SEO (search engine optimization), and then refers visitors to other sites to buy. An affiliate marketer gets paid when someone else buys. There are a few other formulas, but this is the most common method.

Bob & Mary had ridden the wave of real estate appreciation in California. They were disappointed, but not devastated, when it turned. They spent a year or so figuring out where they were going to concentrate their next passive income push. They decided to try out affiliate marketing. Mary found an affordable coaching program with an experienced marketer and made him (and her family) a promise to do exactly what he said for four months.

The result: Mary was consistently making $50 - $100 per web site per month. But she didn't have just one web site, she had over 50. Her plan is to add another 10 per month for as long as the business model works. Her total cost was less than $1000.

Success Story #2: All the People You Know. Jon is a very smart businessman. He can take basically any type of business, if the premise is good, and turn it into a winning proposition within two years. That's because he's good as a businessman. But he was tired of working. He wanted truly passive income.

So Jon spent a few years looking for a network marketing company that had a good business premise behind it. When he found one that made sense, he developed a strategy to work the business for 18 months, then stopped working to let the lines catch up for 2 years. Then he'd go back and work it for 18 months. He's now in his second cycle of growth and on track for hitting $1 million in passive per year in the next few years.

He's used his talent for building and growing businesses, coupled with a solid business premise with his business database.

Success Story #3: Work Once; Multiple Streams of Passive Income. This is one of Diane's favorite approaches toward turning business income into multiple streams of passive income. Everything she does has multiple income potential.

For example, Diane gives monthly FREE teleseminars that are always filled up within hours of the announcement. That's because the teleseminars have timely information that her clients want and her sales pitch is more of an offer on how to participate. So, that's income potential #1: Learning more about Diane's services because you want to become a client of her full service tax firm. Income potential #2: The teleseminar is taped and for a short period, the download is free. After that, the teleseminar is for sale on her site. Income potential #3: the teleseminars are also available through other sites for free, once you click through on one of the sponsors. It doesn't cost the subscriber anything, but there is money paid through to Diane for each click through. Income potential #4: The teleseminars are edited and expanded with a written manual to be part of a packaged home study course.

What passive income streams are possible for your business?

Passive income shows up whether you work or not. It means freedom to work when, where, and how much you want. It means freedom from worry about covering your day-to-day expenses. And it means freedom to try new ideas and pursue your passions. It means having the time to be involved and make a difference.

It's never been easier and quicker to start building passive income. Start today!

The Chinese have a saying:
When is the best time to plant a tree? A: Ten years ago.
When is the second best time to plant a tree? A: Today

Action Steps

Action Step 1: Work through the exercises in this chapter alone or, better yet, with your networking group.

Action Step 2: What action steps do you want to take in the next 90 days to increase your passive income?

Resources

www.MultipleSourcesofPassiveIncome.com. This is a targeted resource site, with links to various passive income opportunities, as well as education resources and more.

www.CashByChoice.com. Owned and operated by a successful and wealthy super-affiliate, this web site also offers coaching and information for people just starting out, growing their affiliate marketing business, or looking to fine-tune their existing business.

Section Seven: The Next Stage

Chapter 29:
When is Your Business Ready for the Next Big Step?

In the beginning of your business, it probably felt a little frantic. You might have had some time to plan for the future before you launched, but once it's going, you're focused on just getting and keeping the business running.

Or, let's even take the other point of view, let's say it's not working, and you're ready to just give up.

Those may seem like very different problems, but they really aren't. In both cases, the question is, "What now?"

If something is working, you want more of it. If something isn't working, you want to quit. Both require change.

This chapter is about questions you can ask yourself about whether you're ready to take the next big step with your business: whatever that might be.

And to be clear, a big step could be starting something new, expanding something old, or changing direction entirely.

Smart Business Goals

(1) Build value.
(2) Create current cash flow.
(3) Build equity for the future.

Smart Business Review

Let's identify each of those key components and see how your business is doing:

(1) What does your business do? This is less than an elevator pitch; it's how you introduce yourself and your business at a cocktail party.

(2) Why do your clients buy from you?

(3) What problem are they solving?

(4) What is their basic need that your business speaks to?

(5) What is the dream that they want your help with?

Now, take a look at your current product and service line:

(1) Which products and services are your best sellers?

(2) Which products and services have the highest profit, after cost of goods are subtracted?

(3) Which products and services are most easily scalable? (In other words, you could most easily ramp up to meet more demand in these areas.)

(4) What are the three things that your clients ask for most that you don't have?

With those ideas in place, and after reviewing your homework from Section 6, where should your business expand?

Are there product lines or services that don't work anymore? If so, why not? Did they ever work?

This is the point where it would be great to have a group or coach, or preferably both, to bounce some ideas off of. If you don't have that group or coach and don't want to find them, then take out a few pieces of paper and write down all your thoughts around these questions:

- What does my business really stand for?
- How do we provide value in our market?
- How can we provide more value, and thus receive more profit, in our market?

As you identify the direction your company needs to move in, think about whether that means changing, expanding or shrinking your current business.

That's just one piece of the "The Next Big Step" calculation for Smart Business.

Bigger Business Means More Controls

How do you want to work with your company through this next phase? If it means less involvement for you, you'll want tight tracking and controls to protect your business as it grows. This might be the time to bring in an expert to review your controls currently in place. Where are the holes? What can you do to fix them?

And if your business changes mean more income, then that likely means it's time to take your tax planning up a notch. In fact, if you've recently complained about the amount of taxes you're paying due to business income, it is certainly time to have a review by a Tax Strategist.

You'll find that there is a point, as your business becomes more successful, where you'll have to let go of more tasks than just those you don't want to do anymore. For example, Diane saves her clients an average of more than $30,000 per year in taxes after just one phone call. Now, think about that. What if you had these average results and waited three years before you made a call? Do you really want to waste $90,000?

These are the new challenges you face as your move from being self-employed and working in the business to being a business owner and working on the business.

That's what the next big step is all about. Are you ready?

Action Steps
Action Step 1: Think about or, better yet, journal about what you want your business to be. You may find your plans change and grow a little as time goes on. That's okay. In fact, it's expected as you and your business adjust to market and life changes.

Resources
Branson, Richard. 1999. *Losing My Virginity: How I've Survived, Had Fun, and Made a Fortune Doing Business My Way.* Three Rivers Press.

Christensen, Clayton M. 2003. *The Innovator's Dilemma: The Revolutionary Book that will Change the Way You Do Business.* Harper Paperbacks.

Chapter 30:
Planning Your Exit Strategy

You build, you nurture, you sweat, you survive, you grow, you thrive, and then what? Unless you're planning to die in the saddle, there's an exit strategy somewhere out there on the horizon. And it's better to think about it at the beginning than after 10 years in business.

Most business owners jump into business without thinking about their exit strategy. At that exact moment, you're probably burdened with more than your share of plans to get and stay in business than you are with your getting out plans. That is, short of just closing the doors and going home. (That can be a smart and viable exit strategy if you do it right).

Have you thought about your personal exit strategy for your business? If not, here are the five most common exit strategies:

Exit Strategy #1: Take the money and run: If your company is a cash cow that has a limited shelf life, requires a very specific market condition, or is built on the brand of you, you might not have a choice. Your entire exit strategy is to maximize the income you can make and then invest it wisely.

This exit strategy works if you're the only owner. It gets tricky if you have a partner, and it is pretty much impossible if you have minority shareholders.

A minority shareholder is someone who doesn't own enough of the business to have a say in how it's run. But minority shareholders do have legal rights. That means you can't bleed the company dry with salary, big bonuses, corporate jets, and retreats. All of your shareholders have the right to dividends and if the money is just going to fund your lifestyle, you're just asking for a lawsuit.

If it's just you, though, there is something to be said for "Keep it small, and keep it all." Keep your overhead at a minimum, don't reinvest for longer term and just crank the cash.

In a memorable quote, the owner of a very profitable manufacturing company was grilled on why he didn't hire some really smart business school guys to grow his company huge. He could then sell it for a ton of money.

His answer is classic. "Excuse me?" he responded. "What part of a 30-hour work week and a $5 million personal income don't you understand?"

If that's your exit strategy, here are a few points to be aware of:

- Keep enough money liquid to help out the business if there is an economic meltdown. Money in your pocket is no longer money in the business. Once you've finally gotten it out, there's something infinitely harder about putting money back in the business.
- If you have investors or private lenders, they won't be happy to see you taking the money before they get paid.
- Use a flow-through entity that allows you to take money out in the most tax advantaged method possible.
- Don't try to use upstreaming methods to reduce tax. If you're pulling all the profit anyway, it won't work.
- Invest the money in something that will provide you cash flow down the road.

Without any prior exit strategy planning, "Take the money and run" is your strategy. You are making the assumption that there is no value in the company, and so you might as well take all the money out now. If you're barely covering the bills now, that can be a very sobering thought. Small cash flow is okay only if you're building an asset to sell down the road.

Exit Strategy #2: Everything Must Go! You may decide to simply shut down and sell the hard assets for what you can get on the open market. The advantage of this as a strategy is that it's simple and it's natural. Everything eventually comes to an end, so why not your business? The disadvantage is, just like taking the money and running, there is a feeling of a real waste of time. Why make the effort to start and build a business if you don't try to sell the hard and soft assets as a complete package? If your business is valid, then it has value to someone.

Both this strategy and the "take the money and run" strategy effectively destroy the value of your soft assets. Gone are your client lists, your business relationships, and business reputation. Chances are, there was more value there than you thought, if only you'd taken the time a few years before to make sure your business value was solid.

Exit Strategy #3: Sell to a Friendly Buyer: A friendly buyer is someone who knows you and knows your business. It could be your best customer or maybe one of your vendors. It could also be employees, children, or family members.

Be careful if your plan is to sell someday to your children or family members. Often, they see the cash flow, but not the business behind it. There's a reason that the average inheritance is gone 18 months after it's received. The person outside the company often has a totally different perspective from the one who is building the fortune or the business. They see the rewards, not the hard work.

And remember that "family business" means family. A family that isn't super functional already isn't going to get better when you throw in a business. Don't give Uncle Joe a break simply because he needs the money. Money never solves money problems.

The friendly buyer sale is often a little sloppier when it comes to agreements and terms. That can be a problem down the road as well. The benefit, though, is that the friendly buyer is often emotionally attached and understands at a deeper level what your business stands for.

Some of the benefits of finding a friendly buyer:

- You know each other, for good or for bad. You don't need to do as much due diligence.
- Your buyer understands your business and will likely preserve what's most important to you.
- If your friendly buyer starts buying in slowly, they'll build up a vested interest to making it all work.

There are some disadvantages as well:

- You're going to be attached to the buyer. That could mean that you leave some money on the table.
- It can be disruptive to your relationship, especially if things go south after you've stepped away.

Exit Strategy #4: Sell to an Arm's Length Buyer: In some ways, selling to someone outside your immediate circle is easiest. You're simply going to negotiate the best price that you can. Whether or not the business succeeds after you leave isn't your concern.

If you choose the right buyer, the price tag might be much higher than if it were based on income alone. Why? A complementary buyer may want to buy your business as a way to expand into a new market, or to offer your products as something new to their existing customers. Or, perhaps your competitor is aiming to dominate the market and buying you is the best way to get rid of you.

If you do wind up merging into another company, watch out for the dark side, especially if you've got staff and management carrying on without you. If there's a bad fit between the two companies, the combined companies can self-destruct. Your management team may wind up contractually obligated to work for the combined company and hate the new management style. It can be horribly demoralizing to watch a company implode.

If you're thinking of positioning your business to be acquired, make it attractive to acquisition candidates, but don't go so far as to cut off your other options. One software company knew exactly whom they wanted to sell to, so they developed their product in a way that meshed perfectly with the prospective suitor's products. Too bad the suitor had no interest in the acquisition. The software company was left with a product so specialized that no one else wanted to buy them either.

Pros:
- If you have strategic value, a buyer may pay far more than you're worth to anyone else.
- If you get multiple buyers involved in a bidding war, you can ratchet your price to the stratosphere.

Cons:
- If you organize your business to be attractive to a specific target, that may prevent you from becoming attractive to other buyers.
- Acquisitions are messy and often difficult when cultures and systems clash in the merged company.
- Acquisitions can come with non-compete agreements and other strings. You'll be rich, but your life may be unpleasant for a time.

Strategy #5: The IPO: Going public is another option. It's a lot like Strategy #4, except that you're typically looking for one of two things: either an angel investor or venture capital company to come in and essentially buy you out after the securities registration is done, or for an existing public company to acquire your business.

Going public takes a lot of time, and a lot of money. It begins with a registration statement at the federal level, and after that, a secondary registration process with a trading outlet, like NASDAQ, the New York Stock Exchange, or the OTB Bulletin Board. You've got to be able to simultaneously keep the business going strong while dumping cash into the registration process. And, once you're through the first phase, you've then got to find brokers and other financiers who are willing to push your company's stocks.

It's also critical to remember that when you engage with venture capital companies, your days with the company are numbered. A new management team typically comes in as part of the registration process. That could spell trouble for your senior management. Remember, a venture capital company is simply buying your idea and the business, not you. If you're closely tied to your company, letting go in this fashion can be an emotional wrench.

The Four D's of an Exit Strategy You Didn't Want

As hard as it may be to consider, there are four D's that might make your exit strategy come a lot sooner than you wanted. Have a contingency plan for these, especially as the income grows in your business.

Death: You most likely don't want to be considering your demise. But if you are the business and your family needs that income, you've got to plan what happens to the business if you do die. Generally, a life insurance policy is a good place to start. However, it's not the only action item. Who takes over after you're gone?

Disability: In some ways, a disability can be even harder on a business. You haven't died, so there isn't a lump sum of cash to help things out. You've got spiraling medical costs, and you can't work.

What is the contingency for your business? Do you liquidate? Take the money and run? Or is there a way for it to continue with you only functioning marginally?

Divorce: If you're married, what happens to the business in case of a divorce? You need to be able to agree on a value for the company if it's going to be part of the pot that gets divided. It's an even bigger issue if both spouses worked in the business.

High Profile Practice, Messy Divorce

One of Diane's clients was a successful medical doctor with a thriving practice. He and his wife were in the middle of a messy divorce. He'd made a lot of money, and they had spent a lot. The only real asset in the whole thing was his medical practice.

But when it came down to it, the doctor never really thought of it as an asset, and especially not a community asset. After all, he was the one with the medical degree!

Their attorneys continued to battle it, until they finally agreed on an appraiser to make the business valuation. He'd never set up a valuation process, so they had to do it the hard way. The appraisal was expensive, and the value of the practice, at over $1 million, surprised him. It wasn't a happy surprise, either. He now owed his ex-wife over $500,000 for her share of the medical practice.

It didn't make sense to him because the asset was only valuable to a doctor. There was no value to her. But it didn't matter. That was the value.

In the end, the doctor just closed down his practice and went somewhere else to start over. He didn't have a half million dollars to pay his ex-wife in cash, and he wasn't interested in being indebted to her for years, working insane hours to meet his debt obligations.

Divorce can devastate a business.

Departure (of a partner): What if you need a business divorce? You have a partner who doesn't want to be your partner anymore and there is no way to work out the differences. Now what?

This is where that Buy-Sell Agreement we told you about in Chapter 9 is going to finally be needed. Make sure your agreement addresses not only the business valuation process, but also outlines how to deal with what's happening in the business right now: work in progress, intellectual property, and accounts receivable and payable. Plus, of course, how will the buyer pay for the purchase: over time in payments or all cash? Is it an asset sale or stock sale?

Tax Planning for Exit Strategies

There's also going to be a tax bill to leave it all behind. The answer to "how much?" is, of course, "it depends." Here are some scenarios and how the tax might be calculated:

Close the Doors. If your business operated as a corporation you'll need to file a liquidation plan and a Form 966 with the IRS. You'll also need to dissolve the company in each state or states where it was registered, by filing a notice with the secretary of state's office that the company is being terminated.

If you have an S or C Corporation, you may also receive something called a liquidating dividend. For example, let's assume you close the doors and take the assets, such as they are. On the books, it shows that you have a net book value of $50,000 of assets and a net book value of $60,000 of liabilities. That means there is $10,000 of negative equity that you assume when you shut down. (In other words, there is $10,000 due to someone).

But a corporation distributes assets out at fair market value. In this case, the $50,000 book value of business assets is really worth $100,000. After deducting the $60,000 in liabilities you've got $40,000 left over. That $40,000 will be taxable.

You have an advantage with an S Corporation here, due to the single taxation structure. You can effectively trade your stock for the assets, which lets you create an offsetting gain and loss (i.e., you get the value of the assets but lose the value of the stock, which equals the value of the assets).

Planning with the C Corporation, though, is trickier because of its dual tax structure. The liquidating dividend from the C Corporation is taxable, just like the liquidating dividend from the S Corporation. But you won't be able to offset a C Corporation loss with the personal income from the dividend. Remember, C Corporation losses can't flow through to you personally. There are strategies to handle just about any tax situation and this is no exception, but you need to plan way in advance to make sure you don't end up with unusable losses and a high tax situation.

You let key employees (or anybody else for that matter) buy into the company with sweat equity. This is a common scenario when business owners want to reward employees for work well done. It's also a great strategy to get someone working in the business first, before buying it. A portion of their pay is contributed towards the purchase price over a period of time.

You will want a very clear written agreement in this scenario. What if you have a serious falling out? What happens if the employee leaves? Is there a way to buy the company back? What if the employee has a financial disaster and can no longer contribute towards the equity? How do you get your ownership back without refunding the money?

There's also a potential tax issue for the person buying in with sweat equity. By trading work for ownership, the employee creates a taxable event for himself. For example, if they end up getting 10% of a company worth $1 million, then that person has received $100,000 worth of stock for their work. That means they have received, and must pay tax on, $100,000 worth of income.

This is where your written business valuation formula is so critical. Your formula should value the company at a fair price, but not so high that employee sweat equity won't work.

Plus, your employees might be focused on what they perceive are the benefits of ownership, yet they are completely unaware of the responsibilities. For example, once someone owns 2% or more of the stock in an S Corporation, they no longer receive medical insurance as a non-taxable benefit. This could be a rude shock to an employee who has never had to pay tax on their medical premiums before.

You sell the assets of the company. This is how most sales happen. For a buyer, the best tax advantages come when they purchase just the assets, and not the company itself. The purchase price assigned to the furniture, fixtures, and equipment will all be depreciable assets. The purchase price assigned to the books that the store sells will be inventory and expensed as a cost of goods as the product sells.

As the seller, you treat the purchase price as ordinary income and/or recaptured depreciation. The recaptured depreciation is taxed at a lower tax rate than the ordinary income is taxed.

Let's say you have a bookstore. You rent a space, but all the furniture, fixtures, equipment, and books are yours. You agree to sell the bookstore for $100,000, and apportion $20,000 to the furniture and fixtures, $70,000 to the books, and $10,000 for inventory. It's a cash sale.

As the seller, you'll need to determine your original basis in the furniture and fixtures, how much you've depreciated so far, and then add that amount back in. If it's less than the $20,000 apportioned, you treat the extra as gain. The $70,000 for book inventory is treated as ordinary income, and the goodwill is considered a capital asset.

So in one transaction, you will have three different tax rates (recaptured depreciation, ordinary income, and capital gains) if the asset sale is done through a flow through entity. If this is an asset sale through a C Corporation, the tax cost will be higher because there is no capital gains tax break.

You sell the stock of the company. As a seller, it's far more advantageous to sell the stock instead of the assets. You get a cleaner sale and pay less tax. The stock sale will simply be the sales price of the stock, less any cost of sale, less your basis in the stock. The net gain is all subject to a capital gains tax rate, which is lower than an ordinary income tax rate.

If you have a C Corporation that qualifies as a small business corporation (it has assets of less than $50 million and you've held the stock for at least five years), then you can exclude 50-75% of the gain right off the top. What's left is then subject to the lower capital gains tax rate.

The Great American Dream Revisited

Business ownership has been part of the American Dream almost since this country was founded. Starting a business, becoming successful, and growing that business into something that provides financial stability and security for you and your family, was all part of the plan. But once you've accomplished those goals, then what? Status quo? Or reach for the next project?

Your small business needs an exit strategy. If your plan is to someday sell, figure out that exit strategy years in advance. Then, focus on building your business into something that someone else would want to buy.

Action Steps

Action Step 1: What is your exit strategy? Are you happy with it?

Action Step 2: What can you do now to ensure the best possible results when you exit?

Resources

Leonetti, John M. 2008. *Exiting Your Business, Protecting Your Wealth: A Strategic Guide for Owners and Their Advisors.* Wiley.

Watkins, Graham. 2006. *Exit Strategy: A Practical Guide to Selling Your Business.* Book Surge Publishing.

Chapter 31:
Increasing Your Business Value

If growing your business into an attractive, purchasable asset is your goal, then make sure you take time to consider your business valuation.

There are some tried and true methods for determining business value that professional business valuators use. We'll talk about those in a little bit. First, though, let's talk about the importance of selecting a method for valuation.

In law, the fair market value of something is defined as what is agreed upon between a willing and informed buyer and a willing and informed seller under usual and ordinary circumstances. Okay, that makes sense. But, what if there isn't a buyer standing there? Do you still need to come up with a value?

Even if you don't plan on selling anytime soon, every business should select a method to value the company. If you don't put the method down in writing, someone else is going to come up with the method for you. That someone else could be the IRS or the court system. Either way, their agenda isn't yours, and you don't want their valuation method.

Here are just a few of the times when you'll need to have business valuation:

- Estate valuation (both for planning and in case of death)
- Divorce
- Buy-Sell agreement
- Lawsuit

None of those reasons are too pleasant, but unfortunately, they are often a reality to doing business in the US.

Your corporate papers should include the way you value your company, not just the current value. If you have a corporation, it would be in your bylaws and organizational resolutions. If you have an LLC, it should be set out in your operating agreement. And, most importantly, it should be stated in your buy-sell agreements with partners. As your business grows and changes, the value will change. The way you calculate the value will not.

Common Business Valuation Techniques

Some common methods for business valuation are:

- **Book Value.** The value of your business is calculated based on your books. Total assets less total liabilities equals equity, or the book value of your business. The problem with this method is that it's not able to accurately reflect the value of your business. It doesn't allow for appreciation and goodwill, plus other intangible assets.

- **Adjusted Book Value.** Two calculations are prepared here, one for the tangible book value of your business and one for its economic book value (also known as book value at market). The tangible book value starts with the hard assets and then values the intangible assets (e.g., goodwill, patents, capitalized start-up expenses, and deferred financing costs). The economic book value calculation analyzes the value of the assets of your business based on current market rates, and it allows for valuation of goodwill, real estate, inventories, and other assets at their market value.

- **Discounted Earnings.** Determines the value of your business based upon the present value of projected future earnings, discounted by the required rate of return (capitalization rate). Usually, the question is how well earnings are projected.

- **Discounted Cash Flow Valuation.** In discounted cash flow, the present value of liabilities is subtracted from the combined present value of cash flow and tangible assets, which determines the value of the business.

- **Price Earnings Multiple.** The price of your company's share of common stock in the public market, divided by its earnings per share. Multiply this multiple by the net income, and you will have a value for the business. If your business has no income, there is no business valuation. And, if your company isn't publicly traded, the valuation becomes purely subjective. This may not be the best choice of business valuation methods, but it can provide you with a benchmark business valuation.

- **Sales Multiple**. The sales multiple and profit multiple are the two most widely used business valuation methods used in valuing a business. You'll need your annual sales and an industry multiplier, which is usually a range of .25 to 1 or higher. You can find the industry multiplier in various financial publications, as well as analyzing sales of comparable businesses. This method is easy to understand and use. The sales multiple is often used as the business valuation benchmark.

- **Profit Multiple.** You need your business's pre-tax profit numbers and a market multiplier, which may be 1, 2, 3, or 4 and usually a ceiling of 5. The market multiplier can be found in various financial publications, as well as analyzing the sale of comparable businesses.

- **Liquidation Value**. This valuation is similar to an adjusted book value analysis. It uses the value of your business's assets at liquidation, which is often less than market and sometimes even book value. Liabilities are deducted from this liquidated asset value to determine the liquidation value of the small business. This method can be used to give you a bare bottom benchmark.

Your company should have a written business valuation formula. If you don't choose the formula, the court or IRS will. You probably aren't going to like their answer.

Increasing Your Business Value

Once you have a formula established, you have a definition of what it takes to increase the value, at least on paper. For example, if you determine your valuation formula is based on a discounted cash flow valuation, then an increase in cash flow will increase the valuation. On the other hand, if the valuation is simply based on the number of assets, then buying more assets will make your company more valuable.

The business valuation formula does not necessarily equal fair market value for your business.

Valuation does not necessarily mean fair market value. The only way you can determine fair market value is with a buyer. So, if your exit strategy is something other than just take the money and run, it makes good sense to figure out what the fair market value for your company actually would be.

Here's a run down of some of the things to consider:

(1) Who would buy your company?

(2) Why would they buy your company? (brand, market position, location, eliminate you as a competitor, gain talent, get assets, access to customer list, etc.)

(3) How many suitors would you have if your business was up for sale?

(4) Is this a growing industry? Is the niche strong?

(5) Would a buyer most be interested in a predictable income stream and ROI?

The sooner you identify who would buy your company and focus on building the company they want, the more money you'll make when you sell.

Six Critical Factors Business Buyers Look For

(1) **Do you have a clear vision and mission for your company that you can communicate?** A confused customer never buys. If a prospective buyer doesn't understand your business, or sees incongruities between what you say and what you do, they are likely to not see a valuable company. A well-defined vision and mission clarifies what you do as long as your systems and procedures support those statements.

(2) **Have an up-to-date strategic business plan, annual budgeting process, accurate financial statements, and specifics statistics that you use to measure the company.** Smart business owners

have a clear-cut business path with certain measurements. They know what's working and what isn't.

(3) **Is your business <u>growing</u> at or above the average rate for a business of your type and size?** If your business isn't keeping up, a buyer is going to want to pay pennies on the dollar for the company. They see the handwriting on the wall. Do you? On the other hand, a company that is growing faster than other similar businesses is going to command a higher price. Typically, a buyer is looking to double or triple their investment dollars within 5 years.

(4) **Is your business operating at or above the <u>gross margin</u> for a business of your type and size?** If your buyer is looking at buying a fixer-upper, they will want to pay less than the market rate. If you have a good profit margin, then you'll attract a different kind of buyer. This buyer is going to be looking at his ROI, and the higher the ROI, the higher the price tag for the business.

(5) **Do you have written strategies for maximizing cash flow?** When cash is the focus, there is more flowing to the owner's pockets. No matter why your buyer wants your company, cash flow increases the value.

(6) **Is your business too weighted with just one customer?** Ideally, no more than 15% of your total sales should come from just one customer. And your range should be diversified, if possible, across different size customers and in different industries. Of course, if you've got a highly specialized niche that might not be possible.

Create a Higher Value for the Future

What can you do to make your business more attractive to a buyer? Here are some thoughts to get you started:

(1) **Procedures.** A prospective buyer is buying your system. They don't want to reinvent the wheel. They want a turn-key solution. Do you have easily accessible procedures manuals that have been updated regularly?

(2) **Systems.** Just like with the procedures, the overall systems need to be clearly outlined. Does everyone know what to do, how to do it and who does it? A buyer will want to know how to run the company if they need to, without your key employees. They want to know what the business does, how customer service is handled, what to do with complaints, how orders are processed, and in general, who is responsible for what.

(3) **Job Descriptions.** Along with procedures and systems, job descriptions help create a more harmonic workplace. When it comes to the back-end of business, the less drama the better. Your buyer will want to know what the key positions are, the skill sets required and what the going salary rate is for those positions. You want to have written job descriptions and pay scales ready to show potential buyers. The fewer surprises, the better.

(4) **Marketing Efforts.** Now is the time to increase your marketing efforts to show that your business is a vibrant, going concern. Plus, if you have an ongoing plan for the company, your buyer will have some momentum to carry him. You want your buyer to succeed, simply because the last thing you want is a protracted litigation months after the fact because he's trying to undo the deal. Now is the time to crank up the volume, update your website, and make your company image shine. More effort = more value = more money in your pocket.

(5) **Owner Dependence.** If you are the company, then there really isn't a lot of value in the business without you. This may be the hardest thing for the average self-employed bootstrapper to understand. The company is really more valuable if you aren't vital. If you find yourself filling all of the roles and also have employees, it's time to step back and delegate your workload. Empower your staff, hand over the work to competent people, hire a bookkeeper, or create a management position. If you plan to hand over your business to someone new, it is better to prepare yourself by letting go of one thing at a time.

Business buyers buy systems and cash flow first, the rest is secondary.

(6) Increase your business value by turning it into a turn-key operation that makes money, creates cash flow, and has systems so that it's never dependent on just one person.

Final Thought on Business Valuation

How much is your company worth? It depends on who's asking! If the IRS or the court wants to know, you need a business valuation formula to point to. If it's a buyer who wants to know, then the answer is often much less clear.

One thing is clear, though, there are things you can do to increase your value right now. And the sooner you focus on those action steps, the more your company will ultimately be worth.

Action Steps

Action Step 1: Do you have a written procedure for determining business value? If so, does the method still accurately represent the valuation process for your type of business?

Action Step 2: There are often two values for a company: What the internal calculation is, and what the value really is, in the hands of a willing buyer. What would someone really pay for your company?

Action Step 3: What can you do to improve value?

Resources

Horn, Thomas W. 2008. *Unlocking the Value Of Your Business: How to increase it, measure it, and negotiate an actual sale price - Valuation in easy, step-by-step terms.* Charter Oak Press, 3rd Ed.

Chapter 32:
Building a Legacy

More businesses are starting now then in any other time in history. Why? It's because people are realizing the need to take control of their own financial future. And, with your own business, you get to choose what it is, what you do, who your customers are, and what you stand for in the world.

It's also an opportunity for you to create positive change in the world. Here are three quick strategies for doing that:

(1) Set up your business so that you leave people better than you found them. Your business itself is a force for good in other people's lives.

(2) Earmark a portion of your profit to support causes that speak to your heart.

(3) Rally your clients, vendors, employees, independent contractors, or anyone associated with your business around your causes. Ask them to give part of their time and most importantly, their talents, to causes you support.

When times are hard, it's tougher to find the time, money, and heart space to do anything other than take care of yourself and your family.

And it's never been more important. When you pledge money, and honor that pledge, you are making a promise to the future. It's demonstrating a belief in yourself and your business beyond today.

It's truly a wealth belief that transcends time. You will be empowered when you do!

Here are the strategies, one by one.

Strategy #1: Set up your business so that you leave people better than you found them. Your business itself stands for something. And the values determine the corporate culture of how you work together and interface with your vendors and clients.

What is the real core of your business? What need are you fulfilling? If you are fulfilling the need in a way that empowers your client, then you are truly leaving them better off then they were before.

The more people you can serve, the richer you will become.

We've heard small business owners sometimes grumble that they would never send one of their employees to one of our seminars. That's because they would learn how their own business can save them taxes plus give them freedom they'd never get in a job.

"What if they all quit?" worried one seminar participant, who was a fledgling business owner.

And what if they all stayed? Or, rather, the ones who were fulfilled in what they were doing, who really signed on for the bigger mission and understood what you were doing at a deeper level stayed. And they stayed because they wanted to, not because they just needed a paycheck.

And even better, what if you educated and trained your employees so that someday they could have a business, maybe even buy into part of yours or start an ancillary branch that pays you a passive income stream.

Teach your employees to think big and expand the pie, rather than worry how big their particular piece of the pie is.

Strategy #2: Earmark a portion of your profit to support causes that speak to your heart. There will come a time when your business gets through the learning curves, and as long as you're watching your expenses and systems, you'll start creating a big cash flow.

This is the critical point: Now what do you do with the money? Too often, people just go nuts with money, buying cars, and a fast life. Hey, we like cars, too! But when having new shiny toys is the only focus for your business, it seldom fulfills in the long run.

If you set up to give a portion of the proceeds to a cause you care about, you've build a heart right into your business. And that will help you make contacts to grow your business and open doors you never thought possible.

**If you chase money, you seldom find what you really want.
If you instead look to enrich others, you
will have wealth beyond belief.**

When do you start with the giving plan? How about right now? Build the giving from the start and it will help your business focus and create more opportunity right when you need it.

Diane's Story

My businesses have always been about empowering others to take control of their own wealth, to keep more of what they earn. That means creating and implementing powerful tax strategies that control when and how much you pay in taxes.

On a personal note, we're emotionally connected to charities related to children in Mexico. We adopted our son David from a Mexican orphanage and ever since that time, we've seen each child just like the son we love so dearly.

We're now living on the coast in Baja California. We're trying it out for a year, and we'll see what happens after that. We're in a more affluent part of Mexico, so there isn't the crushing poverty and hopelessness you see in cities like Juarez where David came from. But still, there isn't a great support system. School is free, but very expensive uniforms are mandatory, and the children have to pay for standardized tests. Plus, the kids have to be immunized and have birth certificates.

Those requirements keep hundreds, perhaps thousands, of kids out of school each year in this area.

Our family toured schools in our area this past year. We saw the free public class (sizes of 30-50 kids), the lower cost private class (sizes of 20-30) and the exclusive private. The exclusive private are phenomenal, by the way. They're the best I've seen anywhere.

Kids aren't starving in the orphanages here, and they have clothes. But not all of the children get to go to school. So, that's how we're helping. We toured a school along with two girls. One was going to start this year if she could get the money for uniforms, books, and get her immunizations caught up. The other should have started last year, but didn't have the money. They were evaluated, met the teachers, got a tour, and got to play on the playground. When it was time to go, the youngest started silently crying. She didn't want to leave. I think the monkey bars might have been more of a draw than the library, but I was still touched by how much she wanted something a lot of us take for granted.

The two girls started school, for the first time for both of them, on August 25, 2009.

What moves you? What difference do you want to create?

We often overestimate what we can get done in a year, and underestimate what we can do in 20 years. Take the first step, however small, today. You may be surprised where it leads you.

Strategy #3: Rally your clients, vendors, employees, independent contractors, or anyone associated with your business to give part of their time and most importantly, their talents, to causes you support. This third strategy actually combines the first two. You will empower the people you work with and benefit a charity at the same time. When you combine the heart of a cause with the money sense of a business, you have an unstoppable combination.

Gratitude for the Past, Promise For the Future

When times are tough, here's an exercise that Diane's family uses. Take a piece of paper and write down three things, people, or events that you are grateful for. These could be related to things that happened today or in something as far back as early childhood.

Next to each item, add a sentence as to why that is important to you.

Then, finally, write what the next step for you is. It could be contacting someone to say thank you, maybe giving to someone else, or just having a moment of gratitude. Whatever that next step is, do it, and then take the action step.

Feeling gratitude for the past will make you feel richer in the present.

Now make a pledge for the next year. How much of your time, talent, and money will you donate to something that you care about?

A pledge that you intend to keep is especially important in the beginning of your business, when you're wondering how you're going to pay the bills or keep the doors open. That's because the pledge is a promise to the future. It's a promise to the future of the people, animals, causes, and whatever it is that you care so much about. You have just gained leverage on yourself to make those hard decisions about business to make sure your business succeeds. That's because you can't let down the things you hold most dear.

A pledge to give is a promise to the future.

Final Thoughts

In business, it's easy to do just enough. As long as you win more times than you lose, you have a winner. For some, that may be enough. It's an honorable thing to have a business that employs people, invests in capital, and creates living wages for you and others.

If you picked up this book, though, you're yearning for more. Everyday you have a choice. You can make your business small, or you can make it big. You can work night and day, and control every aspect; or you can develop systems, find good people, and trust in others. You can avoid accountability with your financial statements and hope there is enough money in the checking account each week to cover your bills, or you could build a legacy. And, finally, you could over pay your taxes, year after year. Or you can realize that a big part of being a smart business owner is paying the least amount of tax legally possible and putting more money in your pocket year after year.

Everyday you have a choice. How big of a game do you want to play?

Now is the time to fulfill the promise of your business and take the next step up to the business you've always dreamed you could have.

Conclusion

Dear Friend,

    There are many pieces to a Smart Business. It means:

- Creating a corporate culture,
- Leading with vision,
- Focusing on the mission,
- Sticking to your values,
- Planning your business,
- Analyzing your wins and losses,
- Protecting your assets,
- Paying the least amount of tax legally possible,
- Hiring the right people,
- Preparing your exit strategy, and
- Many, many more.

    It can feel overwhelming, if you let it. Go through the chapters one by one. Do the exercises at the end. Check out the resources. Being a successful business owner often means being right just one more time then you're wrong.

    Above all else, remember, you're not in this alone. There are mentors, advisors and mastermind partners who would love to work with you. Being a business owner isn't always easy, but it is rewarding.

    The world needs more people just like you.

    Let us know how we can help!

    Please visit us at www.MySmarterBusiness.com.

Warmly,
Diane and Megan

P.S. Don't forget to check out the Bonus, directly following this page. These are tools our clients have used to go on to create better and more efficient businesses. They won't cost you a dime. It's our way of saying Thank You! for reading our book.

Bonus

Your FREE! $997 Bonus From Diane and Megan

Congratulations on finishing the book! It's not everybody who wants to step up and be a Smart Business owner. We're honored that you spent some time with us.

As our way of saying thank you, we've created a very special online program for you that will help you make more money and pay less tax both now and well into the future. Best of all, you do it by building a Smart Business that works, so you don't have to!

Our gift to you is the *Smart Business Fast-Track System*. It's absolutely **FREE** to you as a way of saying we appreciate your commitment to creating a stronger business and better life.

This detailed online business-building program is your fast track system to turn the ideas, strategies, and exercises that you've worked on throughout this book into real-life results.

This valuable gift is only available for a short time. So, please register online right away. We have reserved the right to withdraw this offer at any time or when our program gets full.

Register now by going to www.MySmarterBusiness.com.

You'll see a spot on the website to register your book. Use this access code to get the complete $997 *Smart Business Fast-Track System* for FREE!

SmartBiz888

When you've finished registering online, you'll get immediate access to the entire *Smart Business Fast-Track System*, which includes:

- **Private access to over FIVE hours of in-depth, money-making, how-to online workshops** that will make growing your business *easier* and *faster*!
- **Three FREE! e-books** on wealth, business, and tax strategy!
- **Free downloads** of all the worksheets shown in this book!
- And much, much more!

These tools, and others like them, are designed to help you take the guesswork out of building, growing and protecting your Smart Business.

Four More Special Bonuses When You Register Within 30 Days of Buying This Book

Bonus One: FREE! Guaranteed Seating at Diane's Sold-Out Teleseminar Courses!

Find out why over 1200 people tried to get one of the only 500 spots at a recent teleseminar by Diane. These teleseminars are filled within hours of Diane's first email. Most people can't get a spot. But not you!

When you register your book now, you'll get a front row, <u>guaranteed</u> seat for FREE! And, it's not just for the next teleseminar. You get that spot guaranteed, <u>for life</u>.

Bonus Two: Three Customized FREE! courses on topics that will make your Smart Business even better.

Choose from over 20 courses on topics that are important to you and your business such as:

- Selecting and Operating the Right Business Structure for You
- Building Your Business Value
- Understanding Financial Statements
- Analyzing Your Financial Scorecard
- Creating an Anti-Embezzlement Program
- Planning Your Exit Strategy
- Finding Benefits that Benefit You
- Improving Your PROI
- Creating Ultimate Systems
- Developing Multiple Streams of Passive Income From Your Business
- Building Business Credit
- Finding Your Hidden Business Deductions

You can select up to three courses with lessons that will be delivered weekly to your email box FREE!

Bonus Three: Your Own One-of-a-Kind Smart Business Mastermind Guide

Mastermind groups are all the rage these days. If you don't have a group of like-minded peers, we'll help you find people to join your group. Then, once you've found your group – now what?

The Smart Business Mastermind Guide is packed with real-life exercises, projects and tips for running an effective mastermind group so that you get huge wins. Your business will grow. Your connections will grow. That's all part of having a smart business.

How to Enroll in the *Smart Business Fast-Track System* Right Now—FREE!

Simply go to www.MySmarterBusiness.com and complete the short enrollment form. When you are prompted for the "Book Access Code," enter the following access code:

SmartBiz888

It's really that easy! Just go to the web site, enter in your registration information, and hit enter.

Please remember, this offer is only available for a very limited time, so make sure you don't miss out. Go online and register now that you're thinking about it.

BUY A SHARE OF THE FUTURE IN YOUR COMMUNITY

These certificates make great holiday, graduation and birthday gifts that can be personalized with the recipient's name. The cost of one S.H.A.R.E. or one square foot is $54.17. The personalized certificate is suitable for framing and will state the number of shares purchased and the amount of each share, as well as the recipient's name. The home that you participate in "building" will last for many years and will continue to grow in value.

Here is a sample SHARE certificate:

THIS CERTIFIES THAT
YOUR NAME HERE
HAS INVESTED IN A HOME FOR A DESERVING FAMILY

1985-2005
TWENTY YEARS OF BUILDING FUTURES IN OUR
COMMUNITY ONE HOME AT A TIME

1200 SQUARE FOOT HOUSE @ $65,000 = $54.17 PER SQUARE FOOT
This certificate represents a tax deductible donation. It has no cash value.

YES, I WOULD LIKE TO HELP!

I support the work that Habitat for Humanity does and I want to be part of the excitement! As a donor, I will receive periodic updates on your construction activities but, more importantly, I know my gift will help a family in our community realize the dream of homeownership. **I would like to SHARE in your efforts against substandard housing in my community!** *(Please print below)*

PLEASE SEND ME _____ SHARES at $54.17 EACH = $ $_____

In Honor Of: _____

Occasion: (Circle One)   HOLIDAY   BIRTHDAY   ANNIVERSARY

       OTHER: _____

Address of Recipient: _____

Gift From: _____ *Donor Address:* _____

Donor Email: _____

I AM ENCLOSING A CHECK FOR $ $_____ PAYABLE TO HABITAT FOR HUMANITY OR PLEASE CHARGE MY VISA OR MASTERCARD *(CIRCLE ONE)*

Card Number _____ Expiration Date: _____

Name as it appears on Credit Card _____ Charge Amount $ _____

Signature _____

Billing Address _____

Telephone # Day _____ Eve _____

PLEASE NOTE: Your contribution is tax-deductible to the fullest extent allowed by law.
Habitat for Humanity • P.O. Box 1443 • Newport News, VA 23601 • 757-596-5553
www.HelpHabitatforHumanity.org

CPSIA information can be obtained at www.ICGtesting.com
Printed in the USA
238081LV00004B/80/P